Tony Gwynn

Tony Gwynn
The Baseball Life of Mr. Padre

SCOTT KINGDON

McFarland & Company, Inc., Publishers
Jefferson, North Carolina

LIBRARY OF CONGRESS CATALOGUING-IN-PUBLICATION DATA

Names: Kingdon, Scott, 1950– author.
Title: Tony Gwynn : the baseball life of Mr. Padre / Scott Kingdon.
Description: Jefferson, North Carolina : McFarland & Company, Inc., Publishers, 2023 | Includes bibliographical references and index.
Identifiers: LCCN 2023029161 | ISBN 9781476691459 (paperback : acid free paper) ∞
ISBN 9781476650371 (ebook)
Subjects: LCSH: Gwynn, Tony. | Baseball players—United States—Biography. | San Diego Padres (Baseball team : National League of Professional Baseball Clubs) | Baseball coaches—United States—Biography.
Classification: LCC GV865.G84 K56 2023 | DDC 796.357092 [B]—dc23/eng/20230623
LC record available at https://lccn.loc.gov/2023029161

BRITISH LIBRARY CATALOGUING DATA ARE AVAILABLE

ISBN (print) 978-1-4766-9145-9
ISBN (ebook) 978-1-4766-5037-1

© 2023 Scott Kingdon. All rights reserved

No part of this book may be reproduced or transmitted in any form or by any means, electronic or mechanical, including photocopying or recording, or by any information storage and retrieval system, without permission in writing from the publisher.

Front cover: San Diego Padres right fielder Tony Gwynn at bat (National Baseball Hall of Fame Library, Cooperstown, New York)

Printed in the United States of America

*McFarland & Company, Inc., Publishers
Box 611, Jefferson, North Carolina 28640
www.mcfarlandpub.com*

To Joan

Contents

Acknowledgments — ix
Preface — 1

1. "Sockball" — 3
2. The Gwynn Charm — 8
3. San Diego State — 13
4. "Who the heck is this guy?" — 20
5. Walla Walla and Amarillo — 23
6. Don't Disgrace No. 19 — 27
7. "Captain Video" — 33
8. A Pennant and a Batting Title — 38
9. World Series — 46
10. "Unbelievable" with Two Strikes — 54
11. "If I had nine Tony Gwynns" — 62
12. "I lost to the best" — 68
13. The Selfish Controversy — 76
14. Fire Sale — 84
15. Chasing .400 — 95
16. "I'm just Chris Gwynn's anonymous brother" — 106
17. "Power hitter" — 120
18. "I want more" — 129

Contents

19. The Last 10 Are the Hardest   139
20. Coach Gwynn   153

Epilogue   170
Chapter Notes   175
Bibliography   187
Index   189

Acknowledgments

This book could not have been written without the assistance of archivists and librarians. I especially would like to thank the archivists at the Sumner County, Tennessee, Archives who uncovered information that might have been difficult to locate otherwise. I received invaluable assistance from the library staffs at the Fort Myers, Florida, Regional Library, the Nashville, Tennessee, Public Library, the Florida Gulf Coast University Library, the Indiana State Library, the Allen County, Indiana, Public Library, the Southern Illinois University Library, the San Diego State University Library, the University of California at Los Angeles (UCLA) Library, and the Dalton State (Georgia) College Library.

I also much appreciate the assistance I received from John Horne at the National Baseball Hall of Fame and Andrew Soliday at the Louisville Slugger Museum & Factory. I also learned from comments either by telephone or email from Jack McKeon, Mark Grant, and Seth Vandable. I further appreciate the assistance of Gary Mitchem, my editor at McFarland & Company.

There is no doubt that a biographer of a late twentieth-century or twenty-first-century athlete gains the advantage of wide access to online sources. Baseball-Reference.com features a description of every at-bat in every game of a modern ballplayer such as Tony Gwynn. Once you find Tony on the website, you scroll down to game logs and you can review each game in a particular season. A similar resource is available for the baseball team at San Diego State. For example, if you enter an online search for "San Diego State 1988 Schedule," you will again find a description of every game. If you scroll down to the bottom of the *San Diego Union-Tribune's* website, you will find a reference to "Archives." From there you can locate, via full-text searching, historical articles from the *Union-Tribune*, the *San Diego Union*, and the *San Diego Evening Tribune* in NewsBank (providing you are willing to pay, of course). I also found San Diego State University's college newspaper, the *Daily Aztec*, to be an excellent source of information.

Acknowledgments

On occasion, some of the sources were in conflict. I tried to use the source that seemed most likely to contain the accurate information. Baseball-Reference.com reports Tony's batting average at Class A Walla Walla as .332. However, numerous newspaper sources, as well as Tony's 1986 book *Tony!* co-written with Jim Geschke, state a batting average of .331. It may be nothing more than a mathematical rounding issue but if Tony cited a .331 average in one of his books that seemed good enough for me.

Preface

I first became intrigued by Tony Gwynn during a tour of the Louisville Slugger Museum and Factory. Near the conclusion of my visit, the tour guide asked if anyone had a question. A woman standing behind me raised her hand. Referencing Louisville Slugger bats shipped to major league ballplayers, she asked, "Who pays for the bats?"

"The teams do," the guide answered. She added that she could think of one exception. "Tony Gwynn pays for his own bats. Mr. Gwynn believes if he breaks the bats, he should pay for the new bats." I thought about the tour guide's answer. Why would Tony Gwynn, almost alone among major league players, believe he had a responsibility to pay for his own bats?

In 1999, I was working as an attorney in Fort Wayne, Indiana. I learned the San Diego Padres were coming to town to play an exhibition game against the Fort Wayne Wizards. The Wizards (later renamed the Fort Wayne Tin Caps) are a Class A affiliate of the Padres, and I was a Wizards season ticketholder. Like many Fort-Wayne-area baseball fans, I knew Tony Gwynn was the star of the Padres and a near-certain future inductee into the Baseball Hall of Fame.

I purchased tickets to the upcoming exhibition game. The Padres were headed to Cincinnati for a three-game series against the Reds. But on Thursday, May 13, 1999, the team diverted to Fort Wayne to take on the Wizards.

I harbored doubts that Gwynn or any other Padres starter would suit up for a mid-season exhibition game against a minor league team. In addition, I discovered Gwynn was nursing a hamstring injury. Thus, I expected Gwynn, then in his eighteenth major league season, to take a pass.

I was mistaken. When the starting lineups were announced, Padres manager Bruce Bochy penciled Gwynn into the lineup as the designated hitter, batting fourth. Gwynn came up to bat against Wizards starting pitcher Josh Harris in the top of the first inning. Harris, possibly nervous pitching to an eight-time National League batting champion, walked Gwynn on four pitches. Anxious to watch Gwynn swing the bat, the crowd booed.

Gwynn batted two more times during the game. In his second trip to the plate, he stroked a single off Harris. Batting for the third time in the fifth inning, he rapped a double, again off Harris.

The Padres sent in a pinch runner for Gwynn after his double. The sell-out crowd of 5,589 gave Gwynn a standing ovation. He tipped his hat to the crowd as he trotted off the field. The Fort Wayne fans knew most of the Padres starters rested for the exhibition game. In contrast, Tony Gwynn made an effort. He put on a show for the fans. Once again, it seemed to me, Gwynn displayed an elevated sense of responsibility.

I set out to answer the question who was Tony Gwynn? Part of the answer is easy enough. Gwynn was a gifted athlete. He excelled in baseball and basketball from adolescence through college. After college, he knew he had to pick one sport. He chose baseball, where he was a star player for two decades. But my experiences at the Louisville Slugger Museum & Factory and a Class A baseball stadium told me there was more to the Tony Gwynn story than athletic achievement. He stood for things.

I was surprised to learn there existed no previous full-length biography of Tony Gwynn. Possibly, it was a time-zone issue. Tony toiled in California whereas many of the major media markets lay three hours east.

I was fortunate in my research to locate many contemporaneous accounts of Tony's character. Rich Wolfe issued *He Left His Heart in San Diego* in 2014, the same year Tony passed away. Wolfe's book contains numerous reminisces of Tony written by journalists who covered him, friends, and former teammates. The San Diego State newspaper, the *Daily Aztec*, published a Tony Gwynn Commemorative Issue which included recollections of Tony from college ballplayers that he coached. Tony published three books. The books predominantly discuss instruction on hitting, fielding, and baserunning but they also provide insights into Tony's personality.

I found a few flaws in Tony during my research. What biographer doesn't? Nonetheless, I began this project believing Tony's life offers a message worth savoring. Nothing I discovered changed my mind.

Chapter 1

"Sockball"

When it came to parents, Tony Gwynn hit a home run. Tony's father, Charles Allen Gwynn, was born on August 26, 1932, in Nashville, Tennessee. Tony's mother, Vendella Douglas, was born on August 6, 1935, in Gallatin, Tennessee.

Both Charles and Vendella grew up in and attended schools in Gallatin. The city of Gallatin sits approximately thirty miles north of Nashville. The city now serves as a bedroom community to Nashville. When Charles and Vendella attended schools, Gallatin was in a rural area with a population of close to 5,000. African Americans, Charles and Vendella attended segregated schools. They attended Union High School in Gallatin during the late 1940s and early 1950s.

Charles and Vendella excelled at sports.[1] Charles played quarterback for the Union High School football team. He was originally a guard and later a forward on the high school's basketball team. Vendella competed in volleyball and played guard for the girls' basketball team.

Charles and Vendella were school leaders. They were active in numerous extracurricular activities. Charles was a member of the Music Guild, the Literary Guild, and the Science Club and he was the sports editor for the Union High School yearbook. Vendella was president of her class and joined Union High School's cheerleading squad.

Tennessee law and custom circumscribed the activities of Union High School athletic teams. There were several dozen segregated schools in Tennessee. Union High School athletes were only allowed to compete against other segregated schools. Not until 1965, years after Charles and Vendella graduated, did an all-black basketball team, Pearl High School in Nashville, compete against a team with white players, Father Ryan High School, also of Nashville.

Soon after graduating from high school, Charles enlisted in the United States Air Force. An Airman First Class, Charles served in the Korean War. He was stationed in Korea from July 1951 to July 1955.

Charles and Vendella married on January 11, 1958. Later in the year,

3

their first son, Charles Allen Gwynn, Jr., was born. Charles Sr. mustered out of the Air Force in 1959. Having experienced lives that were limited by segregation, the Gwynns determined a brighter future for their family lay outside the state of Tennessee. They moved to Los Angeles, California.

Charles and Vendella set up shop in a Los Angeles apartment. Their second son, Anthony Keith Gwynn, was born on May 9, 1960. The Gwynn's last child, and youngest son, Chris, was born on October 13, 1964. With three active boys to look after, the Gwynn family moved to a larger apartment in Los Angeles.

Vendella found work with the United States Post Office.[2] She worked an evening shift, from 5:30 p.m. to 3:00 a.m. Charles Sr. worked for a state of California warehouse. He rose to the position of a warehouse supervisor. The warehouse stored and shipped supplies to California school systems. Charles Sr. worked a day shift, from 7:30 a.m. to 5:00 p.m. Because of their differing work schedules, Vendella and Charles were able to work full-time while commuting with one car. During weekdays, both parents were at home with the three boys for little more than a few hours in the early morning. The Gwynns made it work.

Charles Sr. always maintained a close interest in sports. He was a knowledgeable student of baseball history. He admired Willie Mays and a left-handed hitter who had grown up in San Diego, Ted Williams. He knew Williams in 1941 was the last major leaguer to hit above .400 for a season. He held a "special place" in his heart, as Tony later wrote, for Jackie Robinson.[3]

Charles Sr. the former high school athlete, possessed an analytical mind. He amused his three sons while watching Los Angeles Rams football games on television. He would dissect offensive play calling, anticipate blitzes, and excoriate defenders for attempting to tackle a runner high instead of low.[4]

Charles Sr. and Vendella took a keen interest in public policy and current events. Tony was three years old in 1963 but he remembered watching his parents cry when President Kennedy was assassinated in Dallas on November 22, 1963. Tony also recollected his father was knowledgeable about the political climate in Dallas in 1963 and the animus some in the city harbored toward President Kennedy.[5]

Tony's parents were similarly distraught in 1968 when Dr. Martin Luther King and Robert Kennedy were shot and killed. After Dr. King died, Tony remembered his father pacing back and forth in front of the

1. "Sockball"

television worrying about the future of the Black community and the country.[6]

The Gwynn brothers inherited their parents' athletic talents and their analytical ways. The Gwynn's Los Angeles apartment was situated in an urban area. There was little room nearby for athletic facilities. The two oldest boys, Charles Jr. ("Junior") and Tony attempted to solve the problem. They rigged a trash can against the outside wall of the apartment building. They played H-O-R-S-E and practiced shooting a basketball into the trash can.[7] Charles and Vendella recognized their sons' interests in athletics. By 1969, Charles and Vendella decided they had saved up enough money to buy a house. They determined their family should move closer to athletic fields and better schools. The Gwynns packed up their belongings and moved twenty miles south to Long Beach, California.

The Gwynn's home in Long Beach was near Silverado Park. The park is loaded with athletic venues. It features a swimming pool, baseball fields, and basketball and tennis courts.

The Gwynn's house included a backyard. The backyard was long, more than thirty yards, but narrow. In one direction lay a fence that surrounded a neighbor's yard. In the other was a large tree. Nonetheless, Charles Sr. recognized baseball-playing possibilities. He installed a home plate in the backyard.

It was impractical to hit a regular baseball in the backyard. There wasn't enough room. The Gwynn brothers devised a solution. They hit wiffle balls with a broomstick. One of the brothers would pitch to the plate. The other two brothers would bat. Sometimes, Charles Sr. would step outside to pitch to the boys. Other times, he would sit to the side, while enjoying their exploits.

Eventually, when they grew older and stronger and hit the wiffle balls farther, the Gwynn boys' game of wiffle ball encountered a crisis. The wiffle balls would break. In addition, they were hitting too many wiffle balls into a neighbor's yard, where they were unable to retrieve the balls because a less-than-friendly Doberman pinscher awaited them. The game of wiffle ball was getting expensive.

Once again, the brothers discovered an alternative. Junior apparently got the idea while watching a Los Angeles Dodgers–San Francisco Giants game on television. He learned that no baseballs were to be found in Giants pitcher Juan Marichal's poor neighborhood in the Dominican Republic. Instead, Marichal and his compatriots played ball with bound-up socks.

Tony Gwynn

The Gwynns substituted socks for wiffle balls. They bound the socks with rubber bands. They named their invention, "sock ball." That was not all. The brothers noticed fig trees growing in their neighborhood. They gathered up figs that had fallen from the trees. Then, they used figs as makeshift "baseballs."[8]

The Gwynn family would pack up their car and head east for a family vacation during the summers. They would visit Charles Sr.'s and Vendella's parents in Gallatin, Tennessee. While driving, they would tell the boys sad stories about African Americans who were harassed or killed in Jim Crow Tennessee.

The brothers loved both sets of grandparents, but they took special pleasure with Vendella's parents. They lived in a large house with surrounding acreage. There was room for the brothers to run. They noticed walnuts falling from trees. In addition to swatting at bound-up socks, they took turns whacking walnuts.

The games Junior, Tony, and Chris played in their backyard with socks and figs had their limitations. They had to contend with fences and trees. On the plus side, the brothers learned bat control. In addition, Tony and Chris gained experience hitting breaking balls because Junior was an expert at throwing sock balls and figs that darted like the sinkers, sliders, cutters and other junk thrown by major league pitchers.

Meanwhile, their father decided to shore up the boys' defensive skills. He bought them a baseball mitt, a Ted Williams model.[9] Charles and Vendella moved to Long Beach so the family could be closer to athletic facilities and competitive youth sports. Junior led the way.

Junior signed up for both Little League and Kiwanis baseball. Tony and Chris followed the progress of their brother's baseball teams. One time, Junior's team put together a sixteen-game winning streak. When Junior arrived home during the streak, Tony and Chris were anxious to hear a blow-by-blow account.

Tony and Chris followed Junior into youth sports. Tony enjoyed the games of "sock ball" with his two brothers but his real love was basketball. Their father told his sons to "work hard and good things will happen."[10] Tony took his father's advice. He practiced incessantly shooting hoops and dribbling a basketball.

Tony played basketball for his elementary and middle school basketball teams. He learned that players who refused to pass the ball or took too many shots too were known as "glory hogs." Tony refused to be tagged as a "glory hog."[11] He concentrated on setting up teammates for

1. "Sockball"

open shots with his passing and ball-handling. Consequently, he was popular with his teammates.

Though preferring basketball, Tony stuck with baseball. He followed Junior into Little League and Kiwanis ball. Little League and Kiwanis pitchers were no match for the left-handed hitting Tony. He possessed 20-10 eyesight. He pounded the ball, usually hitting to the opposite field (left field).

Tony's elementary school featured a softball team instead of baseball. Tony pounded softballs too. One season, his softball team played for a championship. His team sustained a tough loss. Some of Tony's teammates griped about the defeat. Tony, instead, put the loss behind him. He decided he would be an athlete who looked to the future rather than dwelling on the past. Years later, Tony remembered his decision to think ahead, not so much behind. He adhered to principles preached by his parents: "bounce back, face troubles, and never lose self-respect."[12]

Meanwhile, Junior began playing Police Athletic League (PAL) football and Senior coached the team. Tony sometimes watched his brother's PAL team practice. He winced when he saw Junior and his teammates smash into each other in the "dummy drill." Nonetheless, Tony dabbled in sandlot football. One day, running with the ball, he took a hard hit and broke his arm. His mother rushed him to a doctor's office. The doctor set the break. Then, he had bad news for Tony. He informed Tony that he needed to rebreak the arm for it to heal properly. Tony made a decision after enduring the pain of first, breaking, and then having the doctor rebreak, his arm. "As far as football was concerned," he wrote later, "I was officially retired."[13]

Aside from baseball and football, Junior also took up tennis. He worked on improving his game. Sometimes, he would challenge Tony to a match. Tony, who almost never picked up a tennis racquet, would beat Junior. Junior was distraught. Tony was amazed. His father, however, was not surprised. One day he took Tony aside. You have a natural talent, he informed his second-oldest son.

Chapter 2

The Gwynn Charm

The Gwynn family took advantage of their proximity to professional sports. They lived close to Silverado Park in Long Beach where they watched semi-pro baseball teams. They drove up to Los Angeles to attend Dodgers games. The family preferred to arrive hours before game time at Dodger Stadium to watch pre-game batting and fielding practice.

Tony found a hero in Dodgers outfielder Willie Davis.[1] Tony admired Davis because he was African American and he hit and threw left-handed, the same as Tony. Many major league players, it seemed to Tony, were going through the motions in their pre-game practice routine. Davis, Tony noticed, was different. Davis went through pre-game batting practice and fielding drills with the same intensity and concentration he brought to games. Tony later observed he also admired Davis because he was "aggressive but under control."[2]

By the time he reached middle school age, Tony was an avid reader of newspapers. He followed the batting statistics of some of the game's best hitters—Willie Davis, Rod Carew, and Pete Rose. He regularly checked for the National League and American League leaders in batting average, home runs, and runs batted in.

Junior's interest in baseball grew. In response, Charles purchased *The Science of Hitting* by Ted Williams. A San Diego native and a baseball Hall of Famer, Williams hit for a .344 batting average and socked 521 home runs during his major league career, all with the Boston Red Sox. Williams wrote in his book, first published in 1970, that "Hitting a baseball—I've said it a thousand times—is the single most difficult thing to do in sport."[3]

A good major league hitter, Williams pointed out, bats for a .300 average. That means even the superior hitter fails to hit safely seven out of ten times at bat. Compare that record, Williams wrote, to other sports. No one would think much of a football quarterback who completed three of ten passes or a basketball player who sank three of ten

2. The Gwynn Charm

shot attempts. In addition, neither a football quarterback nor a basketball star had to contend with a fastball sailing toward them at ninety miles an hour.

In *The Science of Hitting*, Williams argued that if there can be a science in sport hitting a baseball was it. He offered technical advice to the aspiring batter. Your weight while batting, Williams indicated, should be balanced evenly between your front and back foot. Your weight should rest on the balls of your feet. The front foot should be slightly open to promote your pivot to the ball. Your stride to the ball should be eight inches. The stride should vary no more than ten degrees from a perpendicular line to the pitcher.

Junior read Williams' book with interest. Tony perused it. Junior's baseball skills continued to improve. He was a star for the Long Beach Tech High School baseball team. After finishing his senior year, he was selected in the 31st round of the Major League Baseball draft. He demurred on signing a professional baseball contract. He decided to attend college. He originally enrolled at Compton College but later he transferred to Cal State–Los Angeles.

Junior set a one-season Cal State school record with 17 home runs. He rewrote the school's record book for career batting statistics. For the 1979, 1980, and 1981 seasons, he was named to the NCAA Division I All-Far West Team. Late in his college career, Junior wrecked a knee. His knee injury might have been repairable had it occurred twenty or thirty years later. Repair was less feasible in the early 1980s. Junior's hopes for a professional baseball career ended. He decided to go into education. He became a teacher for the Los Angeles Unified School District.

Tony followed Junior to Long Beach Tech High School. He started high school during the 1974–75 school year. Tony was already a grizzled veteran of elementary and middle school and summer league basketball and baseball teams. He would be attending a high school that was a perennial powerhouse in basketball and football, but not baseball. Accordingly, Tony concentrated on basketball. Sometimes when he practiced shooting hoops or honing his dribbling skills, Tony would listen to music on a portable radio.

Tony's father liked traditional, smooth jazz. Tony, in contrast, preferred up-tempo funk. He followed artists such as Sly and the Family Stone and Stevie Wonder. One day, Tony's parents bought him a cassette recorder. Tony began recording songs off the radio. He experimented continually with the recorder and the radio to achieve optimum sound quality. He tinkered with the volume controls on the radio and the distance between the microphone on his recorder and the speaker on his radio. Little did Tony or anyone else suspect that Tony's experiments with cassette recording would someday revolutionize baseball.[4]

Meanwhile, Tony competed for the Long Beach Tech junior varsity basketball team most of his sophomore year. He averaged double digit points per game. On occasion, he practiced with the varsity. The varsity qualified for the state tournament that season, 1974–75. Tony made a brief appearance in one tournament game.

Tech had, in Tony's words, "a monster team" returning for Tony's junior year, 1975–76.[5] The team was laden with talent including six-foot-seven Michael Wiley, six-foot-six Johnny Nash, six-foot-four James Hughes, and six-foot-two Clyde Johnson. Tony, at five-foot-eleven, was the fifth starter, and the point guard. Wiley would later star for Long Beach State and play two years in the NBA. Nash became a stalwart for Arizona State.

Surrounded by so much offensive firepower, Tony's role was to feed his teammates. Tony was an effective point guard. He saw the floor well. He was adept at anticipating the movements of his teammates and defensive players and finding open passing lanes.

Tech rolled to a 30–1 record for the 1975–76 campaign. Only a 55–53 overtime loss in the regular season marred the team's record. The Jackrabbits cruised to the California Interscholastic Federation Southern Section 4A championship. They won the title game 69–50 before a crowd of 10,000 at Long Beach Arena. Tony contributed 10 points to the blowout win. Tech finished the year ranked No. 1 in the state of California.

Tony's junior year was also the year his academics improved. Like many students, Tony was inspired by a teacher. In Tony's case, it was his American history teacher.

With the stars of the championship team graduated, Tony expected to be the scoring leader during his senior year, 1976–77. His coaches advised against it. Don't try to change your game, they advised. Be yourself.[6] Tony agreed to stick to the program. The floor general, he led Tech to a 23–7 record. Tech again qualified for the state tournament. For the second consecutive year they reached the Southern Section 4A championship game, but this time they lost. Tony averaged 10.8 points a game his senior year. He dished out 178 assists. He was named Long Beach all-city and to the Southern Section second team.

Tony's focus remained on basketball. But his natural athletic ability

2. The Gwynn Charm

turned him into a star for the Tech baseball team. Unfortunately, the Tech baseball program was anemic. Tony believed many of his classmates were unaware Tech sponsored a baseball program.[7] His classmates might have had good reason. Tech's baseball team almost never won a game during Tony's tenure.

After his junior year, Tony talked about quitting baseball and concentrating only on basketball. His mother counseled against it. You never know, she advised Tony, baseball could be something to fall back on.[8]

Tony stuck with baseball his senior year. His team was lackluster as usual with 3–16–1 record. He batted above .700 for the season. He was named to all-state teams. His baseball coaches marveled at his eye-hand coordination and his ability to adjust his swing path to the location of a pitch. No different from when he swatted at socks and figs in his backyard or walnuts on his grandparents' farmstead in Tennessee, Tony had an inside-out swing and usually hit the ball to the opposite field.

Tony continued to play baseball during the summer. His Police League team captured the 1977 state championship. Junior also competed for Tony's team. Tony set a tournament record with 14 hits during the eight-team double-elimination tournament that decided the state champion. He was voted the tournament's most valuable player.

Alicia Cureton lived a few blocks from Tony. She was a year and a half older than Tony. Alicia's brother competed in the same baseball leagues as Tony. Alicia and Tony struck up a friendly rivalry. Alicia bragged on her brother's teams. Tony razzed her back.

Alicia was an excellent athlete. For one thing, she was fast. Once, Tony jokingly challenged Alicia to a race. The joke was on Tony. Alicia won the race.[9]

Tony mostly avoided the party scene in middle school and high school. Sometimes he was shy. He was reluctant to draw attention to himself. Still, Tony made numerous friends and acquaintances on athletic fields.

Alicia was more outgoing than Tony. She was dynamic. She was smart. She was a person you knew you could turn to in times of trouble. In high school, Tony decided to forego his rivalry with Alicia. It was time, he later remarked, to deploy "the Gwynn charm."[10] According to Tony, he offered Alicia a bet. He bet his high school basketball team would beat the number-one ranked team in Los Angeles. He proposed Alicia go out with him should his team prevail. Alicia took Tony up on his bet. Tony's team pulled an upset.

Tony and Alicia went to a Denny's restaurant on their first date.

Tony Gwynn

Soon, they were inseparable. Alicia's family, the Cureton family, was known to be strict. When boys came calling on Alicia, the family refused to let them in the house. Alicia talked to prospective suitors through the front door. The Gwynn family, however, had a standup reputation. When Tony began calling on Alicia, he was invited into the house.

Tony immediately noticed a difference after he began dating Alicia. She had a high profile at Long Beach Tech. Students who before largely ignored Tony now said hello. Alicia, Tony would later observe, took him to a "new level."[11] Alicia participated in softball, volleyball, and track while at Tech. UCLA offered her a track scholarship. She attended UCLA when Tony was a senior at Tech. That kind of separation has spelled the end of many a romantic relationship. The separation failed to dissuade Tony and Alicia. They remained close.

Like Alicia, Tony entertained college scholarship offers during his senior year. At one point, it appeared Long Beach State intended to offer him a basketball scholarship but the Long Beach coaching staff decided to recruit another point guard.

Texas Christian University was another school that expressed an interest in Tony. He visited the campus. He discovered that TCU had not taken an African American basketball player in thirty years. In addition, TCU wouldn't allow Tony to compete in both college basketball and baseball. Tony passed on TCU.

Cal State–Fullerton tried to recruit Tony. Tony once again insisted on playing both college basketball and baseball. Cal State declined to guarantee Tony participation in both sports.

San Diego State agreed to offer Tony a basketball scholarship and permit him to play college baseball. That sold Tony. He enrolled at San Diego State for the 1977–78 school year.[12]

Unlike Junior, Major League Baseball teams expressed no interest in drafting Tony after he completed his senior year of high school. Baseball scouts appeared to assume Tony's only serious athletic interest was basketball. In addition, Tech's baseball program was terrible. It was easy for a scout to overlook any Tech prospect, Tony Gwynn included.

Tony and Alicia were stationed about twenty miles apart when Tony was in high school and Alicia was at UCLA. With Tony headed to San Diego State, they were now separated by roughly one hundred miles. Tony and Alicia brushed off the increased distance. Their relationship was tight as ever.

Chapter 3

San Diego State

Tony visited grandparents in Gallatin, Tennessee, during the summer of 1977. His two grandmothers were superb cooks. He had been skinny in high school. Aided by his grandmothers' cooking, he packed more than twenty pounds onto to his five-foot-eleven frame. His grandmothers helped to fatten him up for college sports.

Tony came off the bench for Coach Tim Vezie's San Diego State Aztecs during his freshman season of college basketball. Manning the point guard position, he averaged 4.2 points and 1.9 assists per game.

The Aztecs were members of the Pacific Coast Athletic Association (PCAA) conference. The 1977–78 squad finished with a 19–9 record. They tied with Fresno State for the regular season conference championship. The winner of the PCAA's post-season conference tournament qualified for the NCAA tournament. The Aztecs failed to make it. They lost 64–50 to Cal State–Fullerton in the second round.

College basketball ends roughly three weeks into the baseball season. Tony was raring to go. Contrary to their assurances when they recruited Tony, Coach Vezie and the San Diego State athletic department discouraged Tony from joining the baseball team. Reluctantly, Tony went along with the decision. Coach Vezie knew Tony, who was steadily improving at the point guard position, would be a key player for the next season. He wanted Tony to concentrate on basketball. Also, Vezie probably was thinking about State's change of conferences effective for the upcoming 1978–79 season.[1] State was leaving the PCAA to join the Western Athletic Conference (the WAC). The PCAA featured capable basketball programs including Cal State–Fullerton, Fresno State, and Long Beach State. There was no question, however, that the WAC was a stronger conference. In the WAC, State would match up against the likes of New Mexico, which had been ranked in the top twenty in the country for portions of the 1977–78 season, Utah, which reached the Sweet Sixteen of the NCAA tournament in 1977 and 1978, and the fast-rising BYU Cougars led by their All-American, Danny

Tony Gwynn

Ainge. Vezie recognized his team, and Tony, needed to perform at their peak to survive in the WAC.

San Diego State compiled a respectable 15–12 record for Tony's sophomore season, but State struggled in conference play. They were only 4–8 in the WAC. Tony had rounded into a solid point guard. He averaged 9.7 points a game. He led the team with 5.9 assists per contest.

The San Diego State administration was unimpressed by Vezie's coaching performance. The school concluded it required a high-profile coach to compete in the WAC. The administration fired Vezie and the athletic director.

Tony was hoping State would hire Bobby Dye to replace Vezie.[2] Dye was the head coach at Cal State–Fullerton. He had considered recruiting Tony out of high school. Tony was impressed by Dye's coaching. After Cal State–Fullerton defeated San Diego State in the 1978 PCAA conference tournament, Cal State continued on to win the tournament. Then, Dye led Cal State to an amazing run to the Elite Eight of the NCAA tournament.

Instead of Dye, State hired David "Smokey" Gaines. Only thirty-eight years old, Gaines was thought to be a hot commodity in the college coaching profession. He had been an assistant coach to Dick Vitale at the University of Detroit–Mercy. He succeeded Vitale for the 1977–78 season when Vitale accepted the head coaching position with the NBA's Detroit Pistons. Gaines was one of the first African Americans to coach an NCAA Division I basketball team.

Gaines' Detroit–Mercy team was an instant success. His squad went 25–4 and earned a berth in the 1978 NIT, where they lost in the second round. The next season, 1978–79, Detroit Mercy was 22–6 and qualified for the NCAA tournament. They lost in the first round to Lamar.

Gaines and Tony soon discovered they were contrasting personalities. Gaines was flashy, a fast-talker. Tony was laid back, mellow. Gaines was a smart dresser. Tony lounged in blue jeans. Tony told a teammate Gaines was "a PR guy."[3]

Jim Deitz coached the Aztecs baseball team. A former NAIA All-American in baseball, Dietz had been leading State's baseball program since 1972. He consistently fielded winning teams. The Aztecs were a favorite to win the WAC title in 1979, Tony's sophomore year. Injuries had depleted Dietz's outfield. One day, Dietz was discussing his plight with Bobby Meacham, the team's star shortstop. Meacham had played high school and summer league baseball near Long Beach. He knew the better high school players in southern California. Meacham

3. San Diego State

informed Dietz he could find a more than capable outfielder on the San Diego State campus. The outfielder he was thinking of, Meacham indicated to Dietz, is the best player he competed against in summer league baseball. His name is Tony Gwynn.[4]

Meacham helped to convince Dietz. Days after the 1978–79 basketball season ended, Tony donned an Aztecs baseball uniform. He went 4-for-4 in his first college game. Tony was a good hitter, but he was a liability on the defensive end. Consequently, he usually was the team's designated hitter. When he was put in the outfield, he platooned with Kerwin Danley, a promising freshman from Los Angeles.

On a road trip, Tony acquired a lifetime habit. Curtis Burkhead, a pitcher for State, offered Tony a package of smokeless chewing tobacco. Tony gave it a try. He took ill from his first chew. Nonetheless, the next day he approached Burkhead for another chew. After that, Tony was hooked.[5]

In using chewing tobacco, Tony followed long-standing baseball tradition. For decades, college and professional, and even high school, baseball players used a wide assortment of chewing products, from seeds and chewing gum to smokeless and other tobacco products. Continuous chewing and spitting fit the rhythms of the game. Some sports, such as hockey, soccer, and basketball, force continuous action. That is not so in baseball. In baseball, there are moments of down time. Once you bat, you wait for eight more teammates to take a turn before you bat again. If you play in the outfield, like Tony, you might go several innings without making a defensive play.

At the same time, top-flight baseball players, no less than other athletes, are primed for movement. During baseball's inevitable slow moments, players have long searched for an activity to stay focused. For generations, chewing and spitting filled the need. Chewing tobacco worked for Tony. It relaxed him. It helped keep his head in the game.

Tony batted .301 for the 1979 season. San Diego State was loaded with talent. Bobby Meacham, Buddy Black, and Chris Jones were future major leaguers. The Aztecs swept to the WAC title and qualified for the NCAA tournament.

The NCAA baseball tournament is best known for the College World Series, played in Omaha. To qualify for the Series, college teams compete in regionals at various sites about the country. The regionals contain four teams and are double-elimination. The NCAA assigned San Diego State to the East Lansing, Michigan, regional on the Michigan State campus. The Aztecs defeated Miami of Ohio 11–6 to reach the regional final. Pepperdine beat State twice, 15–9 and 13–2, to knock Tony and his teammates out of the 1979 NCAA tournament.

Smokey Gaines was a former Harlem Globetrotter. He preferred to run a high-energy, fast-breaking offense. The success of the offense depended strongly on the point guard—Tony. Tony was hobbled by a broken foot for part of his junior year of basketball, the 1979–80 season. Still, running a fast-paced offense, Tony increased his per game assist production from 5.9 in the previous season to 8.2. In a game against Nevada, Las Vegas, he cranked out 18 assists.

Despite being a focal point of the offense, Tony was unhappy playing for Gaines. The coach frequently harangued Tony about his weight. Tony was quick and by no means slow but Gaines wanted him faster and lighter. Tony feared that he was Gaines' "whipping boy."[6] In addition, the Aztecs' personnel seemed unsuited to the task of 40 minutes of breakneck basketball. The year before, State went 15–12 under Coach Vezie. In their first season with Gaines, they sank to 6–21.

Tony looked forward to the 1980 baseball season. The Aztecs featured another powerful team. The 1980 season was a break-out year for Tony. His batting average soared from .301 to .423. He led the team in batting average. He was named a third team All-American. Tony thought the 1980 San Diego State squad never fulfilled its potential.[7] The team fashioned a solid 40–26 regular season but failed to qualify for the NCAA tournament.

Tony's improvement on the baseball diamond convinced him to pay closer attention to the finer points of the sport. He visited a bookstore and purchased a paperback version of Ted Williams' *The Science of Hitting*.[8] He perused the book when his father bought it for Junior. Now, he carefully read it word for word. He wrote notes in the margins. For the rest of his baseball career, he would periodically review the book and the notations he had inscribed in the margins.

Williams set out three principles for batters in *The Science of Hitting*: one, look for a good pitch to hit; two, proper thinking, meaning do your research on pitchers; and three, "be quick with the bat."

Ted advised hitters to experiment with bats. In a section of his book captioned "Light but Right," he stated his preference for lighter bats. The best hitters, he noted, wait as long as possible before committing to swing at a pitch. Once they judge a pitch and are ready to swing, they react swiftly. To be quick with the bat, Ted argued, you need a light bat.[9]

Williams described the fastidious attention he paid to bats during

3. San Diego State

his major league career. He discarded bats that were marred or marked. These bats are a distraction, he maintained. He contended a bat can gain an ounce of weight in a "surprisingly" brief period of time. To ensure proper weight of his bats, he took his bats to the post office and weighed them. Later, he persuaded the Red Sox to install a scale in the clubhouse.

Tony used a 34 inch, 32 ounce bat during his sophomore year when he hit .301. Early in his junior year, he noticed his bat, an aluminum bat favored by college players, had a dent in it—a distraction. In accordance with Williams' prescriptions, Tony selected a shorter, lighter bat. His new bat was 32 inches long and weighed 31 ounces. Using the bat, he pounded the ball in practice. He first deployed the bat in a game against UCLA. He went 4-for-5. He stayed with the lighter bat for the rest of the season. The results showed. He improved his 1980 batting average by 122 points over 1979.

Coach Dietz was well aware of Tony's budding promise. Dietz coached a summer league team in Boulder, Colorado. He invited Tony to join the team for the summer of 1980.[10] Tony hit well in Boulder. His summer league season was cut short when he dislocated an ankle while rounding first base. Coach Dietz rushed out and re-set Tony's ankle. Several of Tony's teammates in Boulder ended up in the major leagues—Bobby Meacham, Mickey Tettleton, Jim DeShaies, and Matt Williams. He took summer classes at the University of Colorado.

Basketball remained Tony's first love but he dreaded the thought of playing another season for

Tony batting while a player for San Diego State. Here he demonstrates his ability to concentrate on a pitched ball (SDSU Athletics).

Tony Gwynn

Coach Gaines. He and Gaines were like mixing oil and water. By Tony's junior year, Alicia had transferred from UCLA to San Diego State. No longer did they negotiate a geographic separation. Alicia encouraged him to stick it out. Sounding like Tony's high school basketball coaches, she advised him to be yourself and rely on your talent.

Coach Dietz had become a mentor to Tony. Tony had an affinity for nicknames for teammates and coaches. He referred to Dietz as "the Deeker." Dietz joined Alicia in pushing Tony to continue with basketball. You came here on a basketball scholarship, he pointed out.

Gaines' up-tempo style began to click for the Aztecs during the 1980–81 season. The team was helped when Gaines scored a significant recruiting success by bringing in highly-touted six-foot-nine freshman Michael Cage. Reversing the 6–21 disaster of 1979–80, State achieved a 15–12 mark overall and 8–8 in the WAC.

Despite the team's improvement, Tony and Coach Gaines continued to have their disagreements. Late in the season Tony and his coach had a blow-up at practice. Tony had only ten games left to play in his college basketball career. Yet, he wanted to quit. You can't quit, Coach Dietz argued, you only have ten games left. Tony's dad agreed with Dietz. "Go in and talk with the man (Coach Gaines)," he advised.[11]

During his final ten games, Tony played the best basketball of his college career. On Saturday, February 14, 1981, the Aztecs upset Danny Ainge and twentieth-ranked BYU, 72–71. Tony led the way with 21 points and 9 assists.

In the second-to-last game of his college career, Tony made a spectacular play. With the clock running down and State down 72–70 to Texas El-Paso, Tony swished a 55-foot shot that would have tied the game and sent it into overtime. (Tony's basket occurred prior to the NCAA's implementation of the three-point shot rule.) The referees waved off the basket. What happened next once again highlighted the personality chasm between Tony and Coach Gaines. Irate, Gaines chased after the referees, arguing the call. Tony, calm, objective, analytical, contradicted his coach. "Yeah," he said, "it was after the buzzer."[12]

Tony competed in his final college basketball game on Saturday, March 7, 1981, against New Mexico. The New Mexico game was probably the finest performance of Tony's basketball career. He was all over the floor. He ran the show, scoring 16 points and dishing out 16 assists. He led his team to a 92–84 victory.

Tony averaged 9.6 points and 6.3 assists a game his senior year. He

3. San Diego State

was named to the All-WAC second team. He finished his career as San Diego State's all-time leader in career assists.

Years later, Tony mellowed when he reflected on his days playing for Coach Gaines. His coach was just trying to push him to get better, he decided.[13] Gaines, likewise, made a peace with Tony. Gaines was let go by San Diego State after the 1986–87 season. Looking back on his eight-year tenure at State with a reporter for the *Los Angeles Times*, Gaines talked about coaching Tony Gwynn, by then a star in the major leagues. Gwynn is one of the best I've coached, Gaines noted, especially the last ten games.[14]

On Monday, March 9, only two days after his final college basketball game, Tony suited up for the Aztecs baseball team. He drove in the winning run in both ends of a doubleheader.

Tony hit .416 for the 1981 season. Once again, he led the team in batting average. He slugged 11 homers and drove in 62 runs.

The Aztecs had a terrific regular season. They were ranked in the top 10 in the country in the polls. They were a favorite to be one of the eight teams qualifying for the College World Series. The NCAA tournament was a disappointment. Same as 1979, State was eliminated in the regional.

Given his impressive hitting pedigree, Tony knew he would be selected in the June 1981 Major League Baseball draft. In addition, the Houston Astros had expressed interest in drafting him. Tony and Alicia had no illusions about what came next. Alicia, who had graduated from San Diego State, was working for a grocery store in Los Angeles. Once Tony was drafted, they both knew he would embark on the vagabond life of a professional athlete.

Tony and Alicia thought they had to hurry. On June 6, three days before the draft, they were married. They exchanged vows at a Baptist Church in Long Beach. Next followed a reception with family, friends, and former teammates. It was a "heckuva" reception according to one of Tony's friends.[15] After their wedding, Tony and Alicia traveled to Las Vegas for a whirlwind honeymoon. By June 9, they returned to Long Beach to learn Tony's fate in the 1981 draft.

Chapter 4

"Who the heck is this Guy?"

Neither the Houston Astros nor any other Major League team selected Tony during the first two rounds of the 1981 draft. Unbeknownst to Tony, the San Diego Padres coveted him. Padres Vice President of Baseball Operations Jack McKeon knew San Diego State's personnel. Prior to the start of their regular season, the Padres would take on the Aztecs in an exhibition game. McKeon was attending one such exhibition game when Tony rifled a triple off Padres pitcher Steve Mura. His next at bat, Tony scorched a double off Padres middle reliever and sometime starter Juan Eichelberger. "Who the heck is this guy?"[1] McKeon asked his scouts. Tony Gwynn, replied his scouts. They informed McKeon that Tony was a basketball player and had only been on the baseball squad for a week.

McKeon noticed the way Tony carried himself on the field. He liked Tony's aggressiveness and awareness running the basepaths. "You could see," McKeon wrote later, "that he had the stroke and that sixth sense about the game."[2]

The Padres held two picks for the first round of the draft. They had settled on their first-round picks. They drafted Kevin McReynolds, a power-hitting outfielder from the University of Arkansas. McReynolds shattered school home run records for the Razorbacks. He was voted to 1980 and 1981 College All-America teams. Next, they took Frank Castro, a catcher with the University of Miami.

McKeon expected to take Tony in the second round. His scouts resisted. They wanted Bill Long, a pitcher from Miami of Ohio. Is Bill Long better than Tony Gwynn? McKeon asked. His scouts asserted that he was. Thus, the Padres selected Long in the second round. Thereafter, McKeon conveyed a message to his scouts. If he is available and you don't take Tony Gwynn in the third round, he emphasized, you're all fired.[3]

Tony was available in the third round. The Padres grabbed him. Many scouts had Tony low on their radar screen. Most scouts attended

4. "Who the heck is this Guy?"

San Diego State games to look in on Bobby Meacham, an All-American shortstop and a projected first-round pick. Indeed, Meacham was selected in the first round by the New York Yankees. Further, since Tony missed the first several weeks of baseball season because of his commitment to basketball, a number of scouts never saw him play. Lastly, Tony, by his own admission, was "defensively challenged."[4] He had a weak throwing arm. Taking advantage of Tony's arm, some college runners took an extra base on him.

McKeon once observed the secret to scouting is to visualize things other scouts don't see.[5] Every pro scout knows that. The trick is to determine those high school and college athletes with untapped potential. McKeon believed Tony possessed that potential.

While a student at San Diego State, Tony attended several Padres games at the team's Jack Murphy Stadium. The point he most noticed was the Padres' garish brown and gold uniforms.

In 1981, Major League Baseball and the NBA conducted their drafts on the same day. Tony received a surprise when the Los Angeles Clippers took him in the tenth round. (In later years, the NBA draft was limited to two rounds.)

It is unusual for a college athlete to be drafted in more than one professional sport. Over the years, pro sports became more specialized and a year-round commitment for an athlete. Tony had a decision to make. He long had an affinity for basketball. But he couldn't change that he was five-foot-eleven. Anyone could see the early 1980s NBA was trending toward taller guards. Six-foot-eight Magic Johnson of the Los Angeles Lakers, six-foot-seven Reggie Theus of the Chicago Bulls, and six-foot-seven guard/forward Eddie Johnson of the Atlanta Hawks exemplified the trend. Tony had to ask himself: How many seasons could he last in the NBA? He calculated that a third-round baseball pick would receive more bonus money than a tenth-round NBA selection.

On June 25, 1981, Tony agreed to a $25,000 signing bonus with the San Diego Padres.[6] The Padres assigned him to Walla Walla, Washington, the team's affiliate in the Class A Northwest League. Tony was joining a major league organization with a tumultuous history. The major leagues expanded effective the 1969 season. The San Diego Padres and the Montreal Expos were added to the National League. The addition of the Padres and the Expos expanded the National League from ten to twelve teams. Similarly, the American League expanded from ten to twelve by adding the Kansas City Royals and the Seattle Pilots.

The "Padres" team nickname had a long history in San Diego. A

Tony Gwynn

San Diego Padres franchise joined the Triple A Pacific Coast League in 1936. The next season, the Padres won the Pacific Coast League championship. They were led to the title by Ted Williams who hit .291 with 23 homers and 98 RBIs.

The major leagues conducted an expansion draft for the new franchises during October 1968. Expansion drafts typically offer slim pickings for talent. The October 1968 draft was no different. The rules of the draft permitted existing teams to protect 15 veterans from the draft. If one of their unprotected veterans was drafted, the rules allowed a team to protect three more players. The Padres avoided the unprotected veterans. They opted for a "youth movement." They drafted untested minor leaguers, hoping they would develop into reliable major league players.

The youth movement failed. The Padres sagged to a 52–110 record their first season. They finished last in the six-team National League West division. San Diego followed with a 63–99 mark in 1970; 61–100 in 1971; 58–95 in 1972 (a strike-shortened season); and identical 60–102 records in 1973 and 1974. After additional poor seasons in 1975, 1976, and 1977, San Diego broke through at 84–78 in 1978. The 1978 season proved a small reprieve when the team retrogressed to a 68–93 record in 1979 and 74–88 in 1980.

The Padres fired manager Jerry Coleman after the 1980 season. They replaced Coleman with former major league slugger Frank Howard. Under Howard, the Padres were off to a sluggish 22–33 start. On June 9, 1981, Major League ballplayers went on strike. For decades, the "reserve clause" bound players to one team for their careers (unless they were traded). Major League players won the right to free agency (to sign with any team after their contract expired) during the 1970s. The onset of free agency led to labor turmoil in the game. Team owners and the Major League Players Association repeatedly clashed over the terms of free agency. In 1981, the owners were insisting that any team losing a player to free agency should be compensated by a "comparable" player from the team signing the free agent. In response, the players called a strike.

The strike was on when Tony packed his bags for Walla Walla. Minor league players were not members of the Players Association. Thus they were largely unaffected by the strike. Minor league play was still on. That was the scene in professional baseball when Tony began a trek that he hoped would land him a spot on the San Diego Padres roster, garish brown and gold uniforms and all.

Chapter 5

Walla Walla and Amarillo

To Tony Gwynn signing a baseball contract meant more than receiving a bonus and endorsing a piece of paper. It signified his commitment to taking a professional approach to the game.[1] He vowed to ascend to the Major Leagues within three years. Otherwise, he planned to find another line of work.

During the 1970s, college baseball teams began to replace wooden bats with aluminum bats. The results were immediate. Batting averages increased by twenty points. Home run production nearly doubled. The transition from aluminum to the wooden bats used by professional ballplayers had derailed many a minor league career. Wooden bats are constructed with a solid core. Aluminum bats have a hollow center and are, therefore, lighter. College players generated more bat speed with aluminum bats. A 1977 study published in *Research Quarterly* reported that aluminum bats dissipated less energy when struck by a pitched ball.[2] Researchers termed this phenomenon the "trampoline effect." Pitched balls literally rebounded off aluminum bats. In addition, researchers determined that the center of mass, or balance point, is closer to the handle of aluminum bats. Consequently, aluminum bats were more forgiving of batter error. A batter could misjudge a pitch, strike it near the bat handle, and still apply mustard to the ball.

Tony recognized a successful transition to wooden bats was crucial to advancing his professional career. He caught a break because the Major Leagues were on strike.

An outfielder and, occasionally a first baseman, Bobby Tolan competed in the majors between 1965 and 1979. He finished his playing career with the San Diego Padres. Tolan joined the Padres coaching staff after retiring as a player. During the strike, the Padres dispatched Tolan to Walla Walla to work with minor league players. On one occasion, he called Tony to a practice session. Tolan brought a fungo bat, a lighter bat used by coaches to hit balls during fielding practice.[3] A fungo bat can hit a ball far and hard but it is too fragile to last in a game. Tolan

Tony Gwynn

stood to the side of home plate and tossed balls to Tony, who swatted them with the fungo bat. Tolan's drill taught Tony the muscle memory and the bat speed he needed to transition to a wooden bat. Tony had one advantage though. He possessed strong wrists from all his years dribbling a basketball.

Being at the bottom of the pecking order, minor league players are sometimes constrained to take whatever equipment teams give them. Walla Walla furnished Tony with a 35 inch, 33 ounce wooden bat. Tony was off to a good start with the bat. He went 3-for-5 in his first minor league game. He was batting well above .300. Nonetheless, he was dissatisfied. Pitchers were jamming him with inside pitches—the same pitches he might have been able to handle with an aluminum bat.

Tony refused to be fooled by his good start. He knew his weakness on inside pitches would eventually become the book on him. Then, he would see a steady diet of inside pitches from pitchers trying to jam him.

He asked the Padres to ship used bats up to Walla Walla. He found a lighter bat, a Mike Ivy 016 model, that suited his purposes. The change to the Mike Ivy bat worked. He hit a home run in each of his next five games.

Before a road game in Eugene, Oregon, Tony and two of his Walla Walla teammates, first baseman John Kruk and pitcher Greg Booker, visited a sporting goods store. Browsing the store's assortment of wooden bats, Tony found a batch of Mike Ivy 016s, which he purchased.[4]

Tony drew a lesson from his sojourn to the sporting goods store. A professional athlete cannot rely only on equipment provided by a team. Instead, Tony concluded, you have to invest in yourself.[5]

Tony hit .331 for Walla Walla. He led the Northwest League in batting average. Batting leadoff, Tony hit 12 homers and drove in 37 runs for the season. Aggressive on the basepaths, he stole 17 bases. He was voted the League's most valuable player. A few of Tony's 12 home runs were inside-the-park jobs. In a game on July 5, he hit a three-run inside-the-park walk-off homer to win the game for Walla Walla.

An incident in Eugene demonstrated Tony's increasing attention to detail. He slugged what he thought was an inside-the-park homer. After he crossed home plate, the first base umpired called him out. The umpire ruled Tony missed the bag rounding first. Tony ran over to first and checked the bag. He pointed to an imprint of a shoe on the bag. The imprint, Tony argued, matches the bottom of my shoes but not the first baseman's.

The first base ump was unimpressed by Tony's argument. Tony

5. Walla Walla and Amarillo

believed he had proven his point. Typical for Tony, he was chewing a wad of tobacco. Unable to think of a better alternative, he took out a piece of chaw and hurled it at the umpire. That gets you thrown out of any baseball game. Tony was promptly booted.[6] The Eugene fiasco was another lesson for Tony. He would learn to argue his position without being tossed. For the rest of his long playing career, he would be tossed only two more times.

Most minor league players live a modest existence. The Walla Walla players roomed at a Whitman College dorm. Without cars to drive, they pedaled around town on bicycles. Tony and his buddy, John Kruk, were returning to the Whitman College dorm on their bikes when a group passing by in a car yelled racial taunts at Tony. Tony and Kruk were livid. Kruk wanted to jump on their bikes and confront the offenders. Tony was no less furious than Kruk. But, he declined Kruk's offer. Remember why we are here, he stressed to Kruk. Our objective is the Major Leagues. To do so, we should avoid distractions if at all possible.[7]

The Northwest League is a short season Class A league. Many minor leagues begin play in April. The Northwest League starts after the June Major League draft. In 1981, the Northwest League was divided into two three-team divisions. Walla Walla finished last in the Northern Division with a 29–41 record.

The Padres recognized Tony's potential despite Walla Walla's losing record. They shipped him to Class AA Amarillo in the Texas League to finish the 1981 season. Tony discovered the Amarillo outfit was his kind of ball club—loose and fun-loving.[8] In his first Class AA at bat, Tony hit what he derisively described as a "24 bouncer" to the second baseman for an easy out. He returned to the dugout to a chorus of teammates shouting, "That's okay, way to swing, Tony." Tony rolled with the tide. He retorted, "C'mon, I took a crappy swing and you guys know it." Some of his teammates fired back. "Okay," they said, "the hell with you." Then, Tony and his tormentors laughed.[9] And Tony had a world-class laugh. It was as if he put his whole soul into it.

There was no laughing after the "24 bouncer." His second time up, Tony slapped a double. The third time, he smacked another double.

Tony was on the Amarillo team the last three weeks of the Class AA season. He appeared in 23 games. He feasted on Class AA pitching. He hit for a hefty .462 average. The Amarillo Gold Sox caught a hot streak at the end of the season. They swept to a Western Division title.

Tony was making a satisfactory transition from aluminum to wooden bats. Pitchers jammed him up less on inside pitches. His

Tony Gwynn

defense—he primarily was based in center field—was another story. Runners continued to take advantage of his weak throwing arm. Tony's defensive liabilities threatened to retard his march to the major leagues.

After the 1981 season, Padres General Manager Jack McKeon sent Tony to the Padres winter instructional camp in Phoenix. The camp was led by Clyde McCullough, the Padres bench coach. A catcher, McCullough was a fifteen-year veteran of the majors. He spent his entire career with either the Chicago Cubs or the Pittsburgh Pirates.

Every day in camp, McCullough and Tony worked on strengthening Tony's throwing arm. McCullough would take a bag of balls and station Tony near the outfield wall in right field. McCullough would hit balls to Tony who then practiced long throws from near the wall to second or third base.[10]

Chapter 6

Don't Disgrace No. 19

San Diego stumbled through a miserable 1981 season. When players called a strike in June, the Padres were mired in last place in the NL West. The players and owners settled their dispute on July 31. Under their agreement, free agency was restricted to major league veterans with six or more years of service. Teams losing a "premium" free agent were to be compensated by drafting from a pool of unprotected players from all major league teams rather than, as the owners had originally proposed, the team signing the free agent.

Because of the strike, the owners elected to split the 1981 season. The four teams leading their divisions (NL East and West and AL East and West) at the time the strike was called were deemed eligible for the post-season playoffs. The teams in each division with the best record in the second half of the regular season, which commenced on August 10, would also advance to the playoffs. (Wild cards were not added to the playoffs until 1994.) If the same team compiled the best division record in both halves of the season, the team with the second-best record in the second half qualified.

The Padres were equally inept in the second half. They staggered to an 18–36 record. They finished last again in the NL West. Ray Kroc, who built McDonald's restaurant franchises into a fortune, purchased the Padres in 1974. Kroc pledged "a winning team, a fighting team, a personality team."[1] Kroc's pledge had thus far fallen short. On the plus side, he was willing to spend money in free agency and Jack McKeon could spot untapped talent.

The Padres turned it around after the 1981 season. They fired manager Frank Howard. They hired Dick Williams. They signed Williams to a three-year contract. Williams was a proven winner. He also had a proven record of ticking off players and team owners. Players complained Williams was cold and hard. At the same time, he was capable of driving players to their best in all phases of the game.

The Boston Red Sox hired Williams to manage in 1967. He led the

Tony Gwynn

Sox to the 1967 World Series, where they lost in seven games to the St. Louis Cardinals. Williams couldn't get along with Red Sox owner Tom Yawkey or Red Sox star Carl Yastrzemski and the Sox fired him in 1969.

The Oakland A's were the next team to bring on Williams. In 1971, the A's won 101 games with Williams at the helm. In 1972 and 1973, they captured the World Series title. Williams feuded with A's owner Charles Finley, resenting Finley's meddling with his personnel decisions. Despite winning two consecutive World Series championships, Finley sacked Williams.

Williams next had an unsuccessful reign managing the California Angels. Then the Montreal Expos hired him in 1977. Under Williams, the Expos were 95–65 in 1979 and 90–72 in 1980. The Expos were challenging for a second half playoff berth in 1981 when, tired of Williams publicly belittling some members of the Expos pitching staff, they showed Williams the door.

Williams, however, fulfilled all of owner Ray Kroc's requirements. He was a winner, a fighter, and a personality. He wasted no time setting the tone at the Padres 1982 Spring Training Camp in Yuma, Arizona. While directing the team's first drill of the camp, Williams announced, "I don't care if you guys like me or not."[2]

Encouraged by Tony's successful stints at Class A Walla Walla and Class AA Amarillo, the Padres invited him to 1982 Spring Training. Tony continued to work daily with Coach Clyde McCullough on long throws from the outfield. In addition, Tony received valuable assistance from a Padres minor league instructor, Tom House.

House taught Tony the "Captain's Wheel." Tony described the "Captain's Wheel" in his 1992 book *Tony Gwynn's Total Baseball Player: Winning Techniques for Hitting, Fielding, and Baserunning:* "It's as if you're a captain steering the wheel of a boat. When your throwing side goes back, the other side of your body goes up. And when you throw, you pull the nonthrowing side down and the throwing side comes right over the top."[3]

Tony acknowledged in his book that the "Captain's Wheel" dramatically improved the strength of his throwing arm. House made another change when he noticed Tony was gripping the ball incorrectly on his throws. Tony was gripping the ball along the seams. Tony's grip imparted too much spin on the ball, detracting from his throwing accuracy. House instructed Tony to grip the ball across the seams. House also trained Tony on two-hop throws. The first hop is a long bounce. The second hop is a short bounce and thus easier for an infielder to handle.

6. Don't Disgrace No. 19

Tony impressed Williams with his hustle in a Padres Spring Training game. An opposing batter rifled a shot down the first base line. The Padres right fielder, attempting to cut down a runner at third, overthrew the bag. Tony ran in from left field and backed up the play, preventing the runner from scoring. "That's the first time I've seen that in five years," said Williams.[4]

Williams informed Tony he was being sent down to the minors. Williams assured Tony he would advance to the major leagues. It's just a question of time, he indicated. Part of the problem for Tony was that the Padres were loaded in the outfield. Their outfield lineup was set with veterans Ruppert Jones, Sixto Lezcano, and Gene Richards. Tony trudged off to play for the Triple A Hawaii Islanders with spouse Alicia in tow.

Tony got off to a slow start at the plate in Triple A ball. He was batting in the .240s in mid–May when outfielder Gene Richards sustained an injury. Williams wanted to call up Tony. Jack McKeon overruled Williams. San Diego promoted Alan Wiggins instead.

Wiggins had been a baseball enigma. He possessed both talent and a propensity for trouble. The California Angels drafted him in 1977. Wiggins ran like a lightning bug on the bases. In 1977 Class A ball, he stole 25 bases in 63 games. Wiggins got into an altercation with one of his coaches during the 1978 minor league season. The Angels cut him. The Los Angeles Dodgers signed Wiggins in 1979. Wiggins put together a spectacular 1980 season in the Class A California League. He stole 120 bases. Wiggins' season stolen base total was an all-time minor league record. He batted .288 and scored 108 runs. Wiggins' knack for trouble came back to haunt him. He was arrested for possession of marijuana (a greater offense in 1981 than in the twenty-first century).

In December, the major leagues conduct a Rule 5 draft. The Rule 5 draft aims to prevent teams from stockpiling in the minor leagues those players with major league talent. Concerned about Wiggins' drug issues, the Dodgers left him unprotected in the 1980 Rule 5 draft. Deciding Wiggins was worth the risk, McKeon drafted him. Wiggins was hitting .319 for Hawaii when Richards was injured. Wiggins' batting average was nearly eighty points higher than Tony's. What would it say to our minor league players, McKeon argued to Williams, if we bring up Tony Gwynn instead of Alan Wiggins?[5] Wiggins was a fireball for San Diego. He swiped 29 bases in his first 59 games after being called up.

Many baseball writers predicted another last-place finish for the Padres. The Padres fooled them. Wiggins sparked the offensive with his aggressive baserunning. Starters Eric Show, Tim Lollar, and free agent acquisition John Montefusco turned in stellar pitching performances. Catcher Terry Kennedy and the outfield crew of Jones, Lezcano, and Richards (prior to his injury) were rock solid at the plate. San Diego roared to a 50–36 record at the All-Star break. They stood in second place, two games behind the Atlanta Braves. Meanwhile, Tony found his hitting stroke. By mid–July he was batting .328.

On July 18, Hawaii manager Doug Rader summoned Tony to his office. A colorful character, Rader couldn't resist having fun at Tony's expense. Tony expected to be chewed out by his manager. The game before, Tony was late picking up the stop sign from his third base coach. Running through the sign, he rounded third for home. He was thrown out at the plate for the final out of a game that Hawaii lost.

Rader knew Tony expected a dressing down. Rader obliged him. For several minutes he lit into Tony for neglecting the sign. He listened patiently as Tony apologized. Then, Rader nonchalantly informed Tony, by the way, you are going to San Diego.[6] Tony called Alicia. They chatted excitedly on the phone. Tony and Alicia flew overnight from Hawaii to San Diego. Alicia was six months pregnant. She slept on the plane. Tony was too keyed up to doze off.

On July 19, 1982, the Padres were playing a night game in San Diego against the Philadelphia Phillies. Tony arrived at San Diego's Jack Murphy Stadium five and a half hours before game time. The Padres would learn it was Tony's habit to arrive early at the stadium. For the rest of his career, he was usually the first Padre to show up at the ballpark.

Tony was fortunate. The Padres were awful for most of the franchise's thirteen-year history. Now, the team was showing signs of life. Prior to World War II, most professional baseball, basketball, football, and hockey franchises were based east of the Mississippi River. Post–World War II, professional franchises in America expanded from coast-to-coast. With franchises geographically dispersed, it was unusual for a professional athlete to compete near their home town. Tony was an exception. He had been an integral member of a championship high school basketball team in nearby Long Beach. He excelled for San Diego State in basketball and baseball.

By the time he was advanced to the majors, Tony was already a sports celebrity in San Diego. Local newspapers highlighted Tony's promotion to the major leagues. The Padres provided him with 24 tickets for the July 19 game against the Phillies and Tony distributed the tickets to friends, former teammates, Alicia, and his parents.

6. Don't Disgrace No. 19

Padres clubhouse manager Whitey Wietelmann handed Tony his uniform with No. 19 etched on the front and back. Wietelmann explained to Tony the history of uniform No. 19 in San Diego baseball. The number had rarely been worn by either minor league or major league Padres. Ted Williams, Wietelmann noted, wore the No. 19 jersey for the 1936 minor league Padres. He had been a Padres minor league player, Wietelmann added, and he wore No. 19. Wietelmann implored Tony: don't disgrace No. 19.[7]

Manager Dick Williams inserted Tony into the fifth slot in the batting order and stationed him in centerfield. More than 40,000 fans flocked to the stadium for Tony's first major league game. Throughout his long career, Tony often delivered for the fans in big moments. He came through in his first major league game.

Tony was keyed up on the flight to San Diego. Coming up to the plate in the bottom of the first inning, he was calm, focused on the task at hand. Tony batted against Phillies starter Mike Krukow. Padres second baseman Tim Flannery was perched on third base. On a pitch from Krukow, Tony lifted a sacrifice fly to center to score Flannery from third. Tony notched an RBI in his first major league at bat.

Tony batted again in the third against Phillies reliever Sid Monge. Monge came on in the second after a Padres rally chased Krukow. Tony smashed a rocket to Phillies shortstop Ivan DeJesus for an out. Although the ball was caught, Tony's smash was a sign of things to come. A natural opposite field hitter, in the future he would hit safely many times with line drives to the "5.5 hole" between the shortstop and the third baseman.

Sid Monge could throw a nasty sinker. He struck out Tony on one of those sinkers in the fifth inning.

Tony batted for the fourth time in the eighth inning. He blasted a Monge fastball to left center. Phillies center fielder Bob Dernier attempted a diving stab at the ball but came up short, and the ball rolled to the outfield wall. Tony strolled into second base with a stand-up double. The big scoreboard in the outfield flashed, "TONY GWYNN'S FIRST MAJOR LEAGUE HIT."[8] Phillies first baseman Pete Rose was trailing the play. Rose was near second base when he either noticed the sign on the scoreboard or the ball being taken out of play for a keepsake, a typical gesture for a first major league hit.

Rose was number two on the major league's all-time career hits list. He was chasing the all-time leader, Ty Cobb at 4,191 hits. (In later years, an error was found in Cobb's hit totals resulting in his career hit total

Tony Gwynn

decreasing from 4,191 to 4,189.) In the seventh inning, Rose lashed his second hit of the game for career hit No. 3,800.

Next came a moment Tony would never forget. "Hey, I didn't know this was your first game," Rose said to Tony. "Nice going, kid." Rose stuck out his right hand and Tony shook it. A picture of the handshake appeared in the following day's *San Diego Union*.

The Padres–Phillies game was a wild one. The Padres lost, 7–6. Tony had another chance to bat in the bottom of the ninth. He rapped a single to center off Phillies pitcher Ron Reed for his second hit of the game. Rose, at first, provided another memory for Tony. "Hey, kid," said the man with 3,800 career major league hits, "What are you trying to do, catch me in one day?"[9] Tony laughed.

Tony's mother quietly, but strongly, supported the athletic achievements of her three sons. Tony's father, in contrast, had few qualms bragging on his sons' accomplishments. He had good reason. Junior was named to college baseball All-American teams. Tony collected two hits in his first major league game. Youngest son Chris was a star for the Long Beach Tech baseball team.

Tony's father always exuded utmost confidence in Tony's athletic abilities. "Tony," he said to his second-eldest son after the Phillies game, "you made it look easy."[10]

Chapter 7

"Captain Video"

After going hitless in his second major league game, Tony went on a tear. He hit safely in 15 consecutive games. His best performance of the streak was in the second game of a July 27 doubleheader against Atlanta. Tony pounded four hits in five at bats in an extra inning San Diego loss.

On July 21, Alan Wiggins' susceptibility to trouble caught up with him again. The San Diego police arrested him for cocaine possession. The Padres sent Wiggins to a drug rehabilitation facility for 30 days. When Wiggins was released from rehab, Major League Commissioner Bowie Kuhn suspended him for another 30 days. Wiggins finally returned to the lineup in mid–September.

On August 22, Tony hit his first major league home run—a solo shot against the Cubs in Wrigley Field. But the Padres were stumbling after their 50–36 start. They lost the game, 8–7. Dick Williams gave Tony a day off in Pittsburgh on August 25. At least that is what Tony expected. In the eighth inning Williams signaled Tony for a defensive replacement in right field. Tony dived for the first ball hit to him and broke his right wrist. It was a fluke play. Years later, Tony ascribed the injury, in part, to chewing tobacco. He borrowed from a teammate a brand of chew stronger than what he was used to. Tony believed the stronger brand had detracted from his alertness in the outfield.[1]

Tony was out of the lineup for three weeks. He returned to full-time duty on September 16. He went 2-for-4 with a single and a double against the San Francisco Giants.

The Padres were still on the road in San Francisco when Tony and the team received a shock. Clyde McCullough, a mentor who worked tirelessly with Tony on improving his defense, was found dead in his hotel room. McCullough died of a heart attack. He was sixty-five years old.

McCullough's death was emblematic of the Padres' slide after the 1982 All-Star break. With the loss of Wiggins for two months, injuries to Tony and other starters, and decline in the effectiveness of the pitching staff, the Padres sank below .500. Nonetheless, they were in mathematical contention for the NL West division title until September 27—the latest elimination from post-season play in the team's history.

The Padres made a run near the end of the season. They defeated the Atlanta Braves in the final game of the season to finish 81–81 and in third place in the division. Tony contributed one hit in three at bats and scored a run in a 5–1 victory. For the 1982 season, Tony hit for a respectable .289 average with one homer and 17 RBIs. Many a major leaguer would be satisfied with a .289 average. For Tony, .289 would prove to be the lowest season batting average of his career. Never again would be finish a season batting lower than .300.

One day after the 1982 season ended Tony and Alicia were blessed with their first child, Anthony Keith Gwynn, Jr.

The Padres executed two off-season moves of note. On November 18, 1982, they traded pitcher Juan Eichelberger, who faded in the second half of the 1982 season, to the Cleveland Indiana for pitcher Ed Whitson. Whitson pitched to a 4–2 record in 1982 for Cleveland but the Padres believed he could blossom into an effective starter. More significant, the Padres signed free agent first baseman Steve Garvey. On December 28, 1982, Garvey agreed to a five-year, $6.5 million contract. Garvey averaged .301 and hit a total of 211 home runs in 14 productive seasons for the Los Angeles Dodgers. He drove in more than 100 runs in five of those seasons. He hit 16 homers with 86 RBIs during the 1982 season. Garvey was charismatic. He was a leader in the clubhouse.

Eager to solidify his place on the Padres major league roster, Tony participated in winter ball in Puerto Rico. He was hitting well when, on December 30, 1982, he slugged a liner over the head of the center fielder. Charging around first base, Tony tripped over the bag, fell, and broke his right wrist again. Surveying the break, he knew it was worse than the first one. He realized it would take months to heal.

Spring Training 1983 frustrated Tony. He looked forward to Garvey being on the team. Hampered by the wrist injury, he was relegated to running to stay in shape. The wrist kept him out of commission until late May.

San Diego jumped off to an auspicious start. On opening day, they won a slugfest, 16–13. The Padres hovered slightly under .500 for April and May. They began to jell in June, with Garvey leading the way. They ended June with a 38–37 record.

In late May, the Padres sent Tony to Triple A Las Vegas for a rehab assignment. The Las Vegas franchise replaced Hawaii as the Padres

7. "Captain Video"

Triple A affiliate effective the 1983 season. Tony spent three weeks in Las Vegas. He was hitting .347 when the big club called him back. Tony returned to action on June 21. He punched out one hit in four at bats in a 2–0 win over the Dodgers. The next day he collected three hits in four at bats in another Padres victory over the Dodgers.

Thereafter, Tony's hitting began to slide. In a particular bad stretch, he had no hits in 11 ineffective at bats over the course of three games from July 10 to 12. His batting average slipped to .243 on July 19. At the time, the Padres were on the road for a two-game set against St. Louis.

That is when the youngster who loved to tinker with taping songs off the radio onto a cassette recorder got a moment of inspiration. It was a moment that would rejuvenate his career and transform baseball. He called Alicia from St. Louis. He asked her to tape his at bats on their VCR from the home team television feed to San Diego.[2]

After returning to San Diego from the road trip, Tony analyzed his taped at bats on the VCR. In a short time, he discovered the reason for his batting slump. He was opening his hips too soon. By opening up prematurely, he was robbing his swing of power and authority. Correcting batting slumps had been an issue of concern throughout baseball history. Coaches, teammates, even family members, would attempt to advise the wayward batter on surmounting the slump. They would view at bats and theorize on the reason for the slump. The batter would think about it while attempting to visualize the deficiencies in their swing.

Observing at bats on video took analysis of a hitting slump to a new level. Tony could replay the same at bats over and over on video. He could review his swing in slow motion. The capability to repeat and slow down the observation of ineffective at bats added a new dimension to correcting errors at the plate.

At first teammates and opposing players chuckled when they saw Tony hauling video equipment to tape his games. The last laugh was on them. Soon, every team in baseball constructed a video room where players and coaches could analyze at bats. In recognition of his innovation, Tony became known as "Captain Video."[3]

Tony's video review paid dividends. His batting average hit rock bottom at .229 on July 29. Thereafter, his batting proficiency improved throughout the 1983 season. On August 6, the Padres took on the Cincinnati Reds in a doubleheader. In the first game, Tony collected four hits, drove in a run, and scored a run in an 11–4 win. In the nightcap, Tony went 2-for-4 with a triple and an RBI to help the Padres to a sweep. Tony's efforts in the doubleheader raised his average to .288.

Tony Gwynn

From August 21 to September 18, Tony fashioned a 25-game hitting streak. His streak was the longest in the majors for the 1983 season. He registered three hits in five at bats on the final day of the streak to increase his batting average to 313. Tony was proficient at hitting balls to the opposite field but the September 18 game demonstrated his ability to hit the ball to all fields. In the top of the fourth he stroked a single to left. In the sixth, he knocked an RBI single to center. In the thirteenth inning of an extra inning game and with the score tied 2–2, he smashed a single to right. He then scored the winning run on Ruppert Jones' two-run homer.

Tony had another strong game against the Reds on September 23. He went 2-for-3 with a walk and a homer, drove in three, and scored three runs in an 11–8 San Diego loss. San Diego was 41–44 after the All-Star break. The Padres rallied to win the final four games of the season to finish at 81–81 for the second consecutive season.

San Diego got their money's worth out of free agent Steve Garvey. He was hitting .294 with 14 homers and 59 RBIs when on July 29 he dislocated his thumb in a collision at home plate. Garvey's injury put him out for the season. His absence was a contributing factor to the team's decline after the All-Star break.

Alan Wiggins had a fine 1983 season. He stole 66 bases. He batted .276. He stepped up after Garvey's season-ending injury. Brought in from the outfield, he performed capably for Garvey at first base. Recognizing his overall contribution, his teammates voted him the 1983 team MVP.

Thanks in no small measure to his study of video, Tony led the Padres in batting average at .309. His major league leading 25-game hitting streak served notice that there was a new left-handed hitting prospect on the horizon.

Ted Williams wrote in *The Science of Hitting* that a batter must "practice, practice, practice."[4] Ted revealed that when he competed in the major leagues he practiced batting "until the blisters bled." Williams complained that batters fail to get enough practice. "Part of the problem," he indicated, "is there isn't enough time." That was because "A guy doesn't get in the batting cage often enough and doesn't stay there long enough."

A close reader of *The Science of Hitting*, Tony was probably familiar with Williams' complaints about limited practice time. Tony could do the math. Imagine a major league team practice where 18 batters line up to take batting practice. Assume each batter hits in the batting cage

7. "Captain Video"

for fifteen minutes against a batting practice pitcher. Eighteen batters times 15 minutes equals 170 minutes, or nearly three hours of practice time. Williams was right. There wasn't enough time. A batter had to find another way to work on their craft in addition to routine team practice sessions.

Tony learned about the San Diego School of Baseball. The place had batting cages and pitching machines. Tony came to frequent the School of Baseball to "practice, practice, practice." The School of Baseball, according to Tony, became "my office."[5]

Tony lost Clyde McCullough as a coach. But he continued to work hard on his fielding and throwing in the offseason at the San Diego State baseball complex. He deliberately played shallow in the outfield while he practiced chasing down fly balls hit over his head by San Diego State assistant coaches. He grabbed a bag of balls and practiced throws from the outfield to third base and home plate. Knowing of Tony's work inside and outside the Padres ballpark, Jack McKeon remarked he had never seen a ballplayer with more dedication than Tony Gwynn.[6]

Tony learned another lesson from his dad. One day his dad visited the Padres clubhouse. He watched as Tony and other Padres offered their baseball shoes to a clubhouse attendant to shine. "You shine your own shoes," his dad said. "They're your shoes. You shine them." Thereafter, Tony shined his own shoes.[7]

Tony again played winter ball after the 1983 season. Fortunately, he sustained no injuries this time. Injuries had shortened Tony's 1982 and 1983 Major League seasons. He hoped to stay healthy for a full season in 1984. And the Padres made offseason moves to position themselves for a run at the NL West division title and a post-season playoff berth.

Chapter 8

A Pennant and a Batting Title

San Diego manager Dick Williams revamped his outfield for the 1984 season. Sixto Lezcano was gone. The Padres traded him to the Philadelphia Phillies on August 31, 1983. Ruppert Jones and Gene Richards entered free agency after the 1983 season. Jones and Richards departed San Diego for other teams.

Williams shifted Tony from center to right field. He slated Kevin McReynolds for center field. The Padres first-round pick in 1981, McReynolds injured a knee ligament, underwent surgery, and missed the 1981 minor league season. He scorched minor league pitching in 1982 and 1983. In 1982, he hammered 28 homers with 98 RBIS in Class A ball and clubbed 5 homers with 39 RBIs after the Padres promoted him to Class AA Amarillo. In 1983, he hit 32 homers with 116 RBIs for Triple A Las Vegas. He was named Minor League Player-of-the-Year.

The Padres advanced McReynolds to the majors in June 1983 and again in September. He hit .221 with 4 homers in the majors. Despite his desultory major league hitting numbers, Williams and General Manager Jack McKeon (who had been promoted from Vice President of Baseball Operations in 1980) believed McReynolds had the chops to succeed in the majors.

Williams emplaced Carmelo Martinez in left field. Martinez came up with the Chicago Cubs in 1983. He hit six home runs with 16 RBIs in 29 games for the Cubs. Martinez was an average defender, at best, in the outfield but Williams and McKeon liked his power-hitting potential. They acquired Martinez from the Cubs in a trade that involved four players.

Williams' outfield maneuvers left Alan Wiggins in the lurch. Wiggins was an outfielder in 1982 and 1983 before he was temporarily moved to first base after Steve Garvey's 1983 season-ending injury. Williams shuttled the versatile Wiggins to second base. Wiggins had some experience with the position during his stints in the minors.

The Padres engineered two more acquisitions prior to the 1984

8. A Pennant and a Batting Title

season. They signed former New York Yankee reliever Goose Gossage as a free agent on January 6, 1984. In an era when relievers pitched multiple innings, Gossage won 13 games, while losing five, for the Yankees in 1983 with a sparkling 2.27 ERA. He led the American League in saves in 1975 and 1978, and tied for the lead in 1980. There was no love lost between the freewheeling Gossage and the ham-fisted Yankees owner George Steinbrenner. Gossage disdained Steinbrenner as "the fat man upstairs."

Williams and McKeon were convinced they needed to shore up weaknesses at third base. On March 31, 1984, they traded for another disaffected Yankee, Graig Nettles. Nettles was unhappy being platooned at third base in New York. Nettles was thirty-nine years old. His age did not deter the Padres for they thought Nettles' bat still had pop. He hit 20 homers for the Yankees in 1983. Also, Padres management knew Nettles was a stout defender at third.

Williams now had capable talent at every position. There was Garvey at first, Wiggins at second, Garry Templeton at shortstop, Nettles at third, and Terry Kennedy catching. Tony, McReynolds and Martinez patrolled the outfield. Williams considered the acquisition of Gossage consequential. With Gossage on board, he said, we are a pennant contender.

San Diego fans agreed with Williams' assessment. On opening day against Pittsburgh, 44,459 fans flocked to Jack Murphy Stadium. The Padres parking attendants wore tuxedos. The San Diego Chicken, the yellow-hued mascot who had been entertaining Padres fans for nearly a decade, arrived at the ballpark in a limousine. The absence of Roy Kroc was the only downside to opening day. Kroc died at age eighty-one of a heart attack on January 14, 1984. His wife, Joan, assumed ownership of the team.

The Padres fell behind Pittsburgh 1–0 in the top of the first. They came roaring back in the bottom of the inning. With Wiggins on base, Tony cracked a double to drive in Wiggins and tie the game, 1–1. Garry Templeton followed with a single to score Tony for a 2–1 Padres lead. Later in the game, McReynolds and Martinez socked home runs. The Padres rolled to a 5–1 victory.

San Diego zoomed out of the gate with a 10–2 start. It was by far the best opening to a season in franchise history. The Padres' fast start impressed *Sports Illustrated* writer Steve Wulf. An article by Wulf featured the Padres in the magazine's April 16, 1984 issue. The headline to Wulf's piece read, "The Beast Team in Baseball."[1]

Tony Gwynn

Tony hit a torrid .434 for the month of April. He was voted National League Player-of-the-Month. The Padres were 18–11 when vestiges of the past returned to haunt them. They dropped seven in a row to fall to 18–18.

San Diego thus was reeling when it faced the Montreal Expos on May 17. Tony and Alan Wiggins sparked the team. All day, they hectored Montreal pitching. Tony stole two bases and Wiggins stole five to propel the Padres to a 5–4 victory. The win pushed their record back above the .500 mark, at 19–18.

The May 17 game recharged the team. Tony's bat cooled off in May. In June he cranked it up. On June 1, 2, and 3, he had three consecutive three-hit games, with the Padres winning two of the three. On the second weekend of June, San Diego swept the Cincinnati Reds to vault into first place in the NL West.

Tony reveled in the team atmosphere at Class A Amarillo in 1982. He recognized the same loose, fun-loving manner with the 1984 Padres. Music blared in the clubhouse. Tony relaxed playing pool with "Puff" (Graig Nettles), "Tempy" (Garry Templeton), and "Mac" (Kevin McReynolds).

The Padres participated in another notable game on June 27 against the Dodgers. They were losing 5–0 in the top of the ninth. Dodgers ace Fernando Valenzuala had shut them down, scattering three hits.

Dick Williams' brusque manner turned off some major leaguers. Tony wasn't one of them (National Baseball Hall of Fame and Museum, Cooperstown, NY).

8. A Pennant and a Batting Title

Alan Wiggins batted first in the inning and flied out. Tony batted second and grounded out to the first baseman. Valenzuala was one out from a complete-game victory. The Padres staged a furious rally. They clocked five hits, chased Valenzuala out of the box, and closed the gap to 5–4. With runners on first and third, Kevin McReynolds struck out to end the game.

Tony and many of his teammates considered the June 27 contest another turning point in the 1984 season. The two-out rally signified the team's resiliency. Despite losing the game, the players celebrated in the clubhouse. Normally, watching a team celebrate a loss would impel Dick Williams to blow his top. Instead, he took it in stride. "It pulled us together as a team," he believed.[2]

San Diego went 19–10 in June. Tony was leading the National League in batting average. He was voted a starter for the National League All-Star team. Though shy at times, Tony loved to mingle. He chatted up every All-Star player he could find. He knocked out one hit in three at bats with a stolen base in a 3–1 National League win.

Tony believed a four-game series at home in July had torpedoed the Padres division title hopes in 1983. In the 1983 series the Pirates swept San Diego four straight.

Tony had ominous remembrances of 1983 when San Diego traveled to Pittsburgh in July 1984 for a six-game set. The Pittsburgh series got off to a bad start. The Pirates conquered San Diego in the first game, 5–1. The two teams played a doubleheader the next day. The Pirates won again in the first tilt. Things looked grim for San Diego in the second game. For seven innings tough Pirates leftie John Tudor kept the Padres bats in check. San Diego trailed, 1–0. In the top of the eighth, Tony kicked his team out of the doldrums. Reserve catcher Bruce Bochy and Alan Wiggins reached base on infield hits. Batting next, Tony smashed a three-run homer off Tudor. Tony's four-bagger was the game's decisive blow. The Padres held on to win, 3–2. Pirates manager Chuck Tanner praised Tony. "We contained everyone but one guy. It may not be possible to stop Tony Gwynn. He covers the entire plate, hits the ball hard everywhere, and has the speed to beat out the choppers."[3]

San Diego split the Pittsburgh series 3–3. Tony was satisfied with the split given the Pirates' four-game sweep in 1983. He hit a mere five home runs during the 1984 season. But his home run shot in Pittsburgh was another signature point in the Padres 1984 season.

The Padres avoided the second-half slumps they experienced in

Tony Gwynn

1982 and 1983. They posted a 21–9 record for the month of July. On July 31, they led the NL West by eight and a half games.

Tony set a torrid batting pace in July. He hit .398 for the month with 15 RBIs. At the end of the month, he was batting .366 for the season and leading the National League.

The Padres held a nine and a half game lead over the second-place Braves when they headed to Atlanta for an August 10–12 series. The teams split a doubleheader on August 10. San Diego won on August 11 to extend their lead over Atlanta to ten and a half.

On paper, Sunday's August 12 game featured an outstanding pitching matchup between Atlanta's Pascual Perez, 10–4 on the season, and San Diego's Ed Whitson, at 12–5 and fulfilling his potential as a starting pitcher foreseen two years prior by Jack McKeon. The game began under a thick cloud cover. Perhaps, the weather left the players in a feisty mood. Alternately, maybe it was the phase of the moon. In any event, the August 12 Padres–Braves game was among the strangest in baseball history.

On the game's first pitch, Atlanta pitcher Perez plunked Alan Wiggins on the ribs. Perez batted for Atlanta in the bottom of the second. Deciding to retaliate for the pitch that hit Wiggins, Whitson threw a ball behind Perez. After Perez struck out, Padres catcher Terry Kennedy followed him to the Atlanta dugout. Perez turned and raised his bat toward Kennedy. Fortunately, Atlanta reserve Bob Watson defused the possible confrontation. Watson grabbed Perez from behind and pulled him away from Kennedy. Home plate umpire Steve Rippley issued a warning to both teams.

Perez batted again in the fourth. Whitson threw three consecutive fastballs inside in evident attempts to hit Perez. The elusive Atlanta pitcher evaded all three Whitson pitches. Home plate umpire Rippley had seen enough. He ejected Whitson and Dick Williams for presumably ordering Whitson to hit Perez.

Perez batted a third time in the sixth. San Diego's pitching staff had performed capably all season but appeared incapable of tagging Perez. Tony's Class A teammate Greg Booker threw at Perez but the ball sailed over Perez's head. Having a busy day, Rippley thumbed Booker and Padres coach Ozzie Virgil.

The histrionics of the game's first seven innings were merely preliminary. Tempting fate, Atlanta sent Perez to the plate a fourth time in the eighth. What happened next triggered one of the all-time chaotic brawls in major league history. Succeeding where his teammates

8. *A Pennant and a Batting Title*

failed, Padres reliever Craig Lefferts nailed Perez with a fastball. At this point, Tony recalled, "All hell broke loose."[4] Players for both teams emptied their dugouts and charged the field. Wisely, Perez beelined for the safety of the Atlanta dugout with Padres reserve Champ Summers in hot pursuit. Two Atlanta players blocked Summers and wrestled him to the ground, protecting Perez. Meanwhile, players and coaches were pushing, shoving, and punching in all corners of the diamond.

Tony was not the fighting sort. He was, however, an "other-centered" person. He empathized with those he believed were being maltreated. He was offended when he spotted an Atlanta player holding Padres pitching coach Norm Sherry in a headlock. Sherry was not a big man. Of more import to Tony, Sherry had a heart condition. Tony was just under six foot but he was strong and built like a tank. He rushed to Sherry's defense. He threw the Atlanta player off his coach.

Some Atlanta fans decided to join the fun. They threw items at the Padres players. One fan jumped out the stands and entered the field. Players formerly tussling with each other turned and held off the fan.

The melee lasted nearly fifteen minutes. The umpires and the Atlanta police managed to restore order. The umpires' crew chief, John McSherry, tossed three Braves players, two Padres players, and two Padres coaches.

The eighth inning slugfest was epic but it wasn't the last one. Graig Nettles had blasted a home run in the seventh. Apparently sensing an opportunity for further retaliation, Atlanta pitcher Donnie Moore clanked Nettles with a pitch in the top of the ninth. An irate Nettles charged the mound. Two Atlanta players intercepted Nettles and wrestled him down. For a second time in the game, both dugouts emptied. There was more pushing, shoving, and punching. Atlanta's fans weren't done either. They tossed open beers at Padres players. When he was doused with a beer, Padres reserve infielder Kurt Bevacqua, in Tony's words, "went berserk." Bevacqua leaped on top of the San Diego dugout wielding a bat and poised to take on the entire Atlanta fan base. Before it got ugly, Atlanta police restrained Bevacqua.

After order was restored, crew chief John McSherry evicted Atlanta pitcher Moore and Atlanta manager Joe Torre. The Atlanta police arrested several fans. McSherry commanded all players not in the lineup out of their dugouts and back to their dressing rooms.

Through the various calamities of the day, a nine-inning baseball game was completed. Atlanta won, 5–3. Umpire McSherry was distraught after the game. He said the San Diego–Atlanta fiasco was "the worst thing I've seen in my life." He feared the Padres and Braves had "set baseball back 50 years."[5] National League president Chubb Feeney echoed McSherry. The brawl in Atlanta, he asserted, was the worst in baseball history.

Braves manager Joe Torre helpfully informed local sportswriters that "Dick Williams is an idiot with a capital I."[6] Retorted Williams, "You can tell Torre to take that finger he's pointing and stick it."[7] Williams asserted that San Diego had "some honor to defend." Atlanta, he opined, attempted to intimidate his team.

The brawls were intense moments for Tony and all involved. Typical of Tony, later he saw the humor of it. He amused himself on occasion by settling back in an easy chair at home and viewing a tape of the two August 12 brawls.

San Diego was too good a team to be sidetracked by the fisticuffs in Atlanta. They clinched the NL West division title on September 20. That evening, Goose Gossage hosted a raucous victory celebration at his house. There was a swimming pool in the backyard. Eventually, the pool was too much of a temptation for some of the celebrants. They hoisted various patrons into the drink.

Tony excelled in his first full major league season. He batted .351— tops in the major leagues. He won the National League batting title by thirty points. He drove in 71 RBIs and stole 33 bases. He struck out a paltry 23 times in 606 at bats.

Leadoff batter Alan Wiggins energized the offense. He batted .258 but drew 75 walks. He pilfered 70 bases, second-best in the National League.

Tony, who batted second in the batting order, gave Wiggins due credit. He had good reason. He hit for a .412 average during the 1984 season with Wiggins on base. "You talk about a catalyst." he told writers, "It seemed like every time I came up Wiggy was on base. He was Mr. Excitement."[8] Tony explained that he refrained at swinging at pitches when he saw that Wiggins had a good jump on the pitcher and a chance to steal a base. At the same time, because he had good bat control he could aim for holes left by the infielders moving. (Meaning he hit to holes in the defense when infielders were moving to cover a base Wiggins was attempting to steal.) Furthermore, fearing Wiggins' threat to steal, Tony pointed out, pitchers threw him fastballs that were good pitches to hit.

Tony praised Dick Williams. He said Williams was "a winner who taught his players how to play the game, how to win and to be mentally tough."[9]

8. A Pennant and a Batting Title

In 1984 there were no major league wild card or division series in the post-season. The winners of the National and American League East and West divisions clashed for the pennant in a five-game series. The Padres would face the winners of the NL East for the pennant and another franchise with a frustrating past—the Chicago Cubs.

Chapter 9

World Series

San Diego finished the 1984 regular season with a 92–70 record. They won their division by 12 games. The Cubs took the NL East with a 96–65 mark. They bested the second-place New York Mets by six and a half games.

Cubs fans had suffered a long period of futility—longer than the Padres. The Cubs had last won a World Series in 1908. Their most recent World Series appearance was 1945. Some claimed the Cubs were plagued by a curse from a goat. In 1945, a Chicago businessman purchased a ticket to Game 4 of the World Series for himself and his goat. The businessman and the goat were initially admitted into Wrigley Field. After complaints from patrons about the goat's smell, Cubs management evicted the goat and the businessman from the ballpark. The businessman reputedly imposed a hex on the Cubs. They will never win again, he supposedly said.[1]

Curse or not, oddsmakers installed the Cubs as favorites to win their best-of-five game playoff series against San Diego. The two teams met 12 times during the regular season, each team winning six games. Oddsmakers set the Cubs as favorites primarily because of Cubs pitcher Rick Sutcliffe. The Cubs obtained Sutcliffe in a mid-season trade with the Cleveland Indians. Sutcliffe had only won 4 and lost 5 for Cleveland. With the Cubs, the six-foot-seven Sutcliffe went on a tear. He was 16–1 for Chicago and the most dominant pitcher in the National League. Should the series go the full five games, Sutcliffe was expected to pitch Games 1 and 5. He was thought to be the difference between two otherwise evenly-matched teams.

The Cubs hosted Games 1 and 2. They played like the favorites in Game 1. They roasted San Diego, 13–0. Sutcliffe pitched seven innings of two-hit shutout ball, while striking out eight. Cubs reliever Warren Brusstar mopped up in the eighth and ninth.

Tony was a frustrating 0-for-4 in Game 1. He was given one chance to produce in the fifth inning. With San Diego trailing 5–0 and Templeton on third and Wiggins on first, he grounded out to short.

9. World Series

The Cubs forged a 3–0 lead in Game 2. Tony scored San Diego's first run of the series in the top of the fourth. He slapped a double to left field, reached third on a groundout, and scored on a sacrifice fly to cut the gap to 3–1. The Cubs responded with a run in the bottom of the fourth to increase their lead to 4–1. Tony contributed to San Diego's second run of the game in the sixth. His groundout advanced Wiggins from first to second. Wiggins scored on a Garvey single to make it 4–2. Tony had a chance to drive in a run in the eighth. With Wiggins on second and two out, he flied out to left to end a San Diego threat.

The Cubs won Game 2 by a 4–2 count. For the second straight game, Cubs pitching stifled San Diego bats. Cubs starter Steve Trout pitched eight and a third innings yielding only five hits. Cubs reliever Lee Smith retired the final two San Diego batters to seal the victory. With their team holding a 2–0 lead and one victory from a National League pennant, Cubs fans were feeling sprightly. The curse of the goat was tottering.

After losing Game 2, the Padres were in a funk. We can't get anything going, moaned Dick Williams.[2] Tony said to a *Sports Illustrated* writer that it was as if the National League Championship series "was starring" the Chicago Cubs but with an appearance by the San Diego Padres.[3]

Games 3, 4, and 5 were set for San Diego. The Padres team plane was delayed three hours at Chicago's O'Hare Airport. The disposition of the Padres players darkened when they learned air traffic controllers cleared the Cubs plane to take off first.

The mood on the flight to San Diego was somber. Assuming they were about to be knocked out of the playoffs, some players discussed their plans for the offseason. The team's spirits further deteriorated upon their arrival in San Diego. Only a smattering of fans showed up at the airport to greet them. The players trudged to the team buses that would transport them from the airport to their cars parked at Jack Murphy Stadium.

The scene they encountered at Jack Murphy amazed the players and coaches. Despite the late hour, thousands of fans cheered the arrival of the team buses. Long-time San Diego sportswriter Bob Chandler was traveling with the Padres. "I have never seen the mood of a team change as radically," Chandler wrote later, "as when the Padres saw their reception."[4] Players and coaches exited the buses and waded through the crowd high-fiving fans. Dick Williams found a motor scooter and circulated among the throng. Reserve outfielder Bobby Brown grabbed a

Tony Gwynn

bullhorn and repeatedly shouted, "Three in a row." The response of the fans, said Tony, "moved everybody."[5]

A raucous crowd of 58,346 packed Jack Murphy Stadium for Game 3. The fans sang "We ain't afraid of no Cubs," mimicking a song from the hit movie, "Ghostbusters."

Tony tried to spark the Padres in the bottom of the first. He hit a double but he was left stranded at second base. He stroked a single in the fourth but he was scrubbed out by a double play.

The Cubs jumped to the early lead for the third straight game of the series. They led 1–0 on a double by right fielder Keith Moreland and a single by third baseman Ron Cey.

San Diego finally took their first lead of the series in the fourth, scoring three runs. The Padres broke the game open in the sixth. Tony led off with a single for his third hit of the game. He scored on a ground-out and a single by Graig Nettles for a 4–1 Padres advantage. Later in the inning, Kevin McReynolds socked a three-run homer which ended the scoring for the game. San Diego won, 7–1.

Another boisterous crowd attended Game 4. Fans greeted pregame introductions of Cubs players with shouts of "Who cares?"[6] Game 4 was, however, an instant classic. The Padres broke to a 2–0 lead in the third inning. Tony drove in the first run with a sacrifice fly. Garvey's double scored Alan Wiggins for the second run.

The Cubs roared back. They took a 3–2 lead on a two-run homer by catcher Jody Davis and a solo home run by first baseman Leon Durham. Garvey singled in a San Diego run in the fifth to knot the score at 3–3.

The Cubs showed their respect for Tony's bat in the seventh. With a Padre runner on second and first base open, they walked Tony intentionally. That brought up Garvey. He made the Cubs pay. He singled to drive in a run for his third RBI of the game. Tony ran from first to third on Garvey's single. He scored on a passed ball. San Diego led the see-saw contest, 5–3.

Once again, the Cubs scrambled back. They tied the score 5–5 with two runs in the top of the ninth. The Cubs brought in their best reliever and future Hall-of-Famer Lee Smith to pitch the bottom of the ninth. Smith fanned leadoff hitter Alan Wiggins. Batting next, Tony drove a Smith pitch to center field for a single. Garvey had driven in a run in the third, fifth, and seventh innings. Against Smith in the bottom of the ninth, he delivered again. He drilled a Smith fastball into the seats for a 7–5 Padres victory. The series was now tied at two games apiece. The curse of the goat was percolating.

9. World Series

Tony called Garvey's five-RBI effort in Game 4 one of the best examples of clutch hitting he had ever seen. Four times in the game, Garvey notched a hit to drive in a San Diego runner.

The oddsmakers figured the Cubs for favorites because of the pitching of Rick Sutcliffe. It was Sutcliffe who took the hill for Chicago in the series-deciding Game 5. He had stymied the Padres in Game 1 when the Cubs coasted to a 13–0 victory. He had beaten the Padres twice during the regular season.

For the fourth time in the series, the Cubs grabbed the early lead. Leon Durham blasted a two-run homer. Later, Jody Davis clubbed a solo homer. The Cubs were on top, 3–0. With a solid early lead and Sutcliffe on the mound, Cubs fans were optimistic.

Sutcliffe breezed through the first five innings. He limited San Diego to two hits. He mastered Tony, striking him out in the first and inducing a ground out in the third. Leading off the sixth, Alan Wiggins dropped a bunt for a single. Tony nicked Sutcliffe for another single to put runners on first and second. Sutcliffe walked Garvey to load the bases. A sacrifice fly by Nettles scored Wiggins and moved Tony to third. Terry Kennedy's sacrifice fly scored Tony. The Padres sliced the Cubs' lead to 3–2.

Sutcliffe had been the mainstay of the Cubs' division-title winning season. Despite yielding two runs in the sixth, Chicago manager Jim Frey sent Sutcliffe out to pitch the seventh. Said Tony later, "I knew we could get to him [Sutcliffe] because he was getting his pitches up. He was wilting and you could see it happening."[7]

Proving Tony's point, Sutcliffe walked leadoff batter Carmelo Martinez on four pitches. A sacrifice fly sent Martinez to second. The next San Diego batter, pinch hitter Tim Flannery, hit what appeared to be a routine ground ball to first baseman Leon Durham. Flannery should have been the second out of the inning. Instead, the ball skidded off the edge of the infield grass and skipped under Durham's glove for an error. Martinez came home on the play to tie it, 3–3.

Alan Wiggins followed with a single. The Cubs gamely stuck with Sutcliffe. Tony came up with Flannery on second and Wiggins on first. It is hard to fathom that a ball bouncing off the infield was one of the hardest Tony ever hit. Still, it is true. Tony ripped a Sutcliffe pitch toward Cubs second baseman Ryne Sandberg. Had Sandberg snagged the ball the Cubs could have turned an easy double play to end the inning with the game tied. Tony's hit struck the infield turf with such force that it bounded over Sandberg's head and rolled deep into the outfield for a double. Sandberg remarked later that Tony's rocket almost took his face off. Flannery and Wiggins scored on Tony's hit for a 5–3 San Diego lead. The goat was bleating. Garvey singled to drive in Tony and push the lead to 6–3.

Rich Gossage allowed a single in the eighth and a single in the ninth but otherwise shut down the Cubs, completing the Padres' comeback from the 0–2 hole they dug to begin the series. They were National League champs. Some Cub fans scoffed at notions of a curse. Others, however, had much to chew on considering the crazy bounce of Flannery's ball under Durham's glove and Tony's hit that eluded Sandberg. The Cubs would wait another 32 years to win the World Series.

Garvey was voted MVP of the series. He hit .400 with seven RBIs. Tony was close behind with seven hits in 18 at bats for a .368 average. He scored six runs in the series and drove in the winning run in Game 5.

A sixteen-year veteran of the major leagues, Steve Garvey described the Cubs–Padres series as "the greatest playoffs he had ever seen."[8] Tony credited the San Diego fans. Recollecting the fans' reception at Jack Murphy after the Padres lost Game 2 and their frenetic cheering in Games 3, 4, and 5, Tony noted that, "They believed in us, and we started to believe in us."[9]

The Padres' upcoming opponent in the World Series was no bargain. The Detroit Tigers won 35 of their first 40 games in the regular season—the best 40-game start in major league history. They won 104 games. They captured the AL East title by a whopping 15 games. They swept the AL West champion Kansas City Royals three straight to win the pennant.

The Tigers were not laden with superstars. But they had productive hitters at every position. Catcher Lance Parrish hit 33 homers, right fielder Kirk Gibson 27, center fielder Chet Lemon 20, first baseman/third baseman Darrell Evans 16, shortstop Alan Trammell 14, and second baseman Lou Whitaker 13. Eight Tiger batters drove in 50 or more runs in the regular season.

The Tigers also had a deep pitching staff. Their ace, Jack Morris, won 19 games, Dan Petry 18, and Milt Wilcox 17. Their front-line reliever Willie Hernandez went 9–3. He appeared in 80 games with two saves and a 1.92 ERA. Another Tigers reliever, Aurelio Lopez, won 10 games, losing only one.

The 1984 World Series opened on October 9 in San Diego before 57,908 fans. The Padres played from behind for much of their playoff series against the Cubs. They fell behind again early in Game 1 of the

9. World Series

World Series. The Tigers scored a run in the first on Whitaker's double and Trammell's single. As in the Cubs series, San Diego struck back. Alan Wiggins fanned to lead of the first. In his first World Series at bat, Tony flied out to right. Then, the Padres staged a two-out rally. Garvey and Nettles singled. Terry Kennedy's double plated both runners for a 2–1 San Diego lead.

San Diego threatened again in the third. Alan Wiggins singled. Tony walked. Steve Garvey came up next. Garvey had been spectacular in the post-season with runners on base. Detroit starter Jack Morris bore down and forced Garvey to ground into an inning-ending double play.

A two-run homer by Lance Parrish in the fifth swung the lead back to Detroit, 3–2. In the bottom half, Tony responded with his first World Series hit, a two-out single to center. Tony put himself in scoring position by stealing second. Once again Morris put down the clamps, enticing Garvey into another ground out.

Behind 3–2, San Diego took another run at Morris in the bottom of the sixth. Graig Nettles and Terry Kennedy led off the inning with single. It was at that point, Tony observed, when Morris simply decided to throw his best stuff. Morris struck out the next three Padres batters.

Still trying to tie the game or take the lead, Tony drew a two-out walk in the seventh. Tony tried again to steal second but he was thrown out by Detroit catcher Lance Parrish to end the inning. Detroit won Game 1 by a 3–2 count. Jack Morris pitched a complete game.

The Tigers pounded Padres starter Ed Whitson in Game 2. Detroit raced to a 3–0 lead in the top of the first with four singles, a stolen base, and a sacrifice fly. The Padres fought back in the bottom of the first. Wiggins singled. Tony walked, and two sacrifice flies scored Wiggins to make it 3–1. San Diego scored another run off Detroit starter Dan Petry in the fourth. Tony also came up in the fourth. There were two runners on base so he had a chance to tie the game or put San Diego ahead. He hit a long fly ball to right field that Kirk Gibson chased down for the final out of the inning.

The Padres finally broke through in the bottom of the fifth. Kurt Bevacqua smashed a three-run homer for a 5–3 San Diego advantage. That turned out to be the final score. The Padres relievers pitched well in Game 2. After Whitson's shaky start, Andy Hawkins and Craig Lefferts combined for eight and a third innings of shutout ball.

The two teams traveled to Detroit for Games 3, 4, and 5. The Tigers waxed another Padres starter, Tim Lollar, in Game 3. They scored four

Tony Gwynn

runs in the second inning. The game ended with a 5–2 Detroit win. Tony played a role in both San Diego runs. He singled in the third to send Wiggins from first to third. Wiggins scored on Garvey's groundout. Tony singled again in the seventh. He took third on Garvey's double. He scored on Nettles' sacrifice fly. Tony went 2-for-5 in Game 3.

Tigers shortstop Alan Trammell was the star of Game 4. He slugged a two-run homer in the first and another two-run shot in the third. Tony committed an error in the third when he fumbled Lou Whitaker's single. Whitaker took second on Tony's error. The error made no difference in the final tally. Trammell followed with his third inning home run so Whitaker would have scored in any event.

In Game 4 Jack Morris pitched his second complete game of the World Series. He yielded a run in the second and in the ninth in Detroit's 4–2 win. Tony had one hit in four at bats.

Down three games to one in the series, San Diego was one loss from elimination. Tony was having a solid World Series excepting his error in Game 3. He was batting .364 with a .421 on-base percentage.

Tony was ineffective in Game 5. He was 0-for-5. Four times in the game he made an out with a runner on base. The Tigers blew out to a 3–0 lead. San Diego chipped away to tie it, 3–3. In the fifth, Detroit loaded the bases. Detroit designated hitter Rusty Kuntz lofted a fly ball to right. It would have been an easy play for Tony. But, he lost the ball in the sun. Wiggins, the second baseman, covered for Tony and made a running catch of Kuntz's fly ball. Wiggins' back was to the plate when he caught the ball. Taking advantage of Wiggins' awkward position, Kirk Gibson tagged at third and scored to put Detroit ahead, 4–3. Had Tony, running in, caught the ball Gibson would have had no chance to score.

Later in the game, each team scored a run to make it 5–4, Detroit. The Tigers put the game away in the bottom of the eighth. Kirk Gibson blasted a Goose Gossage slider into the right field seats to put Detroit ahead, 8–4. Four years later, injured, and practically standing on one leg, Gibson hit a dramatic homer for the Dodgers in the 1988 World Series. After his equally dramatic home run in Game 5 of the 1984 World Series, Gibson rounded the bases jabbing his right fist into the air.

Tony struck out with Wiggins on base in the first inning, grounded out with Bobby Brown on in the third, and flied out in the fourth with Wiggins on second and the score tied, 3–3. He suffered one more Game 5 indignity in the ninth. With Bruce Bochy on base with a single, he lifted a lazy fly ball to left field for the final out of the World Series. The

9. World Series

Detroit Tigers, one of the best teams of the post–World War II era, were world champs.

Despite the disappointments of Game 5 of the World Series, Tony's first full season in the majors was a success. In addition to leading the majors in batting average, he led in hits with 213. He started for the National League in the All-Star game. He delivered some key hits, including his three-run homer in the crucial regular season series with Pittsburgh and his two-run double in Game 5 of the National League Championship Series against the Cubs. He finished third in National League MVP voting behind Chicago's Ryne Sandberg and the New York Mets' Keith Hernandez.

Tony received a Silver Bat Award from the Louisville Slugger Company for winning the National League batting title. He prized the award. But he was more concerned with his defense, annoyed by his misplay of Whitaker's single in Game 4 of the World Series and losing Kuntz's fly ball in Game 5. He knew he needed to improve his defense.

CHAPTER 10

"Unbelievable" with Two Strikes

Tony informed a *San Diego Union* reporter he doubted he would match or exceed a .351 batting average for the 1985 season. Nevertheless, he understood the expectations fans and team owners set for professional athletes. "You've got to do it every year." he said to the *Union*, "It's not what you did last year. It's 'What you have done for me lately?'"[1]

Tony said he was confident he would bat above .300. "You have to be confident when you go up to the plate," he told the reporter. You have to say, "'This guy can't get me out.'" If not, "you're going down the tubes."[2] Tony was right. He failed to hit .351 but he batted above .300 for the third consecutive season with a .317 average, six homers, and 46 RBIs. He struck out a mere 33 times in 622 at bats. He finished fourth in the National League in batting behind Willie McGee, Vladimir Guerrero, and Tim Raines.

The Padres entered the 1985 season picked by many to repeat as NL West champs. In the offseason they had shored up their starting pitching, which had been pounded by the Tigers in the 1984 World Series. They acquired LaMarr Hoyt in a trade with the Chicago White Sox. Hoyt fell to a 13–18 record for the Sox in 1984. Prior to the 1984 season, however, he had gone 9–3 in 1980 and 1981, 19–15 in 1982, and 24–10 in 1983. With the acquisition of Hoyt the Padres could rely on four dependable starters in Hoyt, Eric Show, Andy Hawkins, and Dave Dravecky.

The Padres were slow out of the gate the first two weeks of the 1985 season. In the meantime, Tony continued to burnish his reputation for being a tough out. On April 21, Dodgers pitcher Orel Hershiser, on his way to the best season of his career with a 19–3 record, was cruising with a no-hitter in the seventh inning when Tony tagged him for a double. Five days later, Hershiser pitched a complete game, limiting the Padres to one hit and one walk—both by Tony.

10. "Unbelievable" with Two Strikes

On April 28, San Diego confronted Fernando Valenzuala, another tough Dodgers pitcher. With the game tied 0–0 and one out in the ninth, Tony slammed a home run off Valenzuala for the only run of the game. The Padres' 1–0 win pushed their record to 10–8 and propelled them into first place in the NL West. Years later, Valenzuala recollected that Tony had nicked him for a number of hits during their careers. Valenzuala couldn't remember all those hits but he remembered Tony's home run blast on April 28, 1985. "What can you do?" said Valenzuala. "You hit one corner [of home plate] and Tony hits it that way. You hit the other corner, he hits it the other way."[3]

Despite taking over first place during their April 25–28 series with the Dodgers, the Padres suffered a blow to their division title hopes on April 25. Their second baseman and team sparkplug, Alan Wiggins, disappeared on April 25. The Padres tracked him down the afternoon of April 26.

Wiggins suffered a drug relapse, apparently from using cocaine. He checked into a drug rehab facility in Minnesota for 30 days. After he was released, the Padres assigned him to Triple A Las Vegas. Wiggins had suffered a similar drug episode when he was with the Padres in 1982. The Padres thus decided to unload him. They traded him to the Baltimore Orioles on June 27.

Wiggins played two and a half seasons with Baltimore. He failed a drug test during the 1987 season. He was suspended by Major League Baseball. Wiggins' once-promising professional baseball career ended. On January 6, 1991, Alan Wiggins died of complications from AIDS, which he contracted by intravenous drug use. He was an early casualty of the AIDS epidemic.

Wiggins varied from the stereotype of a drug addict. He was an intellectual who excelled at mathematics. He knowledgeably discussed religion, economics, and African American history. Wiggins' presence was such, Tony once pointed out, that the Padres divided into "pro–Wiggins" and "anti–Wiggins" factions. For some of his teammates, Wiggins' intellectualism seemed at odds with the tough-guy culture of professional baseball.

Tony stood firmly in the "pro–Wiggins" camp. "To not like Alan Wiggins," Tony said, "is to not know Alan Wiggins."[4] Different or unusual people never bothered Tony. He accepted people as they were. He could get along with a wide variety of personalities.

Wiggins continued to live in the San Diego area after he was traded to Baltimore. Tony stayed in touch. He remained a friend for the rest of

Tony Gwynn

Wiggins' life. It would not be the last time drug addiction would strike down one of Tony's teammates. Wiggins' absence hurt the Padres running game. They stole 60 bases in 1985, worst in the majors, compared to 152 thefts in 1984.

Tony had a banner month of June. Batting in the .280s or the .290s for the bulk of May, he went on a tear in June. He had two-hit games on June 2, 3, 8, 12, and 14 and three-hit games on June 1, 4, 10, and 16. He raised his batting average to .329 after the first game of a June 16 doubleheader.

Tony was also proud of his younger brother, Chris. The baseball career of Tony's older brother, Charles Jr., had been cut short by knee injuries. Chris, in contrast, followed Tony to San Diego State. As a sophomore, Chris excelled during the 1984 college baseball season. He belted 19 home runs and batted .383. He was named a first-team college All-American.

The annual exhibition game between the Padres and San Diego State was held before more than 30,000 fans on April 5, 1985. Before the game, Tony and Chris competed in a home-run hitting contest. Tony prevailed, seven home runs to five. Chris was not surprised he lost to Tony in the home run contest. Most San Diego baseball fans assumed that Chris possessed more power than Tony. Chris wasn't buying it. He knew Tony could hit more homers if he wanted to, but his game was to hit for average and put the ball in play.[5]

In the June 1985 draft, the Dodgers selected Chris in the first round. Tony's fellow participant in backyard games of "sock ball" was charting a path to the Major Leagues.

San Diego battled for first place throughout June and into July. On July 4, they were five games ahead in the NL West. Then, the bottom fell out. They lost eight of their next 11 games. They shuttled between second, third, and fourth place. By early September they were flailing at .500, with a 71–71 mark.

From September 9–12, the Padres were in Cincinnati for a four-game set against the Reds. Pete Rose was on the verge of baseball history. On September 8, he notched hit number 4,191 to tie Ty Cobb for the all-time Major League record in career hits. Rose was poised to break the record against San Diego.

Rose sat out on September 9. LaMarr Hoyt, who would go 16–8 for the 1985 season, shut down Rose on September 10. In his first at bat on September 11, Rose laced a single to left center to break Cobb's record. Tony was stationed in right field. He remembered Rose's generosity in

10. "Unbelievable" with Two Strikes

his first major league game. Rose went out of his way to shake Tony's hand after Tony's first major league hit. He kidded Tony about catching him in one day after Tony's second hit of the game.

Teammates and other well-wishers surrounded Rose after his historic blow. Tony wanted to return the favor to Rose and shake his hand.

Tony could be both gregarious and shy. He could chat up almost anyone—teammates, fans, sportswriters, opposing players, and umpires. At the same time, he did not like to draw attention to himself. He also possessed a strong sense of decorum. He decided, he admitted later, it was not his place to barge into Rose's celebration.[6]

On September 20, Tony drove in four runs to lead San Diego to an 11–1 win over Atlanta. The Padres, from there, went on a late-season surge. They won nine of their final 15 games to finish at 83–79 and in a tie for third.

Tony was being recognized as one of baseball's most consistent hitters. Importantly, his defense was improving. Tony was no speed demon, but, as his first college basketball coach Tim Vezie observed, he was quick with a surprising ability to accelerate. Tony got to balls hit to the outfield easy enough. But throughout his high school, college and early professional baseball careers, baserunners took advantage of his mediocre throwing arm. Tony's hard work with Clyde McCullough, Tom House, and other coaches, and his on-season and off-season workouts practicing long throws from the outfield wall to the third base and home plate was beginning to pay off. He tossed out 14 runners from the outfield, third best in the National League, during the 1985 season.

Tony received another blessing in 1985. His second child, daughter Anisha, was born.

Drug issues continued to dog the Padres in 1986. On February 10, LaMarr Hoyt was caught with marijuana, Valium, and Quaaludes while crossing the border from Mexico to the U.S. Hoyt was stopped for running a red light eight days later. Police discovered marijuana in his car. Hoyt checked in for a 30-day drug rehab. He pitched a full 1986 season for San Diego but he was less effective in 1986 than in 1985. He won eight and lost 11. After the 1986 season, Hoyt was caught again with drugs at the U.S.–Mexican border. He subsequently served a 45-day prison sentence at Elgin Air Force Base in Florida. That was enough for the Padres. They released him. Hoyt caught on with his former team, the Chicago White Sox. When he was arrested yet again for possession of drugs, the White Sox cut him. Thereafter, Hoyt was out of professional baseball.

Tony Gwynn

The commissioner's office and the Major League Players Association quarreled about drug testing players. Having observed the problems experienced by Alan Wiggins and Hoyt, Tony and Padres shortstop Garry Templeton were vocal in their support of drug testing. "I'm tired of talking about drugs," said Tony.[7] Of course, Tony had to know he was hooked on a legal drug—smokeless chewing tobacco, which he used regularly.

The Hoyt fiasco was one of two pre-season dramas for the Padres. Going into the 1986 season, manager Dick Williams had one year left on his contract. When Spring Training opened, Williams was nowhere to be found. San Diego's front office claimed Williams was negotiating for a better contract. Williams contended the front office was trying to force him out, noting the Padres had fired his friend and third base coach, Ozzie Virgil. The *San Diego Union* conducted a poll of the players which found that a majority, perhaps turned off by Williams' gruff management style, wanted him out.[8] Whatever the truth of the dispute between Williams and the front office, he resigned on February 24, 1986. The Padres hired their Coordinator of Minor League Instruction, Steve Boros, to replace Williams.

Tony was one of the players sorry to see Williams go. "People shouldn't forget that Dick Williams taught us how to win. A lot of our success was an extension of his personality because Dick was a perfectionist."[9] It was a compliment from one perfectionist to another. By 1986, Tony had amassed a video library of his at bats that he frequently reviewed. A game against the Montreal Expos on May 28, 1986, further illustrated Tony's quest for perfection. The Padres swamped the Expos, 10–1. Tony came to bat with one out in the ninth. Every Padre starter except Tony had hit sharply in the game. Saving their pitching staff, the Expos brought in second baseman Vance Law to pitch the ninth. The son of former Major League pitcher Vern Law, Vance had pitched in college. His fastball had been clocked at a creditable 86 miles per hour. His groundout against Law embarrassed Tony.[10] His teammates laughed. Tony laughed too, sort of. He generally did not dwell on past games but his failed at bat against Law bothered him for years thereafter.

Williams returned the compliment to Tony in his 1990 book "*No More Mr. Nice Guy: A Life of Hardball*." Reflecting on his managerial career with Boston, Oakland, Montreal, and San Diego, Williams wrote that when the Padres promoted Tony Gwynn to the big leagues it was "the nicest thing that ever happened to me." He added, "I don't think I've ever had a player who worked harder and cared more."[11]

10. "Unbelievable" with Two Strikes

The Padres got off to a decent start to the 1986 season. They were 45–43 at the All-Star break. They faded thereafter—a pattern they had followed in past seasons. They finished at 74–88 and in fourth place in the six-team NL West.

Tony's 1986 season featured several spectacular performances. On May 23, the Padres and the New York Mets were tied 4–4 with two outs in the bottom of the ninth. Facing the Mets' best reliever, Jesse Orosco, Tony clouted a broken-bat, three-run homer for a 7–4 Padres victory. Prior to batting against Orosco in the ninth, Tony told his teammate, John Kruk, he was taking Orosco deep. Tony guessed fastball on Orosco's first pitch. He smoked it.

Tony led the Padres to victories with four-hit games on May 14 and 21. After a 2-for-5 outing on May 24, he was batting .363, best in the National League.

Tony again vexed Dodger pitching in a three-game series between June 20–22. He led San Diego to a three-game sweep, going 9-for-15 in the series. He was 3-for-4 and scored three runs in the Padres' 5–4 win on June 20. He went 4-for-6 with an RBI and scored the tying run in the ninth in the Padres' 8–7 win in 14 innings on June 21. He had two hits in five at bats with a triple and an RBI in their 5–4 victory on June 22.

Tony impressed Dodgers manager Tommy Lasorda. Gwynn is "unbelievable" with two strikes on him, Lasorda said. "You make a good pitch on him and he fouls it off and when you make a bad pitch, he hits it."[12] Tony, at this juncture of the season, still led the league in batting at .346.

Tony had another epic game against the Houston Astros on September 20. He clubbed four hits, his fifth four-hit game of the season and the eighth of his career, scored twice, and drove in one. What's more he tied the modern Major League record by stealing five bases—a feat last accomplished by his friend Alan Wiggins on May 17, 1984. Tony swiped second three times and third twice. Batting in the ninth, Tony was well aware of his chance to break the record. He hit a looper to right, saw his chance to stretch it to a double, and succeeded. John Kruk, Tony's old minor league teammate who had made it to the majors, batted next and flied out to end the game, which San Diego lost, 10–6. "If I had gotten on first on that hit," Tony said after the game, "I would have tried for six." Using a nickname as he liked to do, he added that he remembered "Wiggy" tying the record in 1984. In fact, he said, "I faked bunts four times so he could steal them."[13]

Tony Gwynn

Another notable game occurred on April 14. Employing an effective cut fastball, Dodgers pitcher Bob Welch struck out Tony three times. It was Gwynn's first three-strikeout game of his career, reported Mark Kreidler of the *San Diego Union*. Had Kreidler possessed a crystal ball, he could have called the game historic. Never again would Tony strike out three or more times in one game. Tony maintained he should have been punched out four times by Welch not three because the home plate umpire missed a pitch that should have been a called strike three.[14]

The April 14 game against the Dodgers demonstrated Tony's growing prowess on defense. With the game tied 3-all in the ninth, Dodgers second baseman Steve Sax led off with a double. Catcher Mike Scioscia followed with a single to Tony in right. Scioscia's hit was spinning away from Tony toward the right field line. Tony scooped up the ball, wheeled, and threw a strike to home to nail Sax trying to score. Padres catcher Terry Kennedy threw to second to catch Scioscia in a rundown to complete a double play. The play helped to preserve the 3–3 tie and send the game into extra innings. Reserve catcher Bruce Bochy won it for the Padres with a walk-off home run in the eleventh.

Tony had another outstanding defensive outing in New York against the Mets on August 27. Perched on third base in the first inning, the Mets Darryl Strawberry tried to score after a flyball out to Tony. Tony rifled a throw to home and Strawberry was tagged out. In the second, Rafael Santana attempted to stretch a single to right into a double. He was out on Tony's throw to second base. In the fifth, Keith Hernandez also tried

Tony pictured in a brown and gold Padres uniform he wore from 1982 through the 1990 season. He was not a fan of the color scheme (National Baseball Hall of Fame and Museum, Cooperstown, NY).

10. "Unbelievable" with Two Strikes

to stretch a single into a double but he was out at second on Tony's perfect throw.

In addition to throwing out three runners in one game, Tony collected three hits and stole two bases. "I've never seen anything like it," said Padres manager Steve Boros. "Tony put on a show out there."[15] A headline in the next days' *San Diego Union* referred to Tony as a "complete player."[16]

Tony led the National League in batting for much of the first half of the 1986 season. He faded into the .330s in July. Tim Raines of the Expos caught up with him. Tony and Raines fought for the batting lead throughout July, August, and into September. On September 20, Tony was in the lead at .335, the Dodgers' Steve Sax had made it up to second at .329, and Raines was third at .328. Raines poured it on his final five games to take the batting title at .334. Sax finished second at .332. Tony finished third with .329. Possibly energized by his pre-season home run hitting contest with brother Chris, Tony smacked 14 homers, 33 doubles, and seven triples. He knocked out 211 hits and swiped 37 bases. In later years, Tony would be critical of his approach to the 1986 race for the batting title. He decided he had spent too much time dwelling on the batting statistics of Raines and Sax and not enough on his own.[17]

On December 2, 1986, *The Sporting News* recognized Tony's excellence in the field. He was awarded a Gold Glove as the National League's leading defensive right fielder. Years earlier, Tony's father noted that Tony was a natural athlete in the batters' box. His fielding and throwing improved only from hard work. "I'd be lying if I said it [the Gold Glove] wasn't important to me," Tony said. "I'd be awfully proud of a Gold Glove."[18]

Thus far in his five-year Major League career, Tony had taken one National League batting title with a fourth place and a third place. He was just getting started.

Chapter 11

"If I had nine Tony Gwynns"

Tony's 1987 season was spectacular. His team, in contrast, was dysfunctional.

The Padres front office considered the even-tempered Steve Boros the perfect antidote to the sometimes irascible Dick Williams. The team's 74–88 record during the 1986 season convinced management that the Boros experiment had failed. San Diego fired him on October 28, 1986. The Padres replaced Boros with Larry Bowa. An outstanding defensive shortstop, Bowa competed for 16 seasons in the Major Leagues, primarily with the Philadelphia Phillies, but also with the Cubs, the Toronto Blue Jays, and the New York Mets. Bowa had only one season's experience managing a team but he impressed the Padres by leading their Triple A affiliate, the Las Vegas Stars, to the 1986 Pacific Coast League championship. Bowa's personality approached that of Dick Williams. He had been a fiery competitor when he was a player. Once, after an ineffective at bat, he stormed down the corridor between the dugout and the dressing room and smashed every light in the corridor with his bat.[1]

According to baseball tradition, Spring Training is a time for optimism about the upcoming season. Every team, after all, begins the season tied with a 0–0 record. Not one to mince words, Tony ignored tradition. "This team has got some holes," he informed *San Diego Union* sportswriter Mark Kreidler prior to a 1987 Spring Training game.[2]

Many of the veteran players who were instrumental to San Diego's drive to the National League pennant in 1984 and its challenge for the NL West division title in 1985 were gone from the team or in decline. Beset by his drug woes, LaMarr Hoyt was released on January 7, 1987. The Padres declined to offer Graig Nettles a contract after the 1986 season. The team traded Terry Kennedy to the Baltimore Orioles and Kevin McReynolds to the New York Mets. Steve Garvey was approaching the end of his nineteen-year Major League career—1987 would prove to be his final season. Rich Gossage remained a Padre but his 1986 ERA of 4.45 was his lowest since the 1973 season. Padres General Manager Jack

11. "If I had nine Tony Gwynns"

McKeon warned Bowa the team was going with younger or untested players, including outfielder Marvell Wynne, outfielder Stan Jefferson, third baseman Kevin Mitchell, and rookie catcher Benito Santiago.

Tony had become good friends with Montreal Expos left fielder Tim Raines. Raines was the reigning National League batting champion. He became a free agent on November 12, 1986. Tony pestered the Padres front office to sign Raines. The one-two punch of Alan Wiggins leading off and Tony batting second had helped to propel San Diego to the pennant in 1984. Tony envisioned a similar one-two combination with Raines leading off the top of the batting order.

Neither San Diego nor any other team tendered a serious offer to Raines. With no other viable options, Raines re-signed with the Expos. The Major League Players Association alleged the owners colluded in refusing to sign free agents after the 1985, 1986, and 1987 seasons. Later, in three separate arbitration decisions, arbitrators agreed with the players, finding that the owners had entered into a "gentlemen's agreement" not to pursue a free agent if his current team desired to retain him.

The Padres began their 1987 season with six road games. They lost five.

San Diego played their home opener on April 13 against the San Francisco Giants. Before a crowd of 48,686, Tony and two teammates made Major League history. Leading off the bottom of the first, Marvell Wynne clubbed a 3–2 pitch from Giants pitcher Roger Mason down the right field line for a home run. Batting second, Tony yanked a Mason fastball into the right field seats for another homer. Up next, John Kruk smashed a Mason slider to left for San Diego's third consecutive home run. It was the first time in Major League history that a team led off a game with three consecutive homers. After the game the Baseball Hall of Fame requested the three bats used for the historic home runs for its collection. The Padres quickly complied.

Despite their first inning heroics, the Padres lost their home opener to the Giants, 13–6. The team's anemic start was too much for Bowa. In the sixth inning, Padres second baseman Tim Flannery was forced out at second. The throw to first to complete a Giants double play was wide and the batter was called safe. Second base umpire Bob Engel ruled Flannery had veered outside the basepath while sliding into second. Accordingly, Engel reversed the safe call at first and awarded the Giants a double play. Bowa bolted out of the dugout. He threw down his cap, charged after Engel, and argued with the ump for more than two minutes. He was ejected from the game.

Tony Gwynn

The Padres stumbled to a 12–42 start, the worst in franchise history. He was still going to have fun playing baseball, Tony advised. To succeed in this game, he indicated to writers, you should have fun. Also, you must "work hard."[3]

Tony had fun and worked hard on April 16. Once more, he vexed star Dodgers pitcher Orel Hershiser. Tony nicked Hershiser for two doubles and two singles. Three of the pitches Tony hit were good pitches, lamented Hershiser after the game. Tony finished 5-for-5 for the first five-hit game of his career. The Padres eked out a rare victory, winning 3–2 in ten innings.

On May 10, Tony stepped up for the home crowd on Tony Gwynn Poster Night. Each fan attending the game received a color poster of the Padres star. Before the game, Tony was presented with a Silver Slugger award (best-hitting right fielder in the National League during the 1986 season) and his coveted 1986 Gold Glove. Tony went 2-for-4 with a walk, a home run, two RBIs, and three runs scored. The Padres slaughtered the Cubs, 14–2.

Tony ended the month of May with a .335 batting average. Off the field, he and spouse Alicia were forced into a difficult decision. On May 22, reporting liabilities of $1,147,000 and assets of $690,150, the Gwynns filed a bankruptcy petition with a San Diego federal court. Tony had been led astray by his agent. Apparently, he had co-signed loans for the agent's various business ventures. The ventures busted and the loans went sour.

He had been worrying about family finances for a year, Tony confessed.[4] Alicia would buck him up. She assured Tony it was going to be all right. Even four-year-old Tony Jr. tried to help by offering encouraging words to his dad.

Tony admitted he was embarrassed to file for bankruptcy thus exposing his financial failings to the public. At the same time, he noted, now that his financial woes were out in the open it was as if a mountain had fallen off his back. Tony and Alicia worked their way out of bankruptcy. Thereafter, Alicia was in charge of the family finances.

Tony performed in the month of June like a ballplayer with a mountain off his back. For the first six games of the month, he went, collectively, 15-for-26 with eight RBIs, six runs scored, and four stolen bases. He batted .473 for the month of June. He was named National League Player-of-the-Month. Tony's June hot streak bumped his batting average up to .383. For the first time in his career, but not the last, the talk began. Could Tony Gwynn hit .400 or above for a season? No one had

11. "If I had nine Tony Gwynns"

done it since Ted Williams hit .406 forty-six years before, in 1941. Rod Carew of the Minnesota Twins took a run at .400 during the 1977 season. He finished the year at .388. George Brett of the Kansas City Royals batted .390 in 1980.

Alicia was a believer. If Tony put his "mind to it," she contended, he can hit .400.[5] Sitting casually on a chair in the locker room with his feet propped up, Tony broached the .400 issue with writers. "Everybody's talking about it me but me," he chuckled. Tony reported that on a recent road trip he was hounded with the .400 question in Los Angeles and Chicago.[6]

A July 16, 1987, essay in the *San Diego Union* discussed the obstacles to batting .400. Teams are deploying specialized relief pitchers more than ever, the paper reported. Consequently, batters were forced to adjust mid-game to new pitching styles more frequently that when Ted Williams was playing. Furthermore, the article continued, Tony competed in 162-game seasons while Williams only had 154. Also, there was the strain of travel. That was particularly so, the essay pointed out, for a West Coast team. Tony and the Padres typically crossed two or three time zones on road trips. In addition, the *Union* piece indicated, Tony loathed travel. He hated to be away from Alicia and his children, Tony Jr. and Anisha.[7]

Tony doubted he could hit .400. He conceded that he could hit to all fields which was a necessity to bat .400. You have to walk a lot to hit .400, he maintained. In contrast, he did not walk that often. Also, assuming 650 official at bats (plate appearances without a walk, a sacrifice, or being hit by a pitch), you need 260 hits to bat .400. Tony thought getting that many hits was a lot to ask.

Tony's teammate, Tim Flannery, told the *Union* that Tony had one advantage—he played in the relative obscurity of San Diego. If Tony was on a team in Chicago or the East Coast, Flannery contended, the persistent national media attention would be a distraction to batting .400.[8]

The July 14, 1987, All-Star game appeared to validate Flannery's point. Though he was leading the National League in batting average, the fans declined to vote Tony a starter for the National League team. His only plate appearance was as a pinch hitter with nobody on base in the third inning. He grounded out. It's "a shame" America did not see more of Tony Gwynn, said Padres manager Larry Bowa. "That's an embarrassment to the National League," he insisted.[9]

Tony cooled off, to an extent, in July. His batting average declined to .358 by the end of the month. The .400 talk receded. Nonetheless,

Tony Gwynn

Tony had another outstanding month in August. He hit safely in 25 of the 28 games where he participated. He had 14 multi-hit games.

His performance against Atlanta on August 11 was of particular note. For the second time in the 1987 season, he went 5-for-5. He singled and scored in the first. He singled and scored again in the third. He singled and scored a third time in the fifth to break a 3–3 tie. In his fourth at bat, he slammed a two-run homer for a 6–4 San Diego lead. The home crowd rose for a standing ovation after Tony's home run. The fans yelled for Tony to come out of the dugout and wave to the crowd. Many players would have. Cognizant of the perspective of opposing players, Tony couldn't bring himself to come out of the dugout. "I didn't want to show up anybody," he said after the game.[10]

Tony wasn't done. The game was tied, 6–6, when he led off the bottom of the ninth. He singled for his fifth hit of the game. Next, he stole second. He took third on a sacrifice. He scored the winning run on catcher Benito Santiago's single. "There aren't enough adjectives to describe the man," said Larry Bowa.[11] The Padres began to jell after their 12–42 start. Their August 11 triumph over Atlanta, for example, was their seventh straight win.

August also represented another milestone for the Gwynn family. Tony's younger brother Chris was promoted to the majors. In his Major League debut with the Dodgers, Chris hit safely three times in four at bats. Anticipating Chris's promotion to the majors, Tony had joked that he didn't know what his parents were going to do. They had been coming to his games, he noted, but their home in Long Beach is closer to Dodger Stadium. Accordingly, he speculated, they might start watching Chris play at Dodger Stadium instead of traveling to San Diego.[12] For his part, Tony and Chris's father, Charles Sr., attempted to address the dilemma. He ordered a specially-made baseball cap with half a Padres and half a Dodgers insignia.

Tony was battling several injuries late in the 1987 season. He had a sore thumb, a strained hamstring, and a groin pull. Still, he hit 2-for-4 on September 1 to bring his batting average up to .370. He got it up to .372 on October 2. After finishing the season 0-for-3 on October 3 and 0-for-1 on October 4, he ended the year at .370.

Tony's .370 average in 1987 was the best in the National League since Stan Musial hit .376 in 1948. Tony took the National League batting crown, the second of his career, by 32 points over second-place Vladimir Guerrero. He led the Major Leagues in batting average and in hits (218). He was second in the National League in stolen bases (56)

11. "If I had nine Tony Gwynns"

and triples (13). He finished in the top five in the League in seven offensive categories—batting average, hits, stolen bases, runs scored (119), doubles (36), triples and on-base percentage (.447). He only hit seven homers but because of his gap power to right center and left center and resulting doubles and triples he finished tenth in the National League in slugging percentage (.511).

Despite his stellar 1987 season, Tony finished eighth in National League MVP voting. Those who vote for the MVP apparently prefer batters who hit home runs. Andre Dawson of the Cubs, who slammed 47 homers, won the award. Tony confided to George Will, then in the midst of writing his baseball book *Men at Work: The Craft of Baseball*, that he considered changing his batting style after the 1987 MVP vote. Maybe he should be going for more home runs, he thought. Upon reflection, he elected to stick with the contact hitting approach.[13]

Overcoming their 12–42 start, the Padres went 52–45 in their final 97 games. They finished the 1987 season at 65–97 overall and still in last place in the NL West. The team's solid finish suggested room for optimism for the 1988 season. Rooke Benito Santiago, for example, possessed a gun for a throwing arm—possibly the best of any catcher in the majors. Also, he put together a 34-game hitting streak, then the 15th longest in Major League history, and finished the season with a .300 batting average.

Referring to the upcoming 1988 season Larry Bowa said, "If I had nine Tony Gwynns, I wouldn't have to worry about it. But, no one does."[14]

Chapter 12

"I lost to the best"

In 1988 and 1989 Tony grabbed two more National League batting titles. He won by large margins in 1984 and 1987. He had to grind it out to prevail in 1988 and 1989. Tony struggled at the beginning of the 1988 season. He underwent surgery on March 10 to repair a locking tendon in his left index finger. The surgery put Tony out of commission for most of Spring Training.

Prior to one Spring Training game, which Tony sat out, he was approached by a reporter for the *Seattle Times*. Nearby, a group of fans awaited his autograph. To the reporter, he growled, "I'm tired of answering questions." To the fans he barked, "I'm tired of signing autographs." Tony's comments shocked the reporter and probably the fans too. He had gained the reputation as one of baseball's more approachable stars during his six-year tenure in the Major Leagues. Then, Tony grinned. "Had you worried, didn't I?" he said. He sat down for a long interview with the reporter. Then, he signed autographs for the assembled fans.[1]

Tony insisted his finger surgery was not the reason for his early season hitting difficulties. On April 17, he was hitting .238 when San Diego took on the San Francisco Giants. While he was batting in the third inning with a 0–1 count, home plate umpire Joe West called a strike two on Tony.

In Tony's opinion the strike call wasn't even close. He believed the pitch was low and outside. He let West know it. West ordered him back into the batter's box. Tony refused, still informing West he missed the call. If you don't like what you are hearing, Tony told West, you should throw me out of the game. West did just that.[2]

Having been ejected, Tony knew he had nothing to lose. He continued to jaw at West. Manager Larry Bowa rushed out of the dugout to stand between Tony and West. In a demonstration of Tony's strength, he picked up Bowa and moved him aside all the while giving West the business.

It was the first ejection of Tony's Major League career. "Gwynn has

12. "I lost to the best"

always been a decent ballplayer, pretty quiet," West said after the game. He had the feeling Tony was experiencing "a little bit of frustration in his mind."[3] West was right.

On April 23, Tony garnered the 1,000th hit of his Major League career. He hit a lazy fly ball to left field for a single off future Hall-of-Fame pitcher Nolan Ryan. Tony acknowledged his accomplishment but he was downcast. At this point he was batting .245. "This is the worst stretch I've ever had," he said.[4] He wasn't doing enough for the team. It's as if, he asserted, "We have only eight guys out there."[5]

Meanwhile, Tony was arguing with the Padres front office about building an indoor batting cage underneath Jack Murphy Stadium. The Padres were the only team in the National League without an indoor batting cage. It's "a production" to practice hitting without an indoor batting cage, Tony noted. You need a pitcher, a catcher, and fielders to shag balls that you hit. With a cage, he pointed out, it's just you and a pitching machine.[6]

Tony's 1988 season took another adverse turn on May 7. He was perched on first base when Padres third baseman Chris Brown hit a hard ground ball between first and second. Tony jumped to avoid the ground ball but he landed awkwardly on the artificial turf at Pittsburgh's Three Rivers Stadium and injured a thumb. He was out of the lineup for three weeks.

The Padres fired Larry Bowa on May 28. Bowa's fiery management style had worn out its welcome. The team was 16–30 when Bowa was sacked. General Manager Jack McKeon, who managed the Kansas City Royals and the Oakland Athletics in the 1970s, replaced Bowa. According to Padres pitcher Andy Hawkins, Bowa's firing caused no turmoil. "You can see the team is relaxed," he said.[7]

Tony was struggling with a batting average in the .250s on June 6 when San Diego faced Cincinnati. Reds pitcher Tom Browning was working on a no-hitter with one out in the ninth. Up to bat came Tony. Browning threw three straight balls to run the count to 3–0. Browning had walked Tony twice earlier in the game. This time, he refused to give in and walk Tony. He fired two strikes to run the count to 3–2. After Tony fouled off two pitches, he stroked a single between the shortstop and the third baseman, the "5.5" hole, to break up the no-hitter.

Browning explained after the game why he didn't want to walk Tony in the ninth inning.[8] He had already walked Tony twice. He respected Tony too much to walk him again because Tony was the best hitter on the Padres if not the National League. Added Reds manager

Tony Gwynn

Pete Rose, the all-time career hits leader and witness to Tony's first two Major League hits, "He's going to break up a lot of no-hitters."[9]

Still lagging well below the .300 mark, Tony brought his frustrations home. He was moping around the house, not talking much. Keep battling, don't give up, urged Alicia. Take the weight of the world off your shoulders, suggested Jack McKeon. Finally, something clicked. He realized, Tony wrote later, you have to admit publicly that you "suck." That "takes the pressure off."[10]

Tony reviewed tapes of his 1984 season at bats. He slowed down the action and counted the frames before he opened his right shoulder to hit a pitch. He concluded he was turning his right shoulder a fraction too soon. Reviewing his 1988 season plate appearances, Tony found that he was too often looking to hit inside pitches instead of using the entire strike zone. Realizing that Tony was looking inside, pitchers were jamming him.

Tony believed he kicked out of his months-long slump on July 5 against Pittsburgh. He knocked an opposite field single off a fastball from Pirates pitcher Bob Walk. Tony recognized it was only one hit, but it felt right. He had stayed back with his right shoulder that one instant longer before turning into the pitch.[11]

Tony put together an 18-game hitting streak in July. He had more than one hit in 15 of those games. On July 15, he stroked three hits and drove in four in a 7–3 victory over St. Louis. On July 19, he hit safely three times in the first game of a doubleheader. In the second game, he clubbed a three-run homer in his first at bat to bring his average up to .301.

Tony's attention to preparation was demonstrated prior to the August 17 home game against the Expos. He discovered the Padres were bringing in the San Diego Pops Orchestra for a pre-game concert. Realizing the concert would limit batting practice time, Tony hauled off to the San Diego School of Baseball with his friend and former minor league teammate John Kruk. Tony was a part-owner of the school and he had a key. He and Kruk took about 100 licks apiece against a pitching machine.

Tony was a frequent visitor to the school, which was about two miles from Jack Murphy Stadium. One evening, at approximately 11:00 p.m., a Padres employee drove by the school. He noticed the lights were on. He spotted Tony hitting in the batting cage against a pitching machine with a cup between his legs to eject his ever-present chewing tobacco.

12. "I lost to the best"

The August 17 pre-game jaunt with Kruk paid dividends. Tony had a 3-for-3 evening with two RBIs in a San Diego victory. Kruk chipped in with a single and an RBI.

Tony's fortunes were looking up and, so too, were the Padres.' After their disastrous 16–30 start under Bowa, the team rallied for a 67–48 mark under Jack McKeon. A victory on September 5 brought their overall record above the .500 mark and into the thick of a battle for third place in the six-team NL West. Jack McKeon is "our spark," said Tony.[12]

The Padres' September 24 home game was notable for its pre-game theatrics. The occasion was Fan Appreciation Night. Some fans were not appreciative of Padres president (and former National League president) Chubb Feeney. Feeney had taken a beating in the local press because he made no moves in the free agent market or with trades to improve the team. Prior to the game, two fans paraded around Jack Murphy Stadium with a sign that read, "Scrub Chubb." Sitting in owner Joan Kroc's box, Feeney saw the banner. He gave the two fans the finger.

The next day, Feeney denied offering the offending digit to the fans. He had a problem, however. The entire incident had been caught on camera. Feeney resigned effective the end of the 1988 season. He was leaving anyway, Feeney claimed.

A visitor with a sense of history showed up at the Padres' front offices. He heard that Padres security officials had confiscated the "Scrub Chubb" sign. He wanted to preserve the sign for posterity. The visitor was Tony.[13]

Tony was in a tight race for the National League batting title with the Cubs' Rafael Palmerio. On September 26, with six days left in the regular season, Tony led Palmerio .314 to .306. On September 28 Tony went 0-for-5. Two days later, Palmerio had three hits in five at bats to leave Tony at .311 and Palmerio three points behind at .308. Trying to protect Tony's batting lead, Jack McKeon held him out of the lineup on September 30.

Referring to the upcoming October 1 contest against the Houston Astros, Tony was determined to return to the lineup. He insisted he was going to play even if he had to "choke Jack."[14] Likely he was joking…

On October 1, he hit safely in his first two at bats. McKeon removed Tony from the game after he made an out in the sixth inning. In the meantime, Palmerio had a 1-for-3 effort. Now Tony was at .313 and Palmerio at .308.

McKeon held Tony out of the lineup again on the last day of the season, October 2. Palmerio needed five hits in five at bats to catch Tony for the batting championship. It was a high hurdle and he was not able to surmount it. After going 1-for-5 Palmerio's average fell back to .307.

Tony won his second straight National League batting title. He wasn't about to turn down the honor. At the same time, he wasn't thrilled. His .313 average was the lowest title-winning batting average in the history of the National League. The 1988 title, Tony believed, was one he shouldn't have won.

San Diego won its final three games to finish the season 83–78 and in sole possession of third place. It wasn't a division title, Padres players admitted, but they were proud of their accomplishment. They had come from far back in the standings to take third place. Tony agreed. Said the former high school and college basketball star, the Padres 1988 season turnaround was like hitting "a last-second jumper at the buzzer."[15]

The Padres finally acceded to Tony's demands prior to the 1989 season. They constructed an indoor batting cage underneath Jack Murphy Stadium. The room was austere but large enough to install a cage, a pitching machine, and a home plate at sixty feet and six inches from the pitching machine. The room featured adjustable lighting to replicate day or night game conditions. Tony chipped in by adding a sound system.

Tony took batting practice in the indoor batting cage prior to the Padres 1989 season opener, at home, on April 3. After a crowd of 52,767 watched San Diego lose 5–3 to the Giants, Tony was back in the cage, hacking away. "The cage is really beautiful," Tony said. All you have to do is "flip the switch" and then 250 baseballs would come at you (not all at once).[16]

The Padres made an important acquisition prior to the 1989 season. They traded for hard-hitting first baseman Jack Clark. In addition, the Padres' starting pitching was solid with Ed Whitson, Eric Show, Dennis Rasmussen, Bruce Hurst, and Walt Terrell. Their younger players including catcher Benito Santiago, second baseman Roberto Alomar, and outfielders Marvell Wynne and Bip Roberts were coming on. And, of course, they had Tony, the defending National League batting champion. With the addition of Clark, who hit 27 homers and drove in 93 runs for the Yankees during the 1988 season, the Padres, according to a *Sports Illustrated* preview of the 1989 baseball season, were "armed and loaded."[17]

San Diego held first place in the division on April 11. Thereafter, the team slacked off. They were 39–41 at the end of June and 51–54 at the end of July.

12. "I lost to the best"

Tony Gwynn was not slacking off. He batted in the .330s for most of April and May. Consistent with previous seasons, he caught a hot streak in June. He batted .448 for the month with 16 RBIs. He went 3-for-4 with a home run against the Reds on June 3. He had another 3-for-4 outing against Cincinnati on June 4. The following evening against Houston, he smacked four hits in five at bats to contribute to a 10–2 Padres rout. His best game of the month was on June 25 against the Giants. He had four hits, scored three runs, and drove in four to lead a 10–7 Padres win.

Tony was batting .353 at the All-Star break. Fans voted him a starter. He had a single and a stolen base. The National League lost to the American League, 5–3.

On August 5, Tony was thrown out of a game for the second, and last, time of his Major League career. A substitute umpire, brought up from the Pacific Coast League, was tending to third base. Tony was batting in the top of the first inning when the replacement umpire called a strike three on a checked swing. Reminiscent of his beef with Joe West the season before, Tony believed the strike call wasn't even close. He let the ump know it while walking backwards toward the San Diego dugout. The rookie ump thumbed him.[18]

The Padres shook off their first half of the season doldrums. They commenced to play ball like a team that was "locked and loaded." They swept the Braves three straight in early August. In late August they won six in a row. Tony had five two-hit games during the six-game winning streak. He was at .344 at the end of the month to lead the National League.

San Diego took two straight from Houston the first week of September to jump into second place behind San Francisco. They beat the Giants, 5–3, on September 15 to cut the lead to five and a half games. The Padres were winning consistently but so were the Giants. But, after defeating the Dodgers on September 26, they crept to within four games of first. Both San Diego and San Francisco had four games left in the regular season.

San Francisco played a day game on September 27, and lost. Now the Padres were only three and a half out with a chance to tie for the Division title. First, they had to take care of the Cincinnati Reds. Their last three games of the season were at San Francisco. If they could beat Cincinnati and sweep the Giants, they would tie for first and force a playoff.

The September 27 Reds–Padres contest was a grinder. Cincinnati

Tony Gwynn

took a 1–0 lead into the bottom of the ninth. The Padres scratched out a run to send the game into extra innings. San Diego loaded the bases with one out in the bottom of the 11th but failed to score. The Reds' Eric Davis hit an RBI double off the wall in the top of the 13th to put the Reds ahead, 2–1. Tony singled in the bottom of the 13th. A sacrifice bunt and a ground out moved him to third but shortstop Gary Templeton struck out to end the game, sinking San Diego's division title hopes.

Though first place in the NL West was decided, the three-game season ending series between the Padres and the Giants would determine the National League batting champion. Tony and Giants first baseman Will Clark were neck and neck. Tony had faded somewhat after the All-Star break handing the National League batting lead to Clark. But Clark went 0-for-4 on September 27 which brought his average down from .336 to .333. Tony, aiming for his third consecutive batting crown, was on Clark's tail at .332.

It was advantage Will Clark after Game One of the three-game series. His two-of-four outing compared to Tony's one-of-five left Clark at .334 and Tony at .331. Tony scrambled back in Game Two. His 3-for-4 compared to Clark's 1-for-4 allowed Tony to close the gap to one point with Clark at .334 and Tony at .333.

The batting race came down to the last game of the season. Game 3 of the series would have no bearing on the NL West standings. The Giants had clinched the division title and San Diego secured second place by defeating San Francisco in Game Two. Everything was focused on the battle between Clark and Tony. Clark grounded out in his first at bat. Tony responded with a single to take over the batting lead. He stood at .334, Clark at .333. Both Tony and Clark grounded out in their second at bats. Tony clung to his narrow lead.

Tony batted for the third time of the game in the top of the fifth. He bounded a chopper over the pitcher's mound. Giants shortstop Chris Speier charged the ball and rifled a throw to Clark at first. First base umpire Ed Montague started to give the out sign but reversed himself and ruled Tony safe at first, for a single.

Tony knew Will Clark from sitting next to him on the bench during the 1989 All-Star game. Analytical as usual, Tony turned to Clark and asked, "What do you think?" If it meant anything to the division title race, Clark responded, he would appeal.[19]

There was no appeal, practically speaking, in 1989. The Major League rule allowing teams to request a video review of close plays would not be adopted for many years. That did not stop managers and

12. "I lost to the best"

coaches from vociferously arguing calls in, usually, vain efforts to convince an umpire to reverse the call. Sure enough, Giants manager Roger Craig and a Giants coach, Bob Lillis, scrambled out of the dugout to argue with Montague. Lillis argued too vociferously. He was tossed out of the game. The call stood. Tony thus increased his batting lead to two points, .334 compared to .332.

Clark was not out of it. He singled in the sixth inning to reduce the gap, once again, to one point with Tony still at .334 and Clark at .333.

Tony put it away in the top of the eighth inning. He guided a 2–1 pitch past a diving Giants second baseman for his third hit of the game. The hit brought his average up to .336. Unless the game went into extra innings, Tony's third hit of the game clinched the batting title. Clark had one at bat left, most likely, and could not catch him. Tony was well acquainted with the math and he knew that with that third hit he had won his third consecutive batting championship, and fourth of his career, even without the controversial fifth-inning call by umpire Ed Montague. Tony was relieved. He didn't want an asterisk next to his batting triumph. In fact, replays showed the Montague's safe call was wrong. Tony should have been called out. After his third hit, Tony located Alicia and his children sitting in the stands. He waved.

Typically candid, Tony told reporters after the game, which San Diego won 3–0, that he wasn't even thinking about who won or lost the game. He was primed on the race for the batting championship.[20]

"I lost to the best," said Will Clark.[21] Tony responded that he envied Will Clark. "He's going where I want to go," Tony said. "He's going to the playoffs."[22]

Chapter 13

The Selfish Controversy

The 1990 baseball season delivered a severe blow to Tony's psyche. The Padres' high expectations for the season set the stage for Tony's troubles. The Padres went 47–27 after the 1989 season All-Star break. No team in the majors had a better record after the break, and only the 1989 World Series champion Oakland A's could match their second-half record.

On top of their impressive 1989 finish, the Padres acquired outfielder Joe Carter in a December 6, 1989, trade with the Cleveland Indians. Carter, a good friend of Tony's, averaged 31 home runs and 108 RBIs per season from 1986 to 1989. With the acquisition of Carter, San Diego added another potent home run hitter and RBI producer to go with Jack Clark. Featuring Tony, Carter, Clark, Benito Santiago, Bip Roberts, and Roberto Alomar, *Sports Illustrated* reported the team had "one of the most impressive line-ups in baseball."[1]

Contrary to their pre-season expectations, San Diego stumbled out of the gate. They finished the month of April with a 9–10 record. They bumped their season record up to .500, at 16–16, by defeating Philadelphia 5–1 on May 14. They lost two to the Phillies to fall to 16–18 and 10 and a half games behind first-place Cincinnati. "I'm not going to panic," said Tony. "It's a long season. Lots of crazy things can happen."[2]

In short order, they did. After taking two out of three at home from the New York Mets, San Diego embarked on a road trip to Montreal, New York, and Philadelphia. Prior to the leaving for the road trip, Padres third baseman Mike Pagliarulo assented to an interview with a New York newspaper, the *Daily News*. Always attuned to their weaknesses at third base, the Padres had acquired Pagliarulo from the Yankees during the 1989 season. A *Daily News* reporter asked Pagliarulo if he missed playing in New York. Pagliarulo replied that he did. After all, he had been a Yankee. Then, he added the following: One player on the Padres is selfish. He cares only for his hits. If he goes 0-for-4 and San Diego wins, he's upset. If he gets his hits and San Diego loses, that's all right

13. The Selfish Controversy

with him. The Yankees would have "kicked that guy's" tail. Pagliarulo's comments were reprinted in the May 24 *Los Angeles Times*.[3]

A reporter informed Tony of Pagliarulo's claims. Tony had little doubt to whom Pagliarulo was referring. "I've been pretty professional in the way I try to take care of business," Tony said to San Diego reporters. "To have somebody tell me I'm selfish and I'm thinking about myself and not worried about winning, hey, I've got to speak out about that. I know they're wrong. They've got their signals crossed."[4] Tony continued, "When I stink, I hate it. I always think I could do a little bit better. I get upset at myself. No one else. I hope this is a case where people are misreading me being tough on myself."[5] Tony put his finger on what probably was part of the problem. He noted that everyone expected the Padres to be a better team at this point in the season.

The Padres lost to Montreal on May 22 and May 23. They traveled to New York for a four-game set against the Mets. Prior to the May 24 contest, manager Jack McKeon and his coaches excused themselves from the visiting team locker room. You guys should talk, McKeon indicated to his team.

Team captain Garry Templeton officiated at the players-only meeting. Let's talk about things being said in the newspaper, Templeton began.[6] Jack Clark interjected. He took a soft drink and hurled it across the locker room, splattering its contents. We know why we are having this meeting, Clark insisted. We have selfish players on this team—Tony Gwynn and (pitcher) Eric Show.

According to Tony's account, he was the focus of the meeting for roughly twenty minutes. Clark laid out a bill of particulars against Tony. There were two principal gripes. One, it was alleged that Tony squared around to sacrifice bunt to protect his batting average. A successful sacrifice does not count as an official at bat. Two, it was contended that Tony failed to take pitches when a Padres runner on first base took off to steal second. Instead, Tony swung at pitches in an effort to get a hit in the gap left between first and second when the second baseman ran to second base to take a throw from the catcher. There were, apparently, a few other complaints: that Tony was not vocal enough; that he was too close to the news media; and that he paid too little attention to his weight.

Again according to Tony, he asked Clark: What do you want me to do? Clark never provided a direct answer. Apparently, Clark and Tony almost got into a scuffle. Templeton interceded to break it up.[7]

The players discussed other grievances as well, frustrated with their lagging start to the 1990 season. The meeting lasted some fifty minutes. It forced the team to cancel pre-game batting practice. Missing practice bore little effect. The Padres raced to a 5–0 lead. Tony drove in one of the five runs. The Padres held on to beat the Mets, 5–4.

Tony was greatly troubled by the charges leveled against him. Hadn't he been the one when participating in high and college basketball who set up teammates instead of scoring himself because he didn't want to be a "glory hog?" Didn't he lay off good pitches to hit to help Alan Wiggins swipe 70 bases during the 1984 season? Wasn't he a person who generally thought of others before himself? After the May 24 Mets game, Tony said to reporters "Do me a favor and go talk to someone else tonight."[8]

Details of the contentious team meeting soon leaked. Nick Canepa of the *San Diego Evening Tribune* addressed the matter in a May 26 essay. I've known Tony since he was at San Diego State, wrote Canepa. Tony is one of the most genial guys in sports, "especially one who holds such a lofty position."[9] He tirelessly signs autographs for fans. His fault, observed Canepa, is his self-criticism of his own performance. "I can't recall," concluded Canepa, "ever seeing him pleased in defeat."[10]

This has been the hardest thing he had ever been through, Tony admitted to the media. He never before had been criticized in public by a teammate. He had gone through much soul-searching. He spent several sleepless nights. He listened to his teammates. At the same time, he listened to his agent (John Boggs, who replaced Tony's first agent after the 1987 bankruptcy), his parents, and his wife, Alicia. Fingering part of his dilemma, Tony averred, "I know I want to get along with everybody. That's important to me."[11]

The tempestuous clubhouse meeting appeared to energize the team. They won five of their next six games. On June 10, they were at 30–25 and six games behind first-place Cincinnati. Tony once again caught a hot streak in June. He went 4-for-6 on June 1. Before a home crowd of 53,701 on June 2, he came up to bat in the fourth inning with the bases loaded. The large crowd, by now cognizant of Tony's disputes with Clark and Pagliarulo, shouted encouragement. "Tony, Tony, Tony," they yelled. Tony delivered. He lashed a double to the warning track in left center, driving in three runs. The Padres rolled to a 9–0 victory. Tony followed with two-RBI efforts on June 4, 6, and 8. He raised his batting average to .348.

San Diego beat the Dodgers 2–1 on June 10. Thereafter, the roof caved in. They lost 29 of their next 37. Their lack of team chemistry

13. The Selfish Controversy

was probably a factor. One major leaguer, observing the Padres' faltering 1990 season, noted that just because you have good players does not mean you have a good team.[12]

Jack McKeon had been serving both as the field manager and the general manager. He decided the two jobs had become too much. He resigned his manager position during the 1990 All-Star break. First base coach Greg Riddoch replaced him. In another change in management, Joan Kroc sold the team effective June 14, 1990. A group of fifteen investors led by television producer Tom Werner purchased the Padres for $75 million. Werner's Hollywood production company was responsible for some of television's highest-rated programs, including *Roseanne,* starring Roseanne Barr, and *The Cosby Show,* starring Bill Cosby.

The Padres 1990 season took another bizarre turn on July 25. They were hosting a day-night doubleheader against the first-place Reds. San Diego prevailed 2–1 in the day game. The Padres front office decided to promote one of Werner's television productions for the evening tilt. They brought in comedienne Roseanne Barr to sing the National Anthem before a home crowd of 25,774.

Barr was off-key on the song from the start. Her pitch was too high. She screeched through the Anthem. San Diego is a military town. It has a large U.S. Navy presence and a U.S. Marine base nearby. Barr's singing went over badly with the crowd. Boos rang out. The crowd noise interfered with Barr's ability to hear herself sing. Consequently, she placed her hands over her ears. The crowd misread Barr's gesture as a sign of disrespect. The crescendo of boos grew more boisterous.

Barr managed to wobble through the Anthem. She then inflamed the crowd again. Trying to inject humor, she grabbed her crotch and spat on the ground imitating major league players. Barr's antics aside, a baseball game was contested. The Padres triumphed over the Reds 10–4 to sweep the doubleheader. Tony had a 4-for-5 evening with two doubles and two RBIs.

The Barr fiasco occurred prior to the advent of social media. Nevertheless, news of her National Anthem performance swept across the country. Traveling on Air Force One, President George H.W. Bush termed Barr's performance "disgraceful."[13] New York Opera singer Robert Merrill viewed Barr's rendition of the Anthem and reported that he nearly upchucked his dinner. *Men at Work* author George Will confided that he thought Barr was "a slob."[14] Barr conducted a news conference to defend herself. She retorted that she was not the best singer but not the worst either. Also, she would like to hear Bush sing the Anthem.[15] Tony's take was that Barr's singing, and, in particular, her stunt of grabbing her crotch and spitting "soured a lot of people."[16]

Tony's 1990 season took another adverse turn on September 8. He ambled into the San Diego dugout prior to a home game to conduct a pre-game radio show. He noticed a plastic figure hanging on a hook in the dugout. Upon closer inspection, what he saw angered him. A Tony Gwynn doll was hanging from the hook. Its arms and legs were cut off. There was a chain hanging around its neck. "There's nothing wrong with having a good laugh," Tony said later.[17] But when he saw the doll, it wasn't funny, Padres management vowed to investigate. Jack Clark said the Tony Gwynn doll incident was "disgusting."[18]

A few days later, the perpetrator of the hanging doll purportedly came forward. The city of San Diego, not the team, managed Jack Murphy Stadium. Bill Wilson, the stadium manager, disclosed that a member of the seven-person daytime grounds crew, a city employee, came to him and admitted to the deed. The employee meant no malice, Wilson insisted. The employee was trying to make a joke in reference to the "selfish" Tony Gwyn controversy. Wilson and Padres president Dick Freeman informed Tony of their findings.

The Padres indicated that the grounds crew employee planned to apologize in person to Tony. The apology never came. The employee remained anonymous. Tony didn't believe the story. He suspected a teammate. He had no proof, however. Whom he suspected he never publicly revealed.

Referring to the disfigured Tony Gwynn doll, Alicia said that "It has worn a great deal on him."[19] Alicia must have been right because Tony placed a picture of the lynched Gwynn doll in his locker. He said the doll was an attempt at "voodoo."[20] It won't succeed, he vowed.

Tony's troubles were not over. The Padres headed to Atlanta to match up with the Braves. On September 15, one week after discovering the Tony Gwynn doll, Tony was injured attempting to chase down a long fly ball off the bat of Atlanta second baseman Jeff Treadwell. Tony leaped against the outfield wall to snare Treadwell's drive but the ball eluded him and he smashed his glove (right) hand into the wall. He fractured his right index finger.

"I hate to think what else could go wrong," Tony lamented. "Sometimes the worst experience in your life is the thing you learn the most from."[21]

Tony flew back to San Diego to seek medical attention. The verdict

13. The Selfish Controversy

of orthopedic surgeons was no surprise. He required surgery which would put him out for the rest of the season.

Tony arrived at Jack Murphy Stadium in the mid-morning of September 21 to clean out his locker. The day prior his teammates had arrived in San Diego from a road trip but no players were at the ballpark that early. As Associated Press reporter approached Tony. The reporter asked Tony if he expected to meet up with his teammates. Tony's frustrations with his 1990 season spilled out. "Hell, no," he answered, "Why would I want to hang out with those (bleeps)?"[22]

He remained aloof from his teammates the balance of the 1990 season. He refused to be interviewed by the media until December. Tony's comments did not sit well with his teammates, reported Garry Templeton.[23] He made a mistake Tony admitted in December. He had let his frustrations get to him. His actions were uncharacteristic. He should have mentioned specific players instead of the entire team. Tony disclosed that he had been calling teammates to apologize for his remarks to the Associated Press reporter.[24]

Tony batted .309 for the 1990 season, his lowest average since he also hit .309 in 1983. Nonetheless, he finished tied for sixth in batting in the National League. He drove in 72 runs, the highest RBI total at that juncture of his career. He continued his remarkable record of avoiding strikeouts with only 23 K's in 573 at bats. He led the National League in putouts by a right fielder. He won his fourth Gold Glove.

Tony dealt with yet another problem in February 1991. He discovered a growth on his cheek near his right ear—the same spot where, inside his cheek, he held his chewing tobacco. To remove the growth required a four and a half hour operation. Was the growth related to Tony's chewing tobacco habit? The answer wasn't clear. Nevertheless, as Tony once said, "I'm a tobacco junkie."[25] His chewing tobacco habit would continue.

Because of the various arbitration decisions finding collusion by the major league owners against free agents, Jack Clark became a free agent after the 1990 season. San Diego offered him a one-year contract. He secured a better deal with the Boston Red Sox, a three-year contract for $8.7 million plus incentives that could increase the total payout to more than $10 million. The Padres released Tony's other 1990 protagonist, Mike Pagliarulo. He signed with the Minnesota Twins.

Clark continued to hector Tony during 1991 Spring Training. Speaking to the press from the Red Sox camp in Winter Haven, Florida, Clark maintained that he would have liked to stay in San Diego just to get in Tony's face some more. "He's a good player, not a good teammate," Clark contended.[26] Clark derided Tony's reputation in San Diego. Gwynn is known as "Mr. Padre" in San Diego, Clark pointed out. They cater to Tony because he wins batting titles, Clark added. The Padres are not winners, he concluded.

Tony finally had heard enough from Jack Clark. He fired back from the Padres Spring Training site in Yuma, Arizona. Clark is jealous of me, Tony contended. Also, Tony pointed to some of Clark's deficiencies. He walks too often for a clean-up hitter. He takes too many strike threes. He was disappointed, Tony noted, because Clark is still talking about the 1990 season. Let's move on to the 1991 season, Tony advocated.[27]

When not jousting with Clark, Tony acknowledged it had been a tough offseason. "I was miserable, absolutely miserable," he said to the *Los Angeles Times*. "It was a long winter, let me tell you."[28]

Attempting to explain Tony's problems with the selfishness charge, Jack McKeon noted that Tony is "very intense." There were times when he saw Tony go 3-for-5 and be upset about making two outs. Other times he watched as Tony collected three hits in a game but afterward headed straight to a batting cage.[29]

Tony was far from the first high-average hitter accused of being selfish. Pete Rose, Wade Boggs, and Ted Williams were also thusly accused. Tony noted that batting is inherently a selfish act because no one can come up to the plate help you.

Major league ballplayers interact with numerous people every season. They come in contact with fans desiring an autograph, news reporters, managers and coaches, players on opposing teams, and umpires. During the 1990 season Tony discovered that when you have encounters with so many different people, it is impossible to please them all—even if you are Tony Gwynn.

Tony decided he would not change his personality nor his style of play. He always had tried to lead by example and he would continue to do so. Furthermore, he was determined to laugh more in 1991.[30] In addition, he was delighted the Padres had changed the team uniforms. Navy blue and orange replaced brown and gold. "You think of brown and you think of aaghh. You see blue and you say, 'Aah, blue,'" said Tony.[31]

One day in Spring Training Tony was in the batting cage. He squared around to bunt a pitch from the batting practice pitcher and yelled out, "What are you doing? you selfish bastard." He roared with his signature laugh—a laugh that seemed to rumble through his body. With his Spring Training gesture Tony was sending a message to his

13. The Selfish Controversy

teammates, the fans, and the media He was going to have fun playing baseball in 1991.[32]

Nonetheless, the selfish controversy stuck with Tony. In 2011, the sports news website *SB Nation* published an analysis of Tony's career at bats. The *SB Nation* survey found that Tony attempted 45 sacrifice bunts between 1982 and 1990. After the 1990 "selfish" imbroglio, he attempted but four sacrifice bunts the rest of his major league career.[33]

Tony roared off to a great start in 1991. On April 27, he was batting .375. He was still batting in the .370s in mid–June. He was running away with the National League batting race. For the second time in his career, the talk circulated. Could Tony Gwynn hit .400?

Tony tore a cartilage in his left knee in July. He aggravated the injury in August while sliding into a base. He played through the pain in his knee. He used ice packs to reduce the swelling and, on occasion, his knee was drained of fluid. Tony's knee injury inhibited his ability to turn into pitches and drive the ball with authority. His batting average gradually declined. After a September 12 game, he had to call it quits. He underwent arthroscopic surgery on the knee on September 17. Tony always maintained his 1988 batting title was one he didn't deserve. Prior to his injuries the 1991 title was his for the taking. Instead, his .317 average for the 1991 season placed him third in batting in the National League behind Atlanta's Terry Pendleton at .319 and Cincinnati's Hal Morris at .318.

One reason Tony tried to play through his knee injury was that the Padres were much improved from 1990. They had an outside shot at winning the NL West title when they faced the Braves on September 11, 1991. They had won seven in a row to pull within seven and a half games of the Dodgers. San Diego lost a historic game to Atlanta. Three Atlanta pitchers combined for a no-hitter. The September 11 Braves–Padres game was the first time in major league history two or more pitchers hurled a no-hitter. Prior to that, every no-hitter had come from one pitcher pitching the entire nine innings. In subsequent years, as teams obsessed over pitch counts, multi-pitcher no-hitters became commonplace.

The Padres finished the 1991 season with an 84–78 record, good for third place in the NL West. Tony participated only in 134 games in 1991. Despite the knee, he managed to finish second in the National League with 11 triples. In addition, he earned the fifth Gold Glove of his career.

Chapter 14

Fire Sale

On July 14, 1992, Tony participated in his eighth Major League All-Star game, hosted by the Padres at Jack Murphy Stadium. Typical of Tony, he was chatting with fellow players and representatives of the media prior to game time. He talked hitting with Baseball Hall of Famer and now ESPN broadcaster Joe Morgan. Recognizing Tony's abiding interest in the subject, Morgan introduced Tony to Ted Williams. A San Diego native, Williams was in town to throw out the ceremonial first ball. "I'm Tony Gwynn," said Tony. "I know who you are," replied Williams.[1]

Tony, continued Williams, let me see your bat. Tony fetched his 32 inch, 31 ounce Louisville Slugger model, one of the lightest bats in the major leagues. Taking hold of Tony's bat, Williams pretended to pick his teeth with it. Your bat is a "toothpick," Williams declared.[2]

Tony suppressed a laugh. Still, he understood perfectly well Williams' metaphor. In *The Science of Hitting*, a book Tony reviewed regularly, Williams advocated bats that were "light but right." The "light" bat, Williams advised, enables a batter to react at the last possible moment to a pitched ball. The "right" meant a bat with enough length and weight to propel a baseball with power. In his book, Williams derided a bat that was too light as a "toothpick."

You are a big guy, Williams emphasized to Tony. He was referencing Tony's solid, stocky build. Williams had slugged 521 home runs during his major league career. Now Williams counseled Tony, a ballplayer who thus far had only hit 58, that he should hit more home runs. Go after the inside pitch, Williams urged Tony, and knock it out of the park.

Tony declined to apply Williams' advice. Tony knew he was a natural opposite field hitter, not a pull hitter. He likely recollected the hitting slump he endured during the early stages of the 1989 season. Reviewing tapes of his 1989 at bats, Tony concluded pitchers were getting him out because he was too committed to hitting an inside pitch.

14. Fire Sale

Nonetheless, Ted and Tony were on their way to becoming good friends. They seemed an unlikely pair. Ted possessed a booming voice. Tony's was high-pitched. Ted was rarely shy about offering his opinions—and he had many. Tony preferred not to draw attention to himself. Ted frequently clashed with sportswriters and the Boston Red Sox fan base during his playing days. He probably never would have said, as Tony had, that getting along with everyone was important to him.

Still, it was no surprise that they clicked. They shared a deep passion for hitting a baseball. They studied pitchers relentlessly. During his playing days, Williams would practice hitting till his hands bled. Whenever injury limited Tony's batting practice time, he would complain the callouses on his hands were getting soft.

Minutes prior to game time, Ted positioned himself in front of the pitcher's mound for the ceremonial first pitch to St. Louis Cardinals All-Star catcher Tom Pagnozzi. He uncorked a credible throw, slightly inside to a right-hand batter.

Tony went 0-for-2 during the All-Star game. The Nationals lost to the American League, 13–6. Tony validated his five Gold Glove awards with two outstanding defensive plays. In the top of the first, Baltimore's Cal Ripken slashed a liner down the right field line. Tony cut off the ball before it reached the outfield wall. Ripken should have had a double on the play, but Tony whirled and fired a one-hop throw to nail Ripken at second base. In the sixth, the Tigers Travis Fryman drew a walk. The next American League batter singled. Fryman rounded second, thinking about going to third. Tony threw to second base, behind Fryman, to his San Diego teammate, All-Star shortstop Tony Fernandez, who tagged out Fryman. Tony's two outfield putouts tied an All-Star game record.

Tony's 1992 season sailed to a roaring start. He began the year with three consecutive two-hit games. He batted .474 on a long road trip in May. In one stretch during the trip, he hit safely 12 times in 16 at bats. After a 4-for-5 outing with two RBIS in a 9–2 victory over the Pirates on May 15, he was batting .372.

In 1992, the Padres were in the thick of the race for the NL West division title. Their record was 28–22 on May 31, good enough for a tie for first. The team slipped to third place in June, remaining there the rest of the season but always within range of first place. They were 56–48 on July 31, four and a half games out of first.

Tony caught a finger in a car door in mid–May. He fractured the tip of the finger, forcing him to miss four games between May 19 and 22. He sprained his left knee in July. He aggravated the knee in August sliding into a base. In part because of his injuries, his batting average dropped from the 370s to the 320s.

Chris Jenkins of the *San Diego Union-Tribune* was one of the writers following the Padres in their chase for the 1992 division title. Local writers found Tony both affable and knowledgeable. It seemed he could expound on almost any subject—from sports to trends in music, from public policy to civic events in San Diego. The beat writers jested with Tony. They tried to "stump Tony Gwynn."[3]

One day, Jenkins attempted to stump Tony. He queried Tony on 1992 Democrat presidential candidate Bill Clinton's recently-announced tax plan.[4] Tony wasn't fooled. He knew the details of Clinton's plan, including the proposal to increase taxes on incomes greater than $140,000 while also renewing an expired investment tax credit to spur economic activity. He had been talking to his dad last night about the Clinton tax plan, Tony relayed to Jenkins. His dad criticized the Clinton plan for not taxing corporations enough. But, Dad, Tony had replied, "I am a corporation." (Tony and Alicia had been incorporating their various business activities in music and sales of sports apparel.)[5]

On August 31, the Padres front office dealt a blow to the players. In the midst of the division title race, the team traded starting pitcher Craig Lefferts. Lefferts was leading the team with 13 wins. They players had expected any late-season trades to improve the team not weaken it.

Tony was struggling with his balky left knee. He continued to play on because the Padres were fighting for a division title. The knee was drained of fluid in early September. A few days later, his knee locked up. He was forced to scratch from the lineup. He was out from September 9 to 18. He gave it another go on September 19 but had to exit the game after the fourth inning. He underwent arthroscopic surgery on October 5.

The Padres finished the 1992 season 82–80. Tony's final batting average was .317. It was his tenth consecutive season batting above .300. His teammate, third baseman Gary Sheffield, took the National League batting title with a .330 mark. Another teammate, first baseman Fred McGriff, captured the National League home run crown with 35 round trippers.

The Craig Lefferts trade was the first of bad omens. Blaming increasing player salaries, the Padres were estimating a nine million dollar operating loss for the 1992 season. The front office imposed a salary limit for the 1993 season. On October 26, 1992, they traded All-Star

14. Fire Sale

shortstop Tony Fernandez to the Toronto Blue Jays, saving $2.5 million in salary. They announced they had no interest in signing Padre players who were about to become free agents, including catcher Benito Santiago and pitchers Larry Andersen, Jim Deshaies, and Randy Myers.

The local press blasted Padres management. Are you going to sell the furniture too? asked an essay in the *San Diego Union-Tribune*.[6] Padres president Dick Freeman sought to soothe the controversy. He issued a November 23, 1992, letter to season ticketholders stating that the front office had retained a core group of players to lead the team in the future. The letter identified Darrin Jackson, who had blossomed into one of the best defensive center fielders in baseball, McGriff, Sheffield, and Tony.[7]

Tony published a book in 1992. Working with local scribe Jim Rosenthal, he issued his book *Total Baseball: Winning Techniques for Hitting, Fielding, and Baserunning*. Willie Davis, a childhood role model of Tony's, wrote the book's foreword. "I'm honored," Davis wrote, to learn that Tony Gwynn came to Dodger Stadium to watch my games. Tony is always the first player to arrive at the ballpark, Davis observed. He is a "quiet leader" who motivates other players "by showing them the right way to do things."[8]

In *Total Baseball*, Tony advocated prospective ballplayers use batting gloves, stand in the center of the batter's box, finish their swings high, and most importantly, focus on a pitcher's release point rather than their arm motion. One revelation in Tony's book was his advocacy of batting tees. Batting tees are usually reserved for beginners. T-Ball leagues use them. A batting tee, Tony argued, is a viable tool for every player.[9] A batting tee, he pointed out, requires little more than a $10 investment. Work on hitting the top half of the ball off the tee, he advised. Also, set the tee at different angles to practice hitting the ball to all fields. At baseball camps, Tony noted, he always asked his students if they practice with a batting tee. He tried to take at least 200 to 300 swings a day, he wrote, either by hitting off a batting tee, a pitching machine, or a live pitcher. "Think I won four batting titles on sheer ability?" he asked. "Think again."[10]

There was another development for Tony and his family after the 1992 season. Alicia had founded a music promotion company. She heard a gospel group from Indianapolis that she liked. She traveled to Indianapolis to meet with the group. Tony tagged along.

Lugging around the Indianapolis area, Tony and Alicia liked what they saw. They decided to buy a second home in Fishers, Indiana, a

Tony Gwynn

northeast suburb of Indianapolis. For the next decade, the Gwynns summered in San Diego and wintered near Indianapolis. Tony understood both sides of his personality. He was able to spend hours talking to fellow players or sports writers or signing autographs for fans. At the same time, he craved anonymity. He realized he could be comfortable in the public eye if he also found a place of refuge.

Tony found refuge in Indianapolis. Because of the three-hour time difference with San Diego, the Indianapolis newspapers and television media barely took notice of the Padres games on the West Coast. Tony loved the anonymity he found in Indianapolis. He could shop at grocery and big box stores without being recognized. He could be a regular guy. He even enjoyed shoveling snow off his driveway.

Tony became a fixture on the Indianapolis sports scene. In 1994, the Indianapolis Colts drafted Tony's fellow San Diego State alum Marshall Faulk in the first round of the NFL draft. A running back, Faulk was the team's best player. With Faulk on the roster, Tony became an enthusiastic Colts fan. Prior to one game against the Miami Dolphins that the Colts were expected to lose, Tony delivered a stirring pep talk in the Colts locker room. The Colts pulled an upset over the Dolphins.[11]

He was also attended games of the NBA's Indiana Pacers. Other than Pacers players, coaches, and staff, no one appeared to recognize "Mr. Padre" sitting in the second row behind the Pacers bench.

Meanwhile, back to reality, Tony and his teammates endured more ominous signs in the spring of 1993. The Padres traded Darrin Jackson on March 30, dumping more salary. Jackson's trade contradicted Dick Freeman's assurances in his November 23, 1992, letter to season ticketholders.

Tony knew the Padres 1993 season was going to be a disaster. Nonetheless, on many occasions during the season, he was a human highlight reel. On April 18, he went 5-for-5 for the fourth time of his career in a 10–6 Padres victory over St. Louis.

Before a home crowd of 39,343 on April 30, Tony again went 5-for-5. In the eighth inning with the score tied 6–6 Tony excelled on both defense and offense. In the top half, Tony tracked down a liner off the bat of the Mets' Joe Orsulak. When Orsulak attempted to stretch a single into a double, Tony's throw nabbed Orsulak for an out at second base. Tony's play stifled a potential Mets rally. In the bottom half and the scored still tied with two outs and a Padres runner on third base, Tony hit a hard smash up the middle. Mets second baseman Jeff Kent somehow snagged the ball and attempted to throw Tony out at first.

14. Fire Sale

Tony put every ounce of energy he had to successfully beat out Kent's throw. The runner at third scored on the play to put the Padres in the lead, 7–6. Appreciating Tony's effort, the home crowd erupted with cheers. Tony briefly tipped his hat to the crowd. He didn't want to be too demonstrative. The game wasn't over. But the Padres triumphed, 7–6. Regarding Kent's eighth inning throw to first, Tony relayed to reporters that "I just wasn't going to let him throw me out."[12] Said Padres manager Jim Riggleman (who replaced Greg Riddoch late in the 1992 season), "You see five hits in the box score. But the throw he made [in the top of the eighth], the plays he made, and his hustle on the bases were just outstanding. It was Tony Gwynn night."[13]

Against the Dodgers on June 10, Tony ripped a double, a triple, and a home run. He was one hit away from hitting for the cycle. All he needed was a single, a relatively easy task for a hitter with Tony's bat control. But Riggleman removed Tony from the game after the sixth inning to protect, Riggleman said, Tony's left knee. Hitting for the cycle (a single, double, triple and home run in the same game) is a rare feat in professional baseball. Tony admitted to disappointment after the game. No Padre had ever hit for the cycle. He owned plenty of team records, Tony observed. Furthermore, he believed he would get another chance to accomplish the deed. (He never did.)[14]

The next evening was Tony Gwynn Poster Night at Jack Murphy. The Padres trailed the Dodgers 4–0 going into the bottom of the ninth. They rallied to cut the deficit to 4–2. Tony then came up to the plate with the bases loaded. Dodgers rookie reliever Omar Daal was on the mound. The evening before, Tony had studied Daal. He noticed that Daal was throwing only breaking pitches. Second baseman Jeff Gardner was slated to bat after Tony. Kneeling at the on-deck circle, Tony turned to Gardner and told him he was unlikely to get a chance to bat. Daal hung a slider on a 1–0 pitch. Tony was waiting for it. He cracked a bases-clearing double to drive in all three runners for a 5–4 Padres victory. While jogging off the diamond, Tony was mobbed by teammates. "I told you. I told you," Tony shouted.[15]

The Padres' player dump continued on June 24. The team traded defending National League batting champion Gary Sheffield to the Florida Marlins. The front office further depleted the pitching corps by sending reliever Rich Rodriguez to Toronto. The Padres were receiving little in return for their trades, mostly untested, lower-level minor league players. The local newspapers described the Padres personnel moves as a "fire sale."[16]

Tony Gwynn

For some Padres fans the Sheffield and Rodriguez trades were the last straw. They filed a class action lawsuit alleging fraud and misrepresentation based on the assurances in Dick Freeman's November 23, 1992, letter to season ticketholders. The lawsuit eventually settled. The Padres agreed to pay a refund to any season ticketholder who requested one.

Management delivered another body blow on July 18. They shipped off defending National League home run champ Fred McGriff to the Atlanta Braves. Eight days later they unloaded pitchers Bruce Hurst and Greg Harris. Commencing with the October 1992 trade of Tony Fernandez to the trades of Hurst and Harris, the Padres had shed some $24 million in player salaries. If they couldn't afford it, wondered some of the Padres players, why did Tom Werner and his ownership group buy the team? "They're doing what they've got to do," Tony said to reporters. "I've got no control over that. They're going to do what they've got to do whether I like it or you like it or the fans like it. So just deal with what we've got."[17]

The unsettling of the Padres roster did little to deter Tony. On July 16, he hit one of the longest shots of his career. He scorched a fastball from Philadelphia Phillies pitcher David West 430 feet into the right field seats. Tony's home run, his fifth of the season, provided the game's winning run.

On July 27, Tony went 5-for-5 for the third time of the season at Wrigley Field. He singled in the first, third, and fourth innings. He doubled in the fifth and eighth. Manager Jim Riggleman replaced him with a pinch runner after the eighth-inning double. The Wrigley Field crowd of 32,390 rose to give Tony a standing ovation. Tony was surprised. "The last thing I expected was an ovation here in Chicago," Tony confided to Alan Solomon of the *Chicago Tribune*. "Boy, they're really rough on me out there in the bleachers. I can't describe to you what that feeling was like getting an ovation on the road in Chicago. It's something that kind of hits you. To realize there are that many people who respect what you do is just a great feeling."[18]

Jim Riggleman, who prior to 1993 had not seen Tony in action that often, was becoming a believer. "Everything about Tony Gwynn impresses me," he said. "But No. 1 is his preparation. His studying of video is well-documented. He's in control of what's going to happen because he's so well-prepared."[19]

Tony was again spectacular against the Giants on August 4. He had six hits in the game, the only six-hit game of his career. His sixth hit

14. Fire Sale

was a bloop single to center in the bottom of the 12th inning that somehow eluded several Giants defenders. "How did that one fall in there?" asked Giants first baseman Will Clark. "I'm in the zone," Tony replied.[20] Tony's single sent teammate Ricky Gutierrez to third. Gutierrez scored the winning run on a sacrifice bunt. Tony joined elite company in chalking up his fourth game of the season with five or more hits. Only three other players had done it—Wee Willie Keeler in 1897, Ty Cobb in 1922, and Stan Musial in 1948.

On August 5, he hit a two-run homer in a 5–3 Padres loss. The homer was Tony's 1,996th major league hit. He was four short of 2,000. A crowd of 41,085 wedged into Jack Murphy for an August 6 doubleheader against the Colorado Rockies, an expansion team added to the NL West for the 1993 season. The fans, including 50 of Tony's family and friends, hoped to watch Tony attain the 2,000-hit milestone.

Game 1 of the doubleheader was vintage Tony Gwynn. In the first inning with teammate Jeff Gardner on second base, Tony stroked a single to center for an RBI. In the third while participating in a three-run Padres rally, Tony singled to right. In the fourth with Padres runners on second and third, Rockies manager Don Baylor ordered Tony intentionally walked. The gambit worked. The Padres failed to score in the fourth but they held a 4–0 lead. In the sixth, Tony singled to left for hit number 1,999. He had three hits in the game—one to right, one to center, and one to left. In the seventh with the Padres ahead 5–3 and a runner on second, Baylor ordered Tony walked again. The Padres won, 6–3.

Baylor later explained his strategy ordering that Tony be intentionally walked twice with runners on base. He didn't want to give up any more runs. Gwynn was hitting both right-handed and left-handed pitchers. He decided to let some other Padre batter try to drive runners in.[21]

Tony made an out in his first three at bats in Game 2. In his fourth at bat, he singled up the middle off Rockies reliever Bruce Ruffin for career hit 2,000. Fireworks exploded over the giant scoreboard. The board flashed "2,000." Standing at first base, he pointed to Alicia and his two children who were sitting in the stands behind third base. He collected his fifth hit of the doubleheader in the eighth for hit 2,001. The Padres took Game 2 for a sweep of the Rockies.

Writers asked Tony what it meant to attain 2,000 career hits. "It means," he said, "I've got a thousand to go."[22]

A student of baseball history, Tony knew reaching 3,000 hits was both a signature achievement and almost a sure ticket to the Baseball

Tony Gwynn

Hall of Fame. It means more, Tony argued, if you get all 3,000 hits in one uniform than if you move from team to team.

On August 27, Tony recorded his 37th double of the season, beating out his previous career best of 36 in 1987. He was second in the National League in doubles. He also was leading the League with a .362 batting average. Tony appeared to be gunning for a fifth batting title except for a catch. Colorado Rockies first baseman Andres Galarraga was hitting at a .392 clip on July 24 when he went down with a knee injury. Galarraga returned on August 21. By August 31, his average dropped to .374. A batter needs a minimum of 502 plate appearances to qualify for the batting title. Galarraga was far short. The question was would he reach the minimum prior to the season's end on October 3?

Tony's was battling his own knee problems. He came up lame on September 4. He tried to go on September 5 but found he couldn't run. He had to call it quits for the year. It was his third consecutive season cut short by his balky left knee. On September 12, surgeons at the Scripps Clinic in La Jolla performed arthroscopic surgery to clean out Tony's knee.

Tony was easygoing save for talk about his weight. He was displeased when his college basketball coach "Smokey" Gaines harangued him to lose weight. He didn't like it any better when the press asked manager Jim Riggleman whether Tony's weight, reportedly 230 pounds, contributed to his knee injuries. Tony blasted the writers. It's none of your business, he argued. No one complained about his weight when he was playing well. The 1993 season, he asserted, "is maybe the best year I've ever had."[23]

Tony finished the season with a .358 batting average, the second best of his career. He achieved the requisite 502 plate appearances despite missing the last four weeks of the 1993 season. Andres Galarraga managed to beat him out for the batting title. Playing regularly in September and up to October 3, Galarraga finished with 506 plate appearances, four above the minimum. His .370 average bested Tony's .358.

The Padres 1992–1993 "fire sale" led to predictable results. They finished 61–101 for the 1993 season. The team was so bad it finished in last place in the seven-team NL West and behind the expansion Colorado Rockies. When the Padres did it, a fire sale of a professional team was a relatively new trend. Thereafter, the technique became more common. The Marlins have unloaded their best players several times. The White Sox did it 1997. The Cubs shed their roster in 2012 and 2021. In

14. Fire Sale

contrast to the class action lawsuit filed in San Diego, fans rarely file lawsuits after management strips their team of star players. They have come to expect it.

Tony's dad, Charles Gwynn, Sr., urged Tony to leave San Diego. The Padres aren't even trying to win, he contended. You deserve better. Tony disagreed with his dad. He was happy. His family was happy. He was going to remain in San Diego. The Padres would win when they were supposed to win.[24]

Tony was a fixture in San Diego. He appeared frequently on local radio and television. He was a staple of local and regional television commercials while endorsing everything from cars to fast food. He and Alicia were active with several local charities. Tony often was asked to speak at schools and other civic groups. When he spoke, he proffered the Tony Gwynn creed—do what you want, work hard at it, and strive for consistency at what you do. Tony believed he had built a life that was not possible if you transfer from team to team and city to city.

By the 1993 season, the Padres were the only team in the major leagues without a video room. Demonstrating his commitment to San Diego, Tony determined that they would have one. He contributed tens of thousands of his own money for the construction of a video room at Jack Murphy Stadium. The new video complex would encourage his teammates to watch video, Tony noted. Furthermore, it would take some of the pressure off his wife, Alicia. Heretofore, Alicia had been responsible for compiling and filing his various video tapes. The Jack Murphy video room would free up some of Alicia's time. She manages her own business, Tony pointed out.

Charles Gwynn, Sr., died of a heart attack on November 27, 1993. It was a hard loss. Charles Sr. encouraged athletics and preached hard work to his three sons. All three sons followed in their father's footsteps. Both of Tony's parents were a strong influence. His father said work hard and good things will happen. His mother convinced Tony to remain in baseball even as his high school baseball team lost almost every game it played. Also, his mother shared Tony's strong sense of conscientiousness. Once before a road game with the Dodgers, Tony bragged on his mother's cooking. She makes the best pecan pies, he asserted. He promised his teammates to bring the pies to the dressing room. When he revealed his promise to his mother, she was taken aback. She complained to Tony that he hadn't given her much time. But she went to work. She baked the pies. And, soon after the pies were delivered to the Padres dressing room, the pie bins were empty. Both of Tony's parents emphasized treating people with respect. One time a writer asked Tony about his heroes. "That would be my parents," Tony answered without hesitation. "They're honest. They're outspoken, hard-working people."[25]

Two months after his father passed away, Tony made good on his vow to remain a Padre, despite the team's horrendous 1993 season. He was already under contract for 1994 and 1995. In January 1994 he signed a three-year contract extension for the 1996, 1997, and 1998 seasons. Under the extension, the Padres were set to pay him $4 million a year. The Padres also agreed to pay a $500,000 bonus if Tony had more than 500 plate appearances in 1996 and 1997. The Padres held an option to keep Tony on the team and pay him the $4 million in 1998. Tony received flak from officials at the Major League Players Association for continuing to sign contracts with the Padres instead of testing the free agent market. The officials believed, probably correctly, that Tony could make more money if he applied for free agency after his contracts with San Diego expired. They also suggested Tony was suppressing the money other players could earn. Tony was undeterred.[26]

Tony was thirty-three years old. He had won four batting titles, five Gold Gloves, and put together eleven consecutive .300 hit seasons. He continued to work hard. Good things were about to happen.

Chapter 15

Chasing .400

Tony's 1994 baseball season proved historic. But, at first, he encountered obstacles. He tweaked his left knee during a March exhibition game after planting his leg to make a throw from the outfield. The knee was drained of fluid on March 26.

Opening day was on April 4 before a home crowd of 42,251. He singled in his first at bat through the 5.5 hole between the shortstop and the third baseman. That triumph was short-lived. He strained his left calf in his second at bat while hitting a foul ball down the left field line. He ended the at bat grounding out weakly to the third baseman. He removed himself from the game after the fourth inning.

Next, he waged a running battle with manager Jim Riggleman concerning his return to the lineup. The team doctor reported Tony at 60 percent strength. Riggleman indicated he would never insert a player in the lineup who was at 60 percent, Tony Gwynn included.[1] Tony finally prevailed on Riggleman to return to the lineup on April 12 against Pittsburgh. He went 2-for-5.

Meanwhile, the Padres 1992–1993 fire sale continued to wreak havoc. The team's $13.3 million payroll was the lowest in the National League. It showed. San Diego lost 8 of its first 9 games. Their 1–8 record was the worst in the majors. From May 8–21 the Padres lost 13 games in a row, a franchise record.

Despite the early season frustrations, Tony was clicking at the plate. He hit safely in nine of his first 11 games with five of the nine being multi-hit games. On April 23, he went 5-for-5 against the Philadelphia Phillies. He slugged a double and a home run and drove in three runs to lead the Padres to an 8–2 win. He was batting .426 for the season.

After one of his doubles in the April 23 game, some of the Phillies accused Tony of stealing signs that were being flashed from their catcher to their pitcher. Tony strongly denied it. He yelled to the Phillies players that he was not stealing their signs. After the game, he took a cab home with his son, Tony Jr. Just watch, he told his son, in the next game the Phillies pitchers are going to try to hit me.[2]

The next day, Curt Schilling took the mound for Philadelphia. On Schilling's first pitch to Tony, Schilling plunked him on the right knee, sending him sprawling into the dirt by home plate. Jogging to first, Tony pointed at Schilling. He was convinced Schilling hit him intentionally. Tony's later review of the videotape confirmed his opinion.

Tony wanted to avoid being fined or suspended. So, he didn't charge at Schilling. That didn't mean he couldn't find another way to retaliate. He could make a statement by directing a line drive up the middle near the pitcher's mound.[3] In his second at bat against Schilling, the man who learned bat control as a youngster by swatting a wiffle balls, bound-up socks, and figs, hit a line shot just to the left of the pitcher's mound for a single. Tony followed with a hit in his next at bat. Overall he had collected eight straight hits, counting his previous day's 5-for-5 effort. His batting average soared to .448.

Tony noted he was trying to be more aggressive with inside pitches. On May 3, he hit a two-run homer in an 8–3 win. On May 13 during the Padres 13-game losing string, he hit his fourth homer of the season. His batting average dropped below .400 on May 15, but his average consistently remained in the .380s or .390s.

Tony was hitting the ball hard on nearly every at bat. On May 28, he hit a rocket (not on purpose) at the head of St. Louis Cardinals pitcher Alan Watson. Luckily, Watson barely got a glove on the ball and deflected it away. A game against the Cubs on June 14 provided another illustration of how consistently hard Tony was hitting the ball. He came up to the plate in the bottom of the ninth with one out, Padres runners on first and third, and the score tied, 5–5. Tony intended to hit a line shot or a ground ball to the left of the Cubs first baseman. Had he done so, the runner on third would have scored the winning run. Instead, he sent a hard-hit grounder directly at Cubs first baseman Mark Grace who turned it into an inning-ending double play. Tony's ground out to Grace was the 14th time that season he had hit into a double play. He was leading the National League hitting into double plays. Tony was unconcerned hitting into so many double plays because he was consistently hitting the ball hard.[4]

Tony hit a controversial three-run homer on June 19 to seal a 5–1 Padres victory. The ball hit near to the top of the centerfield wall at Jack Murphy Stadium, Thinking the ball hit another wall in the stands behind the outfield, Umpire Brian Gorman ruled it a home run. Replays

15. Chasing .400

demonstrated Gorman had erred. Still, it counted for Tony's eighth four-bagger of the season. He was well ahead of his typical home run pace.

The young Padres squad turned it around after their horrendous start. They went 18–11 after their 13-game losing streak. Amazingly, they were only nine games out of first. Major League Baseball's 1994 divisional realignment was one reason the Padres were within earshot of first place. Under the new alignment, the National and American Leagues each broke up into three divisions—a West, a Central, and an East. In addition, the majors revamped the post-season playoffs. Besides the three division winners in each league, a wild card team that failed to win a division title but otherwise compiled the best won-loss record among the non-division winners in their league would also qualify for the post-season. Because of realignment, the NL West reduced from seven to four teams—the Padres, Dodgers, Giants, and the Colorado Rockies. None of the four teams was playing well. In late June the Dodgers held first place even though they were only one game above .500. Consequently, bad as the Padres had been, they were still in the race.

Tony believed the team lost four games in June that they should have won. He maintained the Padres should have been five games out of first not nine.[5] His teammates' reactions to close losses displeased Tony. He sensed some of his teammates shrugged off the losses as if the Padres were supposed to lose. Manager Jim Riggleman pushed Tony to assume a more vocal leadership role, particularly since the Padres had so many young players.

Tony always had preferred to lead by example by exhibiting his professionalism, preparation, and striving for consistency. He rarely shied from offering batting advice to individual players, including opponents. One time he passed on hitting tips to Houston Astros third baseman Jeff Bagwell. Like Tony, Bagwell was having a stellar 1994 season. If he played for San Diego, Bagwell claimed, he would arrange to have breakfast with Tony Gwynn and "never leave his side."[6]

Gary Sheffield, the former teammate who won the 1992 National League batting title, also took note of Tony's assistance. A Padre on the 1994 team, Eddie Williams, reported he had benefited from suggestions by Tony and Padres batting coach Merv Rettenmund. They helped revitalize my career, Williams revealed. Williams played for Cleveland, the Chicago White Sox, and San Diego from 1986 to 1990. Beset by troubles at the plate, Williams was out of the majors during the 1991, 1992, and 1993 seasons.

Tony Gwynn

Tony worked with Williams during a January 1994 pre-season workout. Williams, aiming for power, was trying to pull every pitch. Tony advised against it.[7] You won't hit any higher than .220, he told Williams. He urged Williams to work on hitting the ball to all fields. Initially, Williams didn't put much stock in Tony's advice. Later, he embraced it. By June 1994, he was back in the major leagues with San Diego. He had a good 1994 season with 11 homers while batting .331.

Despite his ease in advising individual ballplayers, Tony was nervous about giving a talk to his entire team. He was comfortable judging the mood of one individual but he had less confidence in his ability to accurate gauge the emotions of his two dozen teammates. He feared he would come across as arrogant, as if he knew what was best for everyone. Nevertheless, he agreed to Riggleman's request to deliver a pre-game speech. Tony prepared for his speech much like he prepared for an at bat. He revised and revised his speech. He was up at 1:00 a.m. tinkering with his remarks. He kept Tony Jr. awake. He solicited his son's opinion. Groggily, his son voiced his assent.[8]

Tony preached themes of consistency, intensity, and valuing every game you play in his speech. This team is better than you think, he stressed. In a subsequent game, Tony reached first base in his first at bat. The pitcher promptly picked him off. Trotting back to the dugout, Tony knew he was going to hear it. Nice speech chortled a chorus of teammates. Whether Tony realized it or not, working on his speech prepared him for the career he would pursue upon his retirement from professional baseball.

Tony redeemed himself during a June 28 doubleheader against the Phillies. He hit his ninth home run of the season in the first tilt, though the Padres lost. He contributed to the team's 11–3 victory in the second game with two singles and two RBIs.

Tony had a three-hit evening on July 2 to run his batting average up to .393. That day, he was also named to the National League All-Star team for the 10th time. The fans neglected to vote him a starter. National League manager Jim Fregosi added him to the squad as a reserve. The fans failing to vote Tony Gwynn a starter, said Fregosi, makes no sense "being that he is one of the best hitters ever."[9] Lenny Dykstra, the fans' vote for the National League's starting center fielder, later withdrew from participation in the All-Star game. Dykstra was recuperating from an appendectomy. Fregosi tabbed Tony to start in Dykstra's place. Fregosi's gesture thrilled Tony. Typically, he batted but once or twice in All-Star games. For the 1994 game, he expected Fregosi to allow him more than one or two plate appearances.

15. Chasing .400

With his batting average hovering near .390, Tony knew what to expect when he traveled to Pittsburgh for the July 12 All-Star game. The can you hit .400 questions would keep coming and coming. Tony never liked repetitive questions from reporters. Sometimes in Spring Training he would attempt to beat reporters to the punch. He would tape stock answers to reporter questions to his locker (for example, my knee feels fine).

Eleven-year-old Tony Jr. had become a fixture in the Padres locker room at home games. Alicia would drive him to the game. Tony would bring him home afterward. Tony planned to take his son to Pittsburgh for the All-Star game. This will work, Tony joked.[10] When reporters popped the inevitable .400 questions he could answer, "Gosh, guys, I'd love to talk about hitting .400 but I've got my boy with me here and we've got to play catch." Furthermore, Tony argued, July is too soon to talk about hitting .400. It was more appropriate to wait until September.

The July 12, 1994, All-Star game was Tony's favorite. In his second plate appearance, he came up against Kansas City Royals pitcher David Cone with two runners on base. Years later, a reporter asked Tony to list the ten favorite at bats of his career. Tony's at bat against Cone in the All-Star game came in third on his list. Cone ran the count to 2–0, Tony recollected. He knew Cone rarely threw a slider on a 2–0 pitch. He had a hunch. He guessed slider. Cone threw one and Tony smoked it for a double to right field to drive in two runs for a 3–1 National League lead. Cone was perturbed that Tony had outguessed him. When Tony arrived at second base Cone turned and stared at him. It was all he could do, Tony recalled, not to laugh.[11]

The National League had lost six straight All-Star games to the American League. The Nationals were trailing 7–5 in the bottom of the ninth, on the verge of a seventh consecutive defeat. Tony's former teammate Fred McGriff was called on to pinch hit. McGriff lifted a two-run homer to tie the game, 7–7, sending it to extra innings. The American League failed to score in the top of the 10th. Tony, who played the entire game, led off in the bottom of the 10th. He fought off a tough pitch from Chicago White Sox pitcher Jason Bere. The ball snaked through the middle of the infield for a single. Will Clark was stationed at first base for the American League. After the 1993 season, Clark left the Giants. He signed as a free agent with the American League's Texas Rangers. Tony and Clark loved to talk hitting. They also shared a running joke. By the way, Tony once informed Clark, you are my son Tony's favorite player. After Tony's single, Clark could have been forgiven if he was thinking, as he had when he witnessed previous hits by Tony, how did that one get through there?[12]

Chatting with Clark, Tony predicted Bere would come inside with a pitch to the next National League batter, Moises Alou. Then Alou would turn on it and hit a double to left field giving him an opportunity to score the winning run. Sure enough, Bere threw an inside pitch. Alou turned on it for a double to left. Tony took off like a shot. He stumbled slightly roaring across the bag at second base. He charged around third base not even bothering to look for a stop or go sign from the National League's third base coach. He slid into home just beating the relay throw from Cal Ripken for an 8–7 National League victory to end the losing streak. Tony jumped up and spread his arms wide to indicate a safe sign.

Scoring the game-winning run on national television in the All-Star game had a temporary effect on Tony. He flew with Tony Jr., to his second home in Indianapolis. Tony ordinarily sneaked into Indianapolis unnoticed. On this occasion numerous patrons at the airport recognized him.

Tony was in the midst of the best season of his career. He was within serious reach of .400. He was hitting homers and driving in runs at a faster clip. Also, he was having fun in spite of the Padres' struggles with their won-loss record.

Eddie Williams was a continuing source of amusement. Tony like to imitate Williams' swings in batting practice. Though Williams was hitting to all fields more often, he was prone to taking big licks at inside pitches in an effort to drive the ball out of the park. Tony would mimic Williams' swing in practice. He would swing hard at inside pitches, and he would hit home runs.

In one game, Williams swung so hard at a pitch he spun around and landed in the dirt. Tony carefully reviewed that at bat on video. Confident he had it down pat based on his review of the videotape, in the next batting practice Tony took a wild swing at a pitch, spun around, and thudded into the dirt.[13] Williams gave it right back. Possibly the only person on the planet who could get away with it, Williams needled Tony about his weight and his midsection. Tony just chuckled.

Like manager Jim Riggleman, batting coach Merv Rettenmund urged Tony to become a more vocal leader during the 1994 season. At times, Rettenmund asked Tony to break down the opponent's starting pitcher for his teammates in pre-game meetings. Tony would do so, in detail.

Prior to a July game against the Colorado Rockies, Tony and Retten-

15. Chasing .400

mund were sitting in the visitor's dugout discussing hitting. Padres catcher Brad Ausmus, in his second season in the majors, sat nearby. "Brad," Tony asked, "why do you take so many fastballs right down the middle?" Ausmus stumbled to answer. "Too late," Tony interjected. "If you don't know the answer faster than that, then you don't really know why."[14]

That evening, a Rockies pitcher threw a fast one down the middle. Ausmus drilled it for a home run. After the game, Ausmus asked Tony when I was batting and then hit a home run were you thinking about me taking too many fastballs down the middle? Tony admitted he was thinking that. Well, retorted Ausmus, he hadn't taken that pitch. Tony laughed.

Prior to another Mets game in July, Padres batting coach Merv Rettenmund participated in an old-timer's game. Rettenmund had a creditable major league career. He was in the majors from 1969 to 1981, with Baltimore, Cincinnati, San Diego, and the California (now Los Angeles) Angels. He fashioned a .271 career batting average. His best seasons were 1970 and 1971 when he batted .322 and .318 respectively.

Rettenmund approached his job with a sense of humor. When offering a point of instruction and then watching Padres players execute on it, he would claim that he did it better when he was in the majors. Sensing the significance of the occasion, "Captain Video" lugged a video camera to film the old-timer's game. Tony planned to tape Rettenmund's at bats. If Rettenmund failed in his task, Tony and his teammates would earn bragging rights against the coach who insisted he did it better. Furthermore, they would have it on tape.

Rettenmund outfoxed them. In his first at bat, he singled to right. In his second at bat, he knocked a single down the left field line. Possibly energized by Rettenmund's old-timer's game at bats, the Padres pounded 19 hits to bushwhack the Mets 10–1. Manager Jim Riggleman tasked Tony with awarding the game ball. Tony had multiple choices to choose from. Center fielder Phil Plantier had gone 3-for-5 with three RBIs. Shortstop Luis Lopez was 3-for-4 with an RBI and a sacrifice fly. First baseman Eddie Williams stroked three hits with four RBIs. Instead, Tony promptly awarded the game ball to Rettenmund for his two hits in the old-timer's game. His teammates roared their approval.[15]

Tony's chase for .400 gained a great deal of media attention but trouble loomed. The owners and the players association had battled for years over the terms of free agency. Free agency undoubtedly led to increased player salaries. The owners were determined to effect change.

Tony Gwynn

Under the then-prevailing free agency regime, players could become free agents after six years of major league service. They also could file for salary arbitration in years four and five. In 1994, the owners proposed to eliminate salary arbitration. They further suggested reducing free agency from six to four years providing that a team could match any other team's offer in years five and six and thereby retain their player. Lastly, the owners wanted to impose a salary cap which, in effect, would limit the total salary dollars available to players. While the players association disagreed with all of the proposals, they were dead set against a salary cap. Matters took a turn for the worse in July when the owners delayed a large payment into the players' pension fund. The players association responded by threatening to strike even if it occurred midway through the 1994 season.

Tony knew baseball's labor strife might cut short the 1994 season. He nonetheless supported the players association. This fight is for the future of all players, Tony noted. Besides, he added, his son could be in the majors someday (that prediction came true).[16]

For the time being, games continued. For Tony, a July 15 game against the Mets, represented another highlight of his season. The Mets Bret Saberhagen and the Padres Andy Benes locked up in a classic pitchers' duel. Saberhagen shut out San Diego for 10 innings while Benes shut out the Mets for eight. The game was still tied 0–0 in the top of the 14th inning. Tony batted against Mets reliever Mike Maddux (Greg's brother). Tony rarely tried to hit a home run, except when he was mimicking Eddie Williams in practice. With neither team able to push across a run, Tony came up determined to hit it out of the park. Maddux threw Tony a pitch he liked. He turned on it and hit a long home run to right center. Phil Plantier followed with another solo homer. The Padres held on to beat the Mets, 2–1.

Tony had murdered Philadelphia Phillies pitching all season. He feasted again on the Phils staff during a July 22 doubleheader. He garnered four hits in Game 1, a Padres loss. He hit two doubles with three RBIs in Game 2, a Padres victory. For the season at this point, he was 22-for-35 against the Phils for a .611 batting average. His season batting number climbed to .393.

Negotiations between the owners and the players continued to stall. On July 28, the players laid down the gauntlet. They set an August 12 strike date. The players knew the owners made much of their money during the post-season playoffs. They assumed the prospect of losing the post-season, particularly the World Series, would pressure the owners to settle.

15. Chasing .400

Tony was seven points short of the .400 mark. But with a hot streak between July 28 and the proposed cancellation of play effective August 12, he might get up to .400. That brought up a question: If Tony was batting above .400 and the balance of the baseball season was canceled would he be credited as the first major leaguer to match or exceed the .400 mark since Ted Williams in 1941? The Elias Sports Bureau, the official statisticians of Major League Baseball, settled the matter. Gwynn, they ruled, is meeting the requisite average of 3.1 plate appearances per game to qualify for a batting title. Therefore, if baseball ends August 11 and Gwynn is batting .400 or above, his batting average will be considered official.

Between July 28 and August 1 Tony's average dipped to .386. The Padres set out for a 10-game road trip on August 1. They began with a four-game set against the Dodgers. Tony's final push to .400 was off to a good start. In Games 1, 2, and 3 of the Dodgers series, he went, collectively, 7-for-12 to bump his average to .391. He sat out most of Game 4 but he pinch-hit in the seventh inning and grounded out. His average slipped to .390.

The Padres next took on the Cubs at Wrigley Field for a three-game series from August 5–7. Tony was 2-for-5 on August 5 and 1-for-4 on August 6. His average stood at .389.

Tony's outstanding 1994 season was propelled, in part, by a trusty bat. He began using the bat in June. The bat contained only nine grains, unusually low for a major leaguer's bat. Tony dubbed the bat the "Nine Grains of Pain." He usually hit well with the bat.[17]

The nine grains bat was on full display against the Cubs on August 7. In his first three at bats Tony hit a double, a single, and his 12th home run of the season. He left the bat in the dugout for his fourth plate appearance. The Cubs brought in reliever Chuck Crim. Crim threw hard and inside. Tony feared using "Nine Grains of Pain" against Crim risked breaking the bat. Deploying another bat, he popped out against Crim. Tony was back up for his fifth at bat of the game in the eighth against another Cubs reliever Donn Pall. With the nine-grains bat he smoked a liner down the right field line. Had the ball fallen in for a hit, Tony likely would have made it to third for a triple and hit for the cycle. Instead, Cubs right fielder Sammy Sosa tracked down the ball for an out. Tony's 3-for-5 on August 7 bucked his average to .392.

The Padres were off on August 8. Assuming the strike date held and ended the season, the Padres final three games would be in Houston on August 9, 10, and 11. Predictably, Tony was hounded by the .400

question. He would reply that he didn't think he could do it.[18] Nonetheless, if Tony hit near a .700 pace during the Houston series, 9-for-14 for example, he would reach the elusive .400 plateau.

Tony gave it a try. He was 2-for-4 on August 9, bringing his average to .393. The August 10 game, however, was a disappointment. His 1-for-4 dropped his average back to .391. To pull off .400, he needed to get six hits in six at bats on August 11. He singled in his first at bat. But his ground out in his second at bat ended any serious quest to reach .400 before the strike. He went 3-for-5, still a good game by anyone's standard. He was at .394.

Tony heard rumors of possible progress in the labor negotiations. Perched in a Houston hotel room, he turned on the television set nearly every half hour for news that the strike was off. It wasn't to be. The strike was on.

Baseball's labor strife put Tony's charge to .400 on hold. He was not the only potential record-breaker affected by the strike. The 1994 season was prior to Mark McGwire surpassing Roger Maris's one-season record of 61 home runs. Matt Williams of the San Francisco Giants was on pace with Maris with 43 homers. Ken Griffey, Jr., of the Seattle Mariners was close behind at 40. He was six points shy of .400, Tony noted. But if there is no more baseball in 1994, he had a great year.[19]

The strike dragged on. On September 14 the owners cancelled the 1994 season, including the post-season. The players had hoped losing the post-season would force a settlement of the strike but the gambit failed. For the first time since 1904, there would be no World Series. The cancellation of the Series shocked and angered the fans. The Padres finished their year at 47–70, in last place in the NL West. Again demonstrating the weakness of the division that season, they were but 12 and half games out of first.

Major League Baseball declared Tony the National League batting champion. his fifth batting title. He won by a large margin. Jeff Bagwell finished second 26 points behind at .368. Tony led the majors not only in batting average but with hits at 165. He finished with 12 home runs and his 64 RBIs led his team. He led the National League hitting into double plays with 20. Amazingly, he hit into more double plays than he struck out (only 19 K's).

Could Tony have hit .400 but for the strike? "He might've had a chance at .400. You never know," said Padres outfielder Phil Plantier.[20] Yet it was clear Tony was on an upswing when the season ended. He hit .423 after the All-Star break. He hit .475 in the month of August.

15. Chasing .400

Merv Rettenmund was convinced Tony was going to do it. In fact, Rettenmund contended, Tony had been robbed of three hits by the official scorer when they were ruled errors. Those three hits would have put him at .400 on August 11.[21] Tony's sometimes balky left knee had been healthy all season, Rettenmund pointed out. He was running well. He hit the ball hard. Furthermore, he noted, Tony rarely complained about his batting technique during the 1994 season. That was unusual. Gone, at least that season, were the episodes of Tony collecting two or more hits in a game while insisting that he was "way off" or "pulling off the ball."

Possibly because he did not want to put pressure on himself, Tony denied he could hit .400 when queried about it during the 1994 season. Later, he affected a different tone. He was a speaker at an off-season sports banquet. An audience member popped the question. Would you have hit .400 in 1994 had there been a full season? Tony was emphatic in his answer. "I think I would have done it," he said.[22]

Tony was more emphatic during a discussion with a local sportswriter, Bob Chandler. "I would have hit .400. That year I wasn't being fooled. I wasn't swinging and missing. I wasn't chasing pitches. If that year would have continued, I would have hit .400."[23]

Tony's .394 remains in the books as the best major league batting average post–World War II. In 1994 the average major league batting average was .270. By 2021 the average dropped 26 points to .244. With the decline in overall batting averages and the increasing dominance of pitchers in recent decades, it seems doubtful any major leaguer will soon bat .394, much less .400.

Chapter 16

"I'm just Chris Gwynn's anonymous brother"

Watching another athlete break their records distresses some athletes. Ted Williams was not one of those athletes. He wrote in *The Science of Hitting* that "Baseball is crying out for good hitters."[1] Hitting is the most important part of the game, Williams argued, because it drives the action. Thus, when George Brett, Rod Carew, and Tony chased the .400 mark, Ted cheered them on. Impressed by Tony's run at .400 during the 1994 season, in January 1995 Williams invited him for a chat at the Ted Williams Hitters Museum in Hernando, Florida.

Ted and Tony conversed for half an hour. Sportscaster Bob Costas moderated part of their discussion. Sometimes when he fouled off a pitch, Ted Williams recalled, he smelled smoke. So do I, Tony chimed in. Williams claimed that, on occasion, despite the velocity of a ball thrown by a major league pitcher and the rapid movements in his swing, he could see a ball jump off his bat. Hasn't happened to me, Tony replied. Williams issued a statement Tony would not soon forget. You have to go after the inside pitch, Williams insisted. "That is where major league history is made."[2]

After reeling for two seasons from the fire sale, the Padres began to turn it around. Tom Werner's ownership group, which had struggled financially, sold the team in December 1994 to software entrepreneur John Moores. Moores brought in former Baltimore Orioles president and CEO Larry Lucchino, who agreed to a minority ownership in the team, to oversee the baseball operations. A week after purchasing the team, the new ownership orchestrated a twelve-player trade with the Houston Astros. The twelve-player exchange was the biggest trade in Major League Baseball since 1957. The trade brought third baseman Ken Caminiti and center fielder Steve Finley to San Diego. Both would make valuable contributions to the Padres improvement. In April 1995 the Padres signed pitcher Fernando Valenzuala as a free agent. Valenzuala

16. "I'm just Chris Gwynn's anonymous brother"

first broke into the majors with the Dodgers late in the 1980 season. He was an immediate success. After going 2–0 in 1980, he won 13 games in 1981. He won 19 games and the National League Cy Young Award in 1982. He won 150 major league games prior to signing with San Diego. He struggled in 1993 and 1994 but the Padres hoped he could revive his career. The Padres' various pre-season transactions added in excess of $5 million to payroll, a marked contrast to the penurious Tom Werner era.

There remained the problem of baseball's labor troubles. January and February 1995 passed with no sign of settlement to the players' strike. One barrier to settlement was the absence of a strong commissioner. When a labor dispute broke out in 1990, then-commissioner Fay Vincent shuttled between the owners and the players to help broker a four-year collective bargaining agreement (to run from January 1, 1990, to December 31, 1993). Vincent's intervention perturbed the owners. They fired him in 1992. They installed Bud Selig, owner of the Milwaukee Brewers, as acting commissioner. The commissioner was supposed to be an overarching authority above the owners and the players. Because he was an owner, Selig arguably was restrained by a conflict of interest. In addition, the owners limited the authority of the commissioner to take actions "in the best interests of baseball."

It was a federal judge, not the commissioner, who provided the impetus to settle the strike. In December 1994 the owners unilaterally rescinded salary arbitration and restricted the signing of free agents. In March 1995 the National Labor Relations Board (NLRB) leveled an unfair labor practices charge against the owners. The NLRB filed a lawsuit in the federal southern district of New York to enjoin the owners' unilateral actions. The case was assigned to federal district court judge Sonia Sotomayor. President Barack Obama would appoint Sotomayor to the U.S. Supreme Court 14 years later.

Sotomayor ruled for the NLRB. In her written opinion, she found that baseball's salary arbitration and free agency regimes were subjects for mandatory bargaining under the U.S. labor laws. In other words, the owners lacked the authority to unilaterally revoke or restrict salary arbitration and free agent acquisitions. The labor laws instead required them to bargain those topics with the players association. Sotomayor issued an injunction prohibiting implementation of the owners' unilateral decisions. She further ordered the owners and the players to abide by the 1990–1993 collective bargaining agreement until they could negotiate a new one.[3]

Tony Gwynn

The players agreed to work under the 1990–1993 agreement. They voted to end their strike on March 28. Baseball was back. The Major Leagues scheduled a three-week Spring Training followed by a 144-game regular season (rather than the usual 162). Tony is the odds-on favorite to be the first one to show up for Spring Training, said some of his teammates.

Tony looked forward to another season wielding the remarkable "Nine Grains of Pain" bat. But on a pitch from Padres infield coach Rob Picciolo during Spring Training the bat shattered. "I almost started crying," admitted Tony. Picciolo reported he almost cried too. Later, Tony taped the broken nine grains bat back together and placed it in a trophy case at home. He joked that he should have treated the bat better.[4]

The Padres 1995 season opened on April 26 at Jack Murphy Stadium. They lost 10–2 to the Houston Astros. They bounced back to win the next four, lost seven in a row, then won seven of their next eleven. They were 11–13 but within range of first place. This can be a good ballclub, Tony insisted.[5] He thought the Padres should have won the half the games they lost but mental errors—baserunning mistakes, walking weak hitters, chasing bad pitches—had cost them. Still taking on the role of a vocal leader, Tony revealed that he had spoken with every player on the team. Typical of Tony, he was careful not to exempt himself from criticism. "I'm not trying to be superior," he said. "I've got to be accountable too."[6]

Ted Williams mentored Tony on several occasions. Ted urged Tony to "let it go" on the inside pitch (National Baseball Hall of Fame and Museum, Cooperstown, NY).

Tony was off to a blazing start. He knocked out two hits apiece in his first four games. He collected three hits in his fifth. He went 3-for-5 on May 3. His batting

16. "I'm just Chris Gwynn's anonymous brother"

average stood at .500 for the season. Most players would be content to be batting .500 eight games into a season. Not Tony. He was the consummate perfectionist. "I stink,"[7] he announced. He was pulling off the ball. There must be a "little Irishman" sitting on his shoulder.[8] Tony's friend and teammate Eddie Williams thought Tony was swinging the bat well and doubted the "little Irishman" claim. "I'm not going to argue with him," Williams said. But Tony tried not to let himself be fooled by a temporary bout of good hitting. "If you're going about things wrong and are still getting hits, that will stop," he once said.[9]

Tony's season average declined from .500 to .309 by May 27. Many players would bemoan their slump. In this instance, Tony was elated. There had been a flaw in stride toward the ball, he noted. He corrected it. He pointed to a game on May 25 when he "carved" a single to left field. Tony said he felt like he "was cheating" before when the "little Irishman" explained his hits. Now, he announced, "I feel so much better about myself."[10] Tony's self-analysis was accurate. He went 3-for-5 on May 28. His batting average climbed back.

Unsurprisingly, baseball was struggling from the effects of the strike and cancellation of the 1994 World Series. The strike left some fans in a sour mood. On opening day in Detroit, fans hurled onto the field beer cans, baseballs, cigarette lighters, and, appropriate to the Motor City, a hub cap. Baseball's attendance was down 20 percent compared to 1994.

The new Padres ownership tried hard to bring the fans back. In an effort to improve public relations, the Padres established the Padres Scholars Program. Each year the team planned to award $5,000 scholarships to 25 local students. Tony was approached to help. He wrote a $5,000 check on the spot. He solicited teammates for additional donations.[11]

The Padres swept the Mets on June 9, 10, and 11 to move within three games of first place in the NL West. Next, they headed to St. Louis to face the Cardinals. They lost the first game. Tony's all-around play was instrumental to the Padres victory in the second. With the score tied 0–0 and a runner on first in the seventh inning, a Cardinals batter sent a long liner to right center. Tony got a great jump on the ball, hustled some 70 feet, and snagged it for an out to prevent a run from scoring. In the eighth with the score still tied 0–0, he threw out a Cardinals batter attempting to stretch a single into a double to stamp out another potential Cardinals rally. In the top of the ninth, Tony reprised his performance in a 0–0 game against the Mets the previous season. He led off the inning gunning for a home run. Looking to "turn and burn," as he liked to call it, he clubbed an inside pitch over the wall in right-center for a two-run homer. The Padres won, 3–0.

A 14–3 rout of the Dodgers on June 27 brought the Padres within two games of first. The next day they kept pace on the strength of Ken Caminiti's 4-for-5, two home run, five RBI performance to win, 8–2. Caminiti credited his day to a pre-game tip from Tony. Your batting stance has been more closed than usual, Tony advised Caminiti. Caminiti implemented the adjustment.[12]

Meanwhile, Tony was driving in baserunners at a career-best clip. The Padres embarked on a fourteen-game road trip from June 26–July 9. Tony drove in 15 RBIs in the 14 games. By the July 10 All-Star break he had 52 RBIs for the season, on a pace to drive in more than 100. He was batting .364.

After the All-Star game, where Tony was voted a starter by the fans, going 0-for-2 in a 3–2 National League victory, he maintained his RBI production. On July 31 against the Astros he singled in the third to drive in a run and push the Padres lead to 2–0. He singled in the fifth for another RBI and a 3–0 Padres advantage. He came to bat in the seventh against Astros left-hander Dean Hartgraves. The Padres had runners on first and third. Tony fell behind 0–2 in the count. On his third pitch, Hartgraves threw a wicked slider that likely would have struck out most batters. Tony fouled it off. Hartgraves tried to catch Tony off-balance on his next pitch, a fastball, but Tony directed a line drive through the 5.5 hole for his third RBI of the game and a 4–1 Padres lead. Tony's at bat against Hartgraves amused Padres pitcher Andy Ashby. In that situation, Ashby observed, you as a pitcher think you've got the batter right where you want him. It's not so when you are pitching to Tony Gwynn.[13]

Tony's season took a wrong turn on August 3. Leading off the seventh against the Giants, he fouled a pitch off his big right toe. He hobbled back into the batter's box, barely able to push off his right foot. Despite the injury, he managed to slap a single for his second hit of the game. He was removed for a pinch runner. The sore toe put Tony out of commission from August 4 to August 7. He attempted to come back on August 8 but reinjured the toe while chasing a fly ball hit by the Cubs' Mark Grace. The reinjury tore skin off both sides of his toe. That put him out of the lineup on August 9 and 10.

Tony's toe problem dramatically affected his power production. For the next four weeks he managed only five extra base hits—four doubles and a home run. The home run was significant. He hit the first grand

16. "I'm just Chris Gwynn's anonymous brother"

slam homer of his career on August 22 to lead San Diego to a 5–3 triumph over the Phillies. The Padres were hanging on in the division title race, two games out of first.

Tony was in position to grab his sixth National League batting title but he confronted an issue similar to his 1993 battle with Andres Galarraga. Dodgers catcher Mike Piazza suffered an early-season knee injury. He was out from May 11 to June 3. Piazza was hitting well. He was batting .390 at the end of June but was running far short of the plate appearances needed to qualify for a batting title. He dropped to .347 on July 31. He revived in August. On August 28, having remained healthy, he secured the necessary plate appearances to qualify for the batting title. He was hitting .367. Tony was 10 points back at .357. In six games from September 1–6, Tony poured on the jets. He had three three-hit games, a two-hit game, and two one-hit games. He sailed past Piazza with a .367 average while Piazza declined to .360.

Though he led the league in batting average, Tony complained his sore right toe robbed him of a strong core at the plate. Because he could not push hard off his right, and front, foot, he was, he said, missing the snap in his swing. He was only getting hits, he contended, with a variety of bouncers up the middle, grounders through the 5.5 hole, and what he labeled as "bleeders" to left field.[14] Tony can still hit well, explained Padres manager Bruce Bochy, because he was good at keeping his hands back. Advised Padres reserve catcher Brian Johnson, "We all realize that there is something special going on here. There is something special being around Tony every day, both as a person and as a player."[15]

The Padres began to fall back in the division title race in September. In the meantime, Tony continued to pull away from Piazza. He went 3-for-5 on September 16 while Piazza stumbled to 0-for-4. Tony led Piazza by 10 points, .367 to .357. Piazza finished the season at .346.

San Diego's flagging division title hopes ended for good on September 23. It was a Gwynn who shut the door—Tony's brother Chris. The Padres and Dodgers were locked up 2–2 in the bottom of the ninth at Dodger Stadium. The Dodgers had one on, one out. Dodgers manager Tommy Lasorda sent Chris up to pinch hit. He lofted a long, high drive toward Tony in right field. Tony gazed up at the night sky. He knew it was gone.

The Padres finished their season 70–74, eight games out of first. Still, it was an improvement over their miserable 1993 and 1994 seasons. Their pre-season acquisitions paid dividends. Ken Caminiti clouted 26 homers, drove in 94 runs, and batted .302. Steve Finley added 10 homers and batted .297. Both Caminiti and Finley won Gold Glove awards. Fernando Valenzuala recovered some of his early career magic with an 8–3 won-loss record.

Tony finished the season batting .368, the best in the majors. He captured his sixth National League batting title. He finished with 90 RBIs, the highest of his career thus far, nine home runs, 17 stolen bases, and only 15 strikeouts in 577 plate appearances. At ages 32, 33, and 34, when many baseball careers decline, he hit .358, .394, and .368. He became the first major leaguer since Joe "Ducky" Medwick in the 1930s to bat .350 or higher in three consecutive seasons. With his sixth National League batting title, he was behind only Stan Musial and Rogers Hornsby with seven and Honus Wagner with eight in career National League batting titles. By hitting .300 or above in his 13th consecutive season, he joined seven others in major league history who hit at or above .300 for 13 or more consecutive seasons.

The Padres competed in their final game of the 1995 season on October 1 at home against the Dodgers. Tony flied out his first two at bats. He informed the coaching staff his third at bat would be his final at bat of the season. Afterward, he was coming out of the game. Standing in the on-deck circle, he heard a familiar voice ringing out from the seats behind home plate. It was Alicia. "You had better get a hit," she bellowed.[16] Tony responded by smashing a double to left center. He was taken out for a pinch runner. Referring to the challenge issued by his teasing spouse, he said, "To get a hit in that situation was clutch for me."[17]

Tony's 1995–1996 offseason was eventful. On December 6, 1995, the Rotary Club of Denver named him the recipient of the Branch Rickey Award. The award was given to a player who put "Service Above Self." Tony's support of the Padres Scholars Program barely scratched the surface of his charitable endeavors. He and Alicia were long-time financial supporters of Casa de Ampara (Spanish for "House of Refuge"), a shelter for abused children. Tony was active with the Jackie Robinson YMCA in San Diego. Michael Brunker, one of Tony's former coaches at San Diego State, served as the YMCA's executive director. At one point, Brunker advised, several of the YMCA's vans used to transport children were vandalized. Tony wrote a check for repairs. Tony does more than write checks, Brunker noted. He spends hours playing with the children. The Gwynns were active with other non-profits, including the Police Athletic League and the Neighborhood House Association.[18]

In one respect, however, Tony and Alicia undertook a commitment

16. "I'm just Chris Gwynn's anonymous brother"

greater than many celebrities and athletes who donate their time and money to charities. Over the years, the Gwynns sprawling Mediterranean home in Poway, California, became a haven for underprivileged children. They mentored them, guided them, and sometimes obtained custody. They paid for their educations and other needs. Eventually, Tony and Alicia raised or fostered several dozen children from broken homes.[19]

You would never hear from Tony regarding his charitable activities. Once, the Padres public relations area wanted to film Tony visiting a group of children during the Christmas holidays. Tony would have none of it. "I just don't want to talk about that stuff," he would say.[20]

During the 1995–1996 offseason Tony underwent the fourth surgery on his troublesome left knee. Doctors removed loose particles floating in his knee.

Another focus in the offseason was a new stadium for the San Diego State baseball team. Its long-time coach, Jim Deitz, had never won the NCAA title but he ran a successful program. He led the Aztecs to several appearances in the NCAA tournament. Deitz and his players labored in substandard athletic facilities. The bleachers to their stadium were constructed of wood. It was not unusual to see Deitz, hammer in hand, working on repairs to the stadium. One time, Deitz climbed up on a forklift to repair a light tower. Some of the women living in a nearby dormitory feared Deitz was a "peeper."[21] Tony remembered toiling on one of Deitz's many construction projects. He poured concrete, he recalled, for a barbecue area outside the outfield.

For years Deitz lobbied the San Diego State administration to build a new baseball stadium. In the spring of 1996 Deitz's dream came true. Deitz conferred with Tony, Padres owner John Moores, and San Diego State Athletic Director Rick Bay. Moores pledged $3 million toward a new stadium (later adjusted to $4 million). Moores insisted on one condition. He wanted the new stadium named "Tony Gwynn Stadium." Deitz readily agreed. Tony was his most famous former player. Further, Tony was a loyal alum of the program. On "Alumni Day," Tony and other ex–Aztec players would take on the current San Diego State varsity in an exhibition game. Tony went along with the plan but he was not happy about it. "I would much rather see Coach Deitz's name on it," Tony said. "He's the guy who's been there for 24 years and made the program what it is today." Construction commenced with the new stadium scheduled to open at the beginning of the Aztecs' 1997 season.[22]

The Padres made important offseason acquisitions as they had the year before. On December 23, 1995, they signed free agent outfielder Rickey Henderson. In 1996 Henderson would be heading into his 18th major league season. He was a certain Hall of Famer. He won the American League Most Valuable Player award in 1990. He was one of the game's most dynamic players. He was, by far, the all-time major league leader in career stolen bases. The Padres also acquired first baseman Wally Joyner. A solid bat at the plate, Joyner sported a .290 career batting average for his ten previous years in the majors. Lastly, the Padres picked up Chris Gwynn.

Chris had endured an up-and-down major league career since breaking in with the Dodgers in 1987. He hit respectably. His biggest problem was getting playing time. He was, however, lackluster in 1995 (aside from the game-winning home run against the Padres). He hit .214 while participating in only 67 games. Tony was thrilled to have his brother on board.

The Padres opened the 1996 season on the road. They won four of five. They opened at home on April 8. Ted Williams traveled to San Diego to throw out the ceremonial first pitch before a crowd of 44,470. Before the game, Ted and Tony talked for two hours. Ted again impressed upon Tony to swing aggressively at an inside pitch. Because of a stroke, Ted used a cane. Pretending he was swinging at an inside pitch with his cane, he said to Tony, "You've got to turn on it. You've got to let it go. Let it go."[23]

Tony and Ted rode out to the pitcher's mound in a convertible. Ted was somewhat unsteady from the stroke. He took his place in front of the pitcher's mound. Tony steadied him by placing his hand on Ted's non-throwing shoulder. Ted fired a ball to home plate. The Padres swept past the Florida Marlins, 9–2. Tony doubled in the fourth inning and scored the first run of the game. This is going to be a good team, Tony predicted.[24] He was right. The Padres were either in first place or tied for first for much of the 1996 season. They were never more than two and a half games out of first.

Tony had been thinking about Ted Williams' philosophy to turn aggressively on inside pitches. That is where baseball history is made, Ted had contended. Since Tony was well acquainted with baseball history, Ted's statement resonated. Tony's teammates noted that Tony could hit 20 or more home runs a season if he wanted. Tony worried about adopting Williams' approach. He feared it might retard his overall production. He fretted about being struck out more often, a hard thing for a perfectionist to stomach. Still, Tony had tried to "turn and burn" more frequently in the 1995 season, resulting in 90 RBIs.

16. "I'm just Chris Gwynn's anonymous brother"

Tony cracked six doubles in his first 12 games of the 1996 season. He ran into trouble in his 13th. During a close game with the Colorado Rockies he felt a sharp pain in his right heel. He took himself out of the game. Doctors discovered an inflamed bursar sac on his heel. Tony was out of the lineup for the next 10 days. He was out again from July 1 to the first week of August after an MRI revealed a partial tear and fraying of his right Achilles tendon. His right foot was put in a cast.

The heel injury forced Tony to ditch Williams' advice. He found it difficult to push off his right foot, robbing him of his "gap power" to left center and right center. He hit six doubles in his first 12 games. He hit just one in his next 37. He experienced excruciating pain while wearing regular baseball shoes. He switched to cross-trainers with spikes. The cross-trainers set his feet one inch higher off the ground than baseball shoes. While a relatively small difference, it was one more thing where he had to adjust.

There was one notable exception to Tony's power drain. On June 5 he came up to bat against the Cardinals in the bottom of the ninth. The Padres were down 4–3 with two on and two out. Tony hammered a three-run walk-off homer for a 6–4 Padres win. Tony lumbered slowly around the bases. One of his teammates thought it was a victory trot. Not at all, Tony explained, he just couldn't run.[25]

The Padres were in first place in the NL West by six and a half games on June 6. They faltered the rest of June. For a brief time, they fell back to fourth place. They rallied to battle the Dodgers and the Rockies for first place throughout July and August. Though unable to hit consistently with power, Tony was batting in the .340s most of August. Tony at 50 percent, Padres reliever Trevor Hoffman maintained, is better than most players at 100 percent.

The Padres obtained another cog for their division title drive on July 31. They traded for Milwaukee Brewers outfielder Greg Vaughn. Vaughn was having a spectacular 1996 season. With two months of the season still to go. He had hit 31 homers and driven in 95 runs.

With Vaughn, the Padres now had four veteran outfielders who were used to starting—Vaughn, Tony, Steve Finley, and Rickey Henderson. Henderson had a reputation. Some compared him to Yogi Berra. Berra was a master of the malapropism. (When you come to a fork in the road, take it; you're not mathematically eliminated until you are mathematically eliminated.) Henderson thought the comparison to Berra was overblown. But he did have a propensity to refer to himself in the third person. When the Padres acquired Vaughn, manager Bruce Bochy asked

Henderson if he was comfortable platooning instead of starting. "Rickey is okay with this as long as Rickey knows when Rickey is going to play."[26] Henderson answered. Another time, Henderson left a voice mail message for Padres General Manager Kevin Towers. "This is Rickey calling on behalf of Rickey," Henderson said.[27]

One day, Tony was talking in the Padres clubhouse with *San Diego Union-Tribune* writer Bill Center. Tony and Center were in the midst of a long dialogue on their favorite nicknames for current and former baseball players. Henderson happened to drop by his locker nearby. Tony and Center knew Henderson had a long association with professional baseball. Thus, they asked him: What is your favorite baseball nickname? "Rickey," Henderson replied. Tony laughed so hard he fell backward on his stool and banged his head.[28]

Tony went 4-for-4 in an 8–0 Padres win over the Cincinnati Reds on September 15. It was the 29th time in his career that he hit safely four or more times in a game. Umpires were noticing strange notations on Tony's bats. The bats contained a series of circles, dots, and markings, all in different colors. Those weren't put there by Louisville Slugger noted the home plate umpire, Jerry Crawford, during the September 15 Reds game. He was bored sitting on bench during July and the first week of August, Tony explained to Crawford, so he passed the time by doodling on his bats.[29]

Directing mostly singles and hitting to all fields, Tony's average was up to .357 after his 4-for-4 outing against the Reds. He led the Dodgers Mike Piazza by 10 points for the National League batting title. He confronted the same dilemma as Andres Galarraga in 1993 and Piazza in 1995. Because he missed a large chunk of the season with his heel injury, his prospects were dim for attaining the 502 plate appearances required to qualify for a batting title. He needed to average 4.92 plate appearances in the final 12 games of the season to qualify—a high bar.

The Rockies faded from the division title race. The Padres and the Dodgers, however, were both hot teams in September. On September 18, the Dodgers led San Diego by half a game. Over the past 25 games, the Padres had gone 17–8 while the Dodgers went 19–6. The Padres had nine games left in their season; the Dodgers 10. The two teams were set to play each other in seven of their final games. The teams collided in a four-game series in San Diego from September 19–22. Each team won two. The Dodgers, who at this point in the season had played one fewer games than the Padres, remained a half game up.

The Padres suffered a setback during a two-game series at home

16. "I'm just Chris Gwynn's anonymous brother"

against the Rockies on September 24 and 25. The Padres lost two while the Dodgers beat the Giants twice to extend their lead to two and a half. The Padres were off on September 26. The Giants did them a favor by besting the Dodgers, 6–1. The Dodgers led the Padres by two with the two teams set to square off in Los Angeles for their final three games of the regular season.

The first game of the series was tied 2–2 at the end of nine innings. The Padres pushed across three runs in the top of the 10th. Trevor Hoffman, on his way to becoming one of the top relievers in baseball, shut down the Dodgers one-two-three in the bottom half to seal the victory. The Padres were one back with two to play.

Tony provided the decisive blow in the second game. He batted in the top of the eighth with two outs and the bases loaded. Surveying the Dodgers defensive alignment, Tony decided his best option was to direct a ball through the 5.5 hole. That's exactly where he hit it, driving in two runs for a 4–2 Padres advantage. The lead held leaving the Padres and the Dodgers tied for the division lead with one game to play. That day, both teams qualified for the post-season when the Montreal Expos lost 4–0 to the Atlanta Braves. The winner of the final game would take the division title whereas the loser would qualify for the post-season playoffs as a wild card.

Commenting on Tony's key hit in the second game, Dodgers manager Bill Russell (who replaced Tommy Lasorda mid-season) said, "Tony is a special hitter. We had him defended well right there. The pitch is where we wanted it. And he placed the ball perfectly. I've never seen another hitter able to get hits like that."[30]

The final game was another extra-inning affair. The pitching staffs dominated. The game was 0–0 going into the top of the 11th. The Padres' Steve Finley led off with a single. Ken Caminiti followed with another single. Padres manager Bruce Bochy sent Chris up to pinch hit.

Chris struggled throughout the 1996 season. He was batting .169 coming into the final game of the year. Several weeks prior the Padres considered sending him down to the minors. Bochy had asked Chris to pinch hit in the Padres 5–4 loss to the Rockies on September 24. Chris hit into a game-ending double play. Bochy caught flak from the fans and the media for relying on Chris in a crucial situation in a tight division title race.

Bochy remained confident in his player. This time, Chris came through. He smoked a double to right center to drive in Finley and Caminiti for a 2–0 Padres lead. Trevor Hoffman again shut out the Dodgers in the bottom of the inning to preserve the victory. The Padres were NL West champs. They finished the regular season 91–71. They were back in the post-season for the first time since 1984.

The Padres celebrated their championship in their dressing room in typical fashion. Champagne corks popped. Players drenched each other. Tony had much to say after Chris's division-title winning double. "Watching Chris get that hit was one of the highlights of my life. He's obviously had a tough year but it was his hit that sent us to the playoffs as division champions."[31] He added, proudly, that "Today, I'm just Chris Gwynn's anonymous brother."[32] The wait for a division title was worth it, Tony continued. Tony knew he had made sacrifices to stay in San Diego. Other star players sought free agency and to land with a team they expected to reach the playoffs. In contrast, Tony was a fixture in San Diego. He was "Mr. Padre."

Tony garnered his seventh National League batting title and his third in a row. He won in an unprecedented manner. He finished the regular season with 498 plate appearances, four short of 502. For the first time in its history, Major League Baseball applied a little-noticed rule. A provision in Rule 9 stated that if a batter fell short of the requisite plate appearances, their batting average could be recalculated by assuming they registered an out in all plate appearances below the minimum number. Tony finished at .353. Applying Rule 9, it was assumed Tony failed to hit safely in the four appearances he was short of 502. The recalculation dropped his average from .353 to .349, which was still better than the second-place finisher, the Rockies' Ellis Burks at .344. Tony was declared the batting champion. Officially, his batting average remained at .353. He had hit above .350 for the fourth consecutive season. No major leaguer had accomplished the feat since Rogers Hornsby in the 1920s. Tony was now tied for third all-time with Hornsby in career batting titles with only Honus Wagner at eight and Ty Cobb of the American League at 12 ahead of him.

Tony was proud of winning the 1996 title. He struggled nearly the entire season with his sore right heel. After being out from July 1 through August 5, he hit at a .372 clip the rest of the season (68-for-137). To come back like that, Tony believed, said a lot for his preparation.[33]

Ken Caminiti, who slugged 40 homers, drove in 130, and batted .326 was named National League MVP. He went on a tear after the All-Star break. In the month of August, for example, he hit 14 home runs with 38 RBIs. Later, baseball's dark side appeared. Interviewed by Tom

16. "I'm just Chris Gwynn's anonymous brother"

Verducci for a 2002 article in *Sports Illustrated*, Caminiti admitted that, nursing a sore shoulder, he traveled to Mexico during the 1996 All-Star break to purchase performance-enhancing drugs. Caminiti disclosed he used steroids during his career, which ended in 2001.[34] Two years after publication of the *Sports Illustrated* story, Ken Caminiti died of a drug overdose. Most active players were reluctant to talk about drug use in baseball. Tony was not. "It's like this little secret we are not supposed to talk about," he told reporters. He publicly condemned the use of steroids.[35]

The Padres took on the National League Central Division champion St. Louis Cardinals in a best-of-five series in the first round of the 1996 playoffs. Possibly, the team expended too much energy battling the Dodgers for the NL West title. They lost to the Cardinals three straight.

Chapter 17

"Power hitter"

On paper, the 1997 Padres possessed the talent to repeat as NL West champs. In reality, they failed to live up to expectations. They dropped into fourth place on April 13. They remained in fourth most of the season. Injuries were part of the problem. Steve Finley, Wally Joyner, and pitcher Joey Hamilton went on the disabled list in April. Rickey Henderson, Ken Caminiti, and pitcher Andy Ashby went down in May. The Padres had little difficulty scoring runs. They scored 795 runs during the season, a club record. The pitching staff lagged. The staff posted a 4.98 ERA, the second worst in the National League. San Diego finished the season 76–86, leaving them 14 games behind the first-place San Francisco Giants.

At thirty-seven years old, Tony posted the greatest season of his career. He exceeded 1994, when he batted .394. The stage for his spectacular year was set during the preseason. He underwent surgery on October 23, 1996, to repair the bursar sac and the partial tear on his right Achilles tendon. The tear was worse than originally anticipated. It proved to be a 30 percent tear, but it was repairable. Tony was grateful. The Achilles could have "blown" completely, he said.[1]

Like most professional athletes, Tony worked out in the offseason. The close call with his Achilles provided additional motivation. Once he was cleared by doctors, Tony shot one hundred jump shots every day. He hustled up and down stopped escalators at Jack Murphy Stadium. He ran with a parachute tied to his back.

Hampered by injuries in 1995 and 1996, Tony was mentally and physically prepared to follow Ted Williams' advice to "let it go" on inside pitches. It is not as easy as it sounds, Tony explained. When you "let it go" you are apt to miss the ball or get out in front and foul it off. He had perfected a move with his right foot to offset the tendency to whiff or foul off a ball.[2] Timing the maneuver with a pitcher's release point, he had worked on lifting his right foot and softly bringing it down. In addition, Tony noted, he improved his hip movement. When he was trying

17. "Power hitter"

to hit to the opposite field, he would be sliding his hips. When he went hard after an inside pitch, he concentrated on turning, not sliding, his hips.[3]

Tony also had no worries about his status with the Padres. He had accepted a three-year, $12.9 million dollar contract extension to cover the 1998, 1999, and 2000 seasons. In 1997, he was being paid $4 million. Tony is being paid good money, wrote *San Diego Union-Tribune* reporter Wayne Lockwood. Nonetheless, Lockwood pointed out, 75 major league players earn more money than Tony, none of whom have won seven batting titles. Tony Gwynn could be "the most underpaid player in the history of baseball," Lockwood asserted.[4] Tony largely ignored the issue. My family is a team, he said. "We love it here. Anyone who wants to leave here [San Diego] is crazy."[5]

Tony was batting a respectable .313 eight games into the 1997 season. He had hit no homers and one double. His power surge from "letting it go" commenced on April 9. He hit a two-run shot against the Pittsburgh Pirates when he pulled an inside pitch over the right field wall. He clubbed his second home run of the season on April 15. He followed the next day with another one. Both homers came on an inside pitch pulled to right field.

The Padres lost 12–3 to the Houston Astros on April 22. Tony drove in all three Padres runs, two of them on a two-run homer in the eighth inning. Noting Tony's unusual home run production, first-base umpire Joe West needled Tony during the Houston game. "I'm going to check your bat," he said.[6]

Tony smashed his fifth home run of the year on April 25 during a 5–4 loss to Atlanta. "Power hitter," joked Atlanta first baseman and Tony's former teammate, Fred McGriff.[7] On May 2, Tony "turned and burned" on an inside pitch from Montreal Expos pitcher Anthony Telford. Tony's blast tied the score, 4–4. The Padres pitching staff faltered. San Diego lost, 5–4. Tony collected three hits in the game. His second hit, a single, put him at career hit number 2,600.

May 3 was a banner day for Tony. In the afternoon, he attended the dedication of San Diego State's Tony Gwynn Stadium. The new facility boasted skyboxes, seating for 3,500, air-conditioned clubhouses, a museum, and two large batting cages. That evening against Montreal, Tony socked his seventh homer, a liner to right center for a 1–0 San Diego lead. It turned out to be the only run of the game. The pitching staff held on for a 1–0 victory.

In seventeen games from May 13–30, Tony hit safely 33 times in 62

Tony Gwynn

at bats. He hit two homers, seven doubles, and drove in 15 runs. On May 30, his batting average was at .408.

In one game during that stretch in May, Tony tortured Atlanta Braves pitcher Greg Maddux. Maddux was an 11-year veteran of the majors. He was well on his way to one of the great pitching careers. He won 155 games in his first ten seasons. He would eventually win 355 games in his career, eighth best in major league history. He would have one of his better years in 1997, by going 19–4. Some of baseball's premier pitchers, for instance Walter Johnson, Bob Feller, and Randy Johnson, relied on a blazing fastball. Maddux threw his fastball at an average speed, but the ball had great movement. What made Maddux tough was his pinpoint control. He threw a variety of pitches, including a 2-seam fastball, a 4-seam fastball, a changeup, a sinker, and a cutter. Because he had such good control of so many pitches, Maddux was adept at keeping batters off balance.

Tony was not one of those batters. Thus far in his career, Tony was batting above .400 in his plate appearances against Maddux. On May 27, Maddux failed to get Tony out. Maddux threw a fastball on the outside corner during Tony's first at bat. Tony smashed it to right center for a double. Typically, when a batter jumps on a pitch, a pitcher avoids throwing it during the next at bat. Tony guessed Maddux would try to fool him by again relying on the fastball on the outside corner. Tony was looking for it. He cracked a single to center. Maddux threw a nasty changeup in Tony's third at bat. Tony fought it off for a line drive single to center. Having studied Maddux's pitching patterns, Tony knew the one pitch Maddux hadn't thrown to him all day was a fastball that runs into a hitter. Tony was ready for that one too. He lined a single to center for his fourth hit of the game.

On the mound, Maddux was shaking his head and cursing a blue streak.[8] Tony's four-hit performance was not enough to carry the Padres. They lost, 9–2.

Tony was batting .411 on June 1, inviting the inevitable talk of hitting .400. "Tony Gwynn can do it," said Ted Williams. "I wish him luck. I really do." Had he known hitting .400 was such a big deal, Williams advised, he would have tried to do it more often.[9] On June 8 Tony tied Williams on the career hits list with hit number 2,654. Tony doffed his hat to Ted. "Ted Williams is a hell of a lot better player than I'll ever be," he declared.[10]

Tony belted three doubles against the St. Louis Cardinals on June 10. He came up in the bottom of the ninth with two on and two outs and

17. "Power hitter"

the Padres trailing 5–3 and on the brink of defeat. He hit a two-run double to tie the score 5–5. The game went into extra innings. Tony came up in the bottom of the 11th with two outs and a Padres runner on second base. The score was still tied, 5–5. Cardinals manager Tony La Russa wanted nothing to do with Tony. He ordered Tony intentionally walked. The strategy worked when the next batter, Steve Finley, grounded out. The Padres prevailed in the end when they pushed across a run in the bottom of the 12th to win, 6–5.

Tony produced another hot streak in seven games from June 22–30. He clocked 12 hits with three homers and four doubles and drove in 17 runs. In one of those games, at Dodger Stadium on June 26, he came up in the seventh with the score knotted at 4–4. The bases were loaded. He hit a slicing liner to left center. Dodgers left fielder Brett Butler attempted a diving stab at the ball. He came up short. Tony and all three Padres baserunners scored on the play for an unusual inside-the-park grand slam home run. Butler was hurt on the play. He had to leave the game with a strained neck and shoulder. "It's one of those plays," Tony said, "where you have mixed emotions." Tony respected the 40-year Butler who had overcome throat cancer and torn cartilage in his shoulder to remain in the majors. "Tell Tony I'm okay," Butler responded.[11] After the game with the Dodgers, Tony had 13 homers, 67 RBIs, and a .399 batting average.

Tony had company chasing the .400 mark. Larry Walker of the Colorado Rockies was also in the mix. He was batting .408 on June 30.

The major leagues adopted interleague play between the American and National Leagues effective for the 1997 baseball season. San Diego played a two-game set in Oakland on June 30 and July 1. Tony had his second four-hit game of the season on July 1. His RBI single in the sixth inning put the Padres in front, 5–1. Once again, the pitching fell apart. San Diego lost, 8–6.

The fans voted Tony a starter for the 1997 All-Star game. He participated in the 13th All-Star game of his career on July 8 at Cleveland's Jacobs Field. For the most part, he had not fared well in All-Star games, He went 0-for-3. The National League lost, 3–1.

Tony notched his third four-hit game of the year against the Colorado Rockies on July 11. With the Padres down 5–1 in the eighth, he blasted a solo shot to make it 5–2. Down 5–3 with two outs and a runner on in the ninth, he hit a long home run, 425 feet to right field, to even the count at 5–5.

Once again, a manager avoided pitching to Tony in extra innings with runners on base. Greg Vaughn led off the 11th with a double. Rockies pitcher Jerry Dipoto retired the next two Padre batters. Rockies manager Don Baylor ordered Tony intentionally walked. The strategy succeeded. Ken Caminiti grounded out to end the threat. The Rockies scored in the bottom half to prevail, 6–5.

After a three-hit performance at home against the Giants on July 14, Tony was batting .402. Larry Walker was at .411.

Having observed Tony's outstanding 1997 season, Florida Marlins manager Jim Leyland told the press that you're not going to stop Tony Gwynn. Leyland compared shutting down Tony to stopping the Detroit Lions' all-pro running back Barry Sanders. Forget about it, he asserted.[12]

During the week of July 23, *Sports Illustrated* featured Tony on its cover. The best hitter since Ted Williams declared the magazine. Gwynn, *Sports Illustrated* reported, has thus far drilled 15 homers with 84 RBIs and there were 64 games remaining in the season. "It's the kind of year that I've dreamed about my whole career." Tony said to *Sports Illustrated* reporter Tom Verducci.[13]

Verducci sought to locate Tony's place among baseball's all-time greatest hitters for average. It's difficult to compare players from different eras, Verducci conceded. For example, he wrote, in the past week Tony Gwynn has competed in six games in four times zones and faced 16 different pitchers in 28 plate appearances. The extensive travel and confronting so many relief pitchers was not an issue for players in previous eras. Verducci's approach was to compare how the best hitters of each era compared to their peers. Employing this formula, Verducci rated Tony the sixth-best hitter for average of all time, behind Ty Cobb, Ted Williams, Rogers Hornsby, Nap Lajoie, and Wee Willie Keeler.

Another analyst attempted a more detailed approach. Dr. Michael Schell was a professor of biostatistics at the University of North Carolina. Schell specialized in using statistics to determine the most effective treatments for cancer. He was also a devoted baseball fan. Schell decided to use his knowledge of statistics to calculate baseball's best hitter for average. In undertaking his analysis, Schell calculated four statistical adjustments.

First, he considered "hitting feasts and famines." He noted that batters hit for high averages in the 1920s and 1930s while batters in recent years hit more often for power. Schell developed a mathematical adjustment to batting averages to account for the trends of different eras of baseball.

Second, he considered the "ballpark effect." He pointed out that

17. "Power hitter"

batters play half their games in their home ballpark. In some parks, it is easier to hit home runs. In others, because of foul lines placed close to the stands leaving little room for foul outs, it is easier to get hits.

Third, Schell accounted for the talent pool of different eras. For example, how strong was the overall level of talent?

And lastly, Schell restricted his analysis to what he labeled as a ballplayer's "productive career." Most players decline near the end of their careers, he indicated. After reviewing numerous career batting numbers, Schell determined that a batter's first 8,000 major league at bats best represented a player's "productive career." Having made the aforementioned four adjustments, Schell punched the numbers.

Tony Gwynn, Schell announced, is the greatest hitter for average of all-time. According to Schell, Tony's statistically-adjusted career batting average was. 343, beating out Ty Cobb by one percentage point.[14]

Schell visited the Padres dugout during the 1997 season. So you're the one who is putting the pressure on me, Tony joked. Tony was one of the few major leaguers who paid for his own bats. One reason was that he broke the bats. Another reason was he wanted to control disposition of the bats, not the team. He might have as many as one hundred bats at his disposal. Some of the bats were broken. Others he rejected because they were not up to his specifications. He preferred to sign broken or unused bats and donate them to charities. On occasion, Tony would donate a bat he was using currently. He shocked Schell when he presented him a bat that had marks and clearly had been used. That bat has hits on it, Tony pointed out to Schell.[15]

Tony experienced problems with a hamstring as the season wore on. At times his left knee would swell up. Possibly because of injuries, his power production waned by mid–August. His batting average was still excellent, around .380, but he ceased hitting as many home runs and doubles. During an August 8–10 series at Wrigley Field in Chicago, Tony had a 1-for-11 streak. Tony was holed up in a Chicago hotel room reviewing video and looking for answers to his cold streak when he felt a sharp pain. The problem turned out to be a kidney stone. While the rest of the team traveled to their next stop, Tony underwent surgery at a Chicago hospital to remove the stone. Professional athletes learn to play through pain. Tony was no different. But the pain he suffered from the kidney stone, he declared, was the worst feeling of his life. The aftereffects of the surgery also may have retarded Tony's ability to hit with power.

Tony was still a dangerous hitter. He drove in four runs against

Tony Gwynn

Atlanta on September 4. With the Padres down 4–3 in the fourth inning, he crunched a three-run homer to put San Diego ahead 6–4. It was his first home run since July 29. The game was even at 7–7 in the eighth. Padres second baseman Quilvio Veras was on second with two outs. With Atlanta battling for the NL East division title, Braves manager Bobby Cox was taking no chances. He followed a strategy that increasingly was being used against Tony in tight games in the late innings. He ordered Tony walked intentionally. Then, in an unusual move, he ordered Ken Caminiti walked to load the bases. The next batter, first baseman Archi Cianfrocco, grounded out to end the inning. Cox's strategy paid off when the Braves pulled out an 8–7 victory in extra innings.

Tony came to bat on September 10 against the Florida Marlins in the bottom of the ninth at Qualcomm Stadium. (Earlier in the 1997 season the name of Jack Murphy Stadium in San Diego was changed to Qualcomm Stadium.) The game was tied at 3–3 with two runners on base. The Marlins were fighting for a playoff spot. Earlier in the year Marlins manager Jim Leyland commented that you can't stop Tony Gwynn. He didn't. Tony rapped a single through 5.5 hole to drive in the winning run. With the walk-off single Tony had driven in 111 RBIs for the year. It was his 199th hit.

Two days, later Tony collected hit number 200 with another RBI single. It was the fifth time in his career he accumulated 200 or more hits in a season but the first time since 1989. Tony was forthright with reporters after the game. Still, he was sensitive to being called selfish about his individual accomplishments, a charge that had been leveled against him by Jack Clark and Mike Pagliarulo during the 1990 season. "I'm happy" about the 200 hits, he said. He realized the fans and his teammates didn't want to hear about it. Nonetheless, getting to 200 hits was "the one thing" he wanted to accomplish, statistically, during the 1997 season.[16]

Both Tony and the Rockies' Larry Walker had lost sight of .400 weeks earlier. Yet by any standard both were having outstanding seasons. As of September 17, Walker clung to the National League batting lead with a .371 average. Tony was five points back at .366. Walker had already hit 45 home runs for the year. Tony's season home run and RBI totals were already the best of his career.

Tony indicated that he had one advantage over Walker in the race for the batting title. He had been in this position before whereas Walker had not. Furthermore, he had learned a lesson in 1986 when he paid

17. "Power hitter"

too much attention to the batting numbers for Tim Raines and Steve Sax. Based on that experience, he learned to concentrate on what he could do and forget about his competitors. Walker's advantage, Tony went on, is that Walker finishes his season at home while he finished his season on the road.[17]

Walker's advantage failed to pay off. Tony once again poured it on when it counted. He collected three hits apiece on September 19 and 20 while Walker went 1-for-7. Tony forged to a narrow lead for the batting title, .3699 to .3695. He put it away on September 22. He had his fourth four-hit game of the season to raise his average to .373. When

Tony swinging the bat. He was a natural opposite-field hitter but he was gifted at hitting to all corners of a ballpark (National Baseball Hall of Fame and Museum, Cooperstown, NY).

Walker went 1-for-4 in his next game on September 24, his average declined to .366. Both players competed in their final game of the year on September 26. Tony finished at .372; Walker at .366.

Tony took his eighth batting title overall and his fourth consecutive. He was now tied for second all-time with Honus Wagner and only behind Ty Cobb. "From the start of Spring Training to mid–August," Tony recounted, "was the best I've ever felt."[18] His .372 batting average led the majors. His .459 batting average with runners on base was the best in the majors. He also led the majors in hits with 220, the highest hit total for a season of his career. He clubbed 17 homers and 49 doubles and drove in 119 runs—all career bests. His fear of too many strikeouts by "letting it go" on inside pitches failed to materialize. In 1997 he whiffed 28 times compared to 17 in 1996. But he also had more plate appearances in 1997 compared to 1996. He had 651 appearances in 1997, but only 498 in 1996. He finished the year with 2,770 career hits, 230 shy of 3,000. The 3,000 hit milestone is one baseball's best hitters strive for. Again being candid, Tony said to the *San Diego Union-Tribune*, "For the kind of hitter I am, I think 3,000 is necessary to have the respect I want to take away from the game."[19]

Tony spoke at a post-season sports banquet in San Diego. Ted Williams attended. Tony gave Ted credit for his breakout 1997 season. He finally understood what Mr. Williams was trying to tell him, Tony announced to the crowd. Go after the inside pitch to force pitchers to pitch to his strength on balls on the outside portion of the plate. Tony glanced toward Ted who was sitting in the audience. Ted Williams winked.[20]

Chapter 18

"I want more"

Working with journalist Roger Vaughan, Tony published another book in 1998. Tony persuaded his childhood hero, Willie Davis, to write the foreword to his book *Total Baseball: Winning Techniques for Hitting, Fielding, and Baserunning*. He turned to his friend and sometime mentor, Ted Williams, to author the foreword to *The Art of Hitting*. "I am a great admirer of Tony Gwynn as a hitter and as a person," Williams wrote in his foreword. "I'm flattered that he [Tony] read my book *The Science of Hitting* and said it helped him just as I know his book is going to help a lot of young hitters."[1]

Williams praised Tony as a "contact hitter who can drive the ball." Tony is not, Williams added, "a singles hitter."[2] Williams, however, disagreed with Tony that hitting was an art. Instead Williams contended that "hitting is a science and the more we understand about it and practice what we learn, the better we get."[3]

In *The Art of Hitting*, Tony advocated using a light bat, wearing batting gloves, leading the swing with the bottom hand, and landing "softly" on the front foot to promote balance.[4] As he had in his 1992 book *Tony Gwynn's Total Baseball Player*, Tony strongly encouraged use of batting tees. When he was struggling, Tony advised, he practiced with a wiffle ball and a batting tee.[5]

Tony located the art of hitting in a batter's approach to the pitcher. Tony's message was to never give in to the pitcher, even with two strikes on you. Tony relayed the following story to emphasize his point to never give in to a pitcher. During a 1996 playoff game against the St. Louis Cardinals, he hit a hard ground ball that should have gone through the middle of the infield for a key hit in the game. Instead, Cardinals relief pitcher Dennis Eckersley snagged the ball and threw him out at first base. Celebrating his defensive play, Eckersley cocked his fist and yelled, "Yeeaahhh." The next season, Tony wrote, the Padres were playing the Cardinals. The Cardinals were leading by two runs. He came up, Tony noted, with runners on first and second. He hit a pitch from Eckersley to left center for a double to drive in both baserunners and tie the game. When he arrived at second base, Tony revealed, he imitated Eckersley from that 1996 playoff game. He cocked his fist and yelled "Yeeaahhh."[6]

As usual, Tony was the first of the Padres to show up at Spring Training camp in Yuma, Arizona. Only this time, Tony surprised team officials by arriving at 7:30 a.m., one day early. The Padres underperformed during the 1997 season. Tony saw the prospects for a turnaround in 1998. Padres left fielder Greg Vaughn hit 18 home runs in 1997 while batting only .216. Tony had been working with Vaughn. Greg, Tony observed, is improving his knowledge of swing mechanics. Also, Tony knew, the Padres made a significant offseason acquisition to a pitching staff that had struggled during the 1997 season. The Padres pioneered the modern baseball "fire sale" in 1992 and 1993. After the 1997 season they profited from a player dump by another team. The Florida Marlins won the 1997 World Series. Marlins owner Wayne Huizenga complained fielding his World Series–winning team was too expensive. He was losing money. He directed a "fire sale." The Marlins agreed to trade starting pitcher Kevin Brown to the Padres for rookie first baseman Derek Lee. It was not close to an even swap. Brown went 16–8 for the Marlins in 1997. The season prior he led National League starters in ERA. Derek Lee had participated in just 22 major league games. To be fair to Lee, eventually he put together a distinguished major league career with a .282 career batting average over 15 major league seasons. The Padres also signed free agent pitcher Mark Langston. While Langston was nearing the end of his career, he was a capable performer who had won 10 or more games in 11 different seasons.

On opening day in Cincinnati, the Padres rocked the Reds, 10–2. Their new pitching ace, Kevin Brown, dominated. He scattered five hits in six and a third innings, yielding one run. Tony hit a home run and contributed three RBIs to the Padres offense. After dispatching the Reds again in the second game of the season, San Diego split a four-game series against the Cardinals in St. Louis. They returned home with a 4–2 record and in a tie for first place in the NL West. They reeled off seven consecutive victories during the ensuing home stand. San Diego sported a 16–4 record, the best in the majors for the time being, after defeating the Cubs 4–1 in Chicago on April 23.

Tony was off to a reasonable start. He was batting .316 on April 23 when Cubs pitcher Mark Clark plunked him on the right knee with a fastball. The ball cracking bone on Tony's knee could be heard in the Padres dugout. Batting coach Merv Rettenmund feared serious injury.

18. "I want more"

X-rays, however, proved negative. Tony wore a large bandage on the knee for several days. Whether caused by the hit ball or not, the knee also was required to be drained of fluid.

Tony returned the favor to Clark five days later when the Cubs took on the Padres in San Diego. Tony put on a clinic on hitting to all fields. He singled to left off Clark in the first inning. He followed with an RBI single to center off Clark in the second. Tony clubbed a single to right in the fifth as the Padres rallied to a 5–3 lead, chasing Clark out of the game. Tony wasn't finished. He notched his fourth hit of the day by sending a single through the 5.5 hole. He completed a 5-for-5 outing by smashing a solo home run down the right field line. Tony's home run shot completed the scoring. The Padres won, 7–3. Tony accumulated five or more hits in a game for the ninth time in his career. And true to his word in *The Art of Hitting*, he had refused to let a pitcher get the best of him.

Though still battling periodic episodes of fluid build-up in his right knee, Tony had another great outing against the New York Mets on May 14. In the first game of a doubleheader he singled to drive in San Diego's first run and tie the game, 1–1. The Padres prevailed, 3–1. In the second tilt, he drove in four runs, most of them on a three-run homer, his sixth of the season, to lead a 6–2 victory and a Padres sweep. He was now batting a hefty .377 for the season.

Tony continued to be dogged by injuries. He twisted his right knee while batting against the Philadelphia Phillies on May 15. He had to come out of the game. He was having a good evening against the Arizona Diamondbacks on May 27. He doubled in the first to drive in Padres center fielder Steve Finley for a 1–0 lead. His RBI sacrifice fly in the fifth broke a 3–3 tie. Batting in the seventh he fouled a ball off his right big toe. He stumbled back into the batter's box. Ignoring for the moment the pain in his right toe, he lined a single to right to again drive in Finley and extend San Diego's lead to 5–3. The Padres eventually beat the Diamondbacks, 6–4.

Tony incurred another injury in early June when he strained his right calf. He was missing games off and on because of his various injuries but still batting near .350. The Padres, who had been in first place nearly all season, fell into second place behind the San Francisco Giants. Then, they poured it on. They beat the Giants three straight June 12–14 to grab a three-game lead in the division. They were at 57–31 when the All-Star break began on July 5. They were five and a half games in front.

Tony Gwynn

The fans voted Tony a starter for the July 7 All-Star game, the 14th of his career, at Colorado's Coors Field. Tony was off to a good start when he singled off Roger Clemens in the third inning to drive in two for a 2–0 National League lead. But his troubles in All-Star games continued. He tweaked a hamstring, forcing him out of the game. The National League lost, 13–8.

The accumulation of injuries appeared to catch up to Tony after the All-Star break. He went 2-for-28 at the plate during one stretch. He set a personal career record for most at bats without a hit, going hitless 19 in a row. His previous record hitless streak was 14. Everyone on the team is hitting but me, Tony complained.[7] For his entire major league career it had always been Tony who encouraged teammates battling through a hitting slump. For once, the tables were turned. Teammates patted Tony on the back after he made an out. If he hit a ball hard but right to a defender, they would say you really put the screws to that one. Tony hated the slump but he could see the irony, even the humor, in his situation. Nonetheless, he said, "I can't find a hole right now."[8]

Tony showed signs of breaking out of the doldrums on July 17. He hit two home runs, both balls pulled to right field, against the Cincinnati Reds as the Padres rolled to a 13–3 win. After defeating the Reds, the Padres were 28 games above .500, a club record.

Tony overcame the slump for good during four games between July 28–31, going 11-for-19. His batting average was back up to .320, good enough for seventh best in the National League. Tony concluded his slump, as usual when he was struggling, had been a question of balance. He wasn't centering the bat properly, he noted. Instead, he was flailing at the ball forcing him to lean too far forward during his swing.[9]

The injury bug returned to haunt him against Atlanta on August 12. First, however, he gained another triumph against Greg Maddux. He hit a double off Maddux in the fourth inning with Atlanta leading, 1–0. Ken Caminiti followed with a 2-run homer. The Padres beat Atlanta, 5–1. Tony injured an Achilles tendon running out the double. He came out of the game one inning later. Asked by a reporter to explain the injury, Tony couldn't resist a tongue-in-cheek reply, "I'm getting old."[10] The Achilles injury forced Tony out of the lineup the rest of August.

The Padres were still clicking though. Their record stood at 88–47 after they won a sixth consecutive game on August 28. They led the NL West by 16 games.

Tony returned to the lineup from September 1–8. In seven games during that period, he went 9-for-24 with two homers and five RBIs. His

18. "I want more"

average for the year was .326 after play concluded on September 8. But he suffered another injury when he chipped a bone in his right thumb. His thumb was put in a splint. Consequently, Tony could only watch from the dugout when the Padres clinched the NL West title in dramatic fashion on September 12. They clinched against their arch-rivals, the Los Angeles Dodgers. The Dodgers raced to a 7–0 lead, disappointing a crowd of 60,823, which had jammed San Diego's Qualcomm Stadium hoping to watch San Diego sew up the title. The Padres staged a furious comeback. They scored three runs in the bottom of the fifth and five runs in the bottom of the sixth to forge to an 8–7 lead. The San Diego pitching staff shut out the Dodgers the rest of the way to preserve the victory.

Afterward, the Padres dressing room consisted of the usual champagne-spraying festivities. Tony was nowhere to be found. He hid in a trainer's room. He explained his reluctance to join the celebration. He remembered what happened in 1996. After the Padres won the division title on the last day of the season, they were swept three straight in the post-season by the Cardinals. Tony thought it was too early to celebrate.[11] Nonetheless, he praised his teammates. "They're going to hate me off the '84 team," he said, "but this team is far more talented than that team was." In his opinion the 1998 Padres were both more athletic and featured better pitching.[12]

Tony scrambled back into the lineup on September 13, remaining there the balance of the season. Priming himself for the post-season, he hit a game-winning home run against the Dodgers on September 23, his 15th homer of the season. He hit his 16th, and final home run of the regular season, on September 26 during a 3–2 loss to Arizona. He went 2-for-4 on September 27, the final day of the regular season, as the Padres bounced back to beat Arizona, 3–2.

The Padres finished the 1998 regular season with a 98–64 record. They were in first place for all but six days. Limited by his injuries, Tony participated in only 127 games. His .321 batting average led the team. He finished eighth in the National League in batting. He had finished in the top ten every season since 1984. Tony's pre-season observations on left fielder Greg Vaughn's improving swing mechanics proved accurate. Vaughn slugged 50 homers, drove in 119 runs, and batted .272, which was 56 points higher than his .216 average in 1997. Third baseman Ken Caminiti contributed 29 homers and 82 RBIs; center fielder Steve Finley 14 homers and 67 RBIs, and first baseman Wally Joyner 12 homers and 80 RBIs.

Tony Gwynn

The pitching staff turned it around. The staff's 4.98 ERA was the second-worst in the National League in 1997. Their 3.63 ERA was the third-best in the league in 1998. Kevin Brown validated the Padres off-season trade. He went 18–7 with a 2.38 ERA. He was second in the National League with 257 strikeouts. Andy Ashby was 17–8. Trevor Hoffman led the majors with 53 saves.

The oddsmakers considered the Padres underdogs for the post-season playoffs despite the team's lofty 98–64 regular season record. On paper at least, they were upstaged by the NL Central Division-winning Houston Astros and the NL Eastern Division champ Atlanta Braves. Houston won 102 games in the regular season. Atlanta took 106. In addition, the Padres faded during the month of September when they won 9 but lost 15.

San Diego faced the Astros in the first round of the playoffs. Because of their superior regular season record, the Astros held the home field advantage for the best-of-five series. Kevin Brown and future Hall-of-Famer Randy Johnson, the "Big Unit," locked up in a pitcher's duel in Game One. Tony broke the ice on a 0–0 tie in the sixth inning. The six-foot-ten Johnson was a tough foe for Tony but he slammed a double off Johnson. He later scored on a sacrifice fly for the first run of the game. Greg Vaughn's home run sent the count to 2–0. Trevor Hoffman gave up a run in the bottom of the ninth but recorded a save as the Padres won, 2–1. With his team behind 3–0 in Game Two, Tony helped fuel a Padres rally. Tony and Steve Finley each drove in a run to make it 3–2. Later, the Padres tied in 4–4. The Astros pushed across a run in the bottom of the ninth to take Game Two, 5–4.

The Padres won Game Three before a crowd of 65,235 in San Diego by a 2–1 score. Tony went 0-for-4 at the plate but make a key defensive play in the seventh inning. San Diego was ahead 1–0 when Astros left fielder Moises Alou led off with a single. The next Astros batter also singled. Alou tried to take third base on the play but Tony's throw from right field nailed him for the first out of the inning. The Astros tied it at 1–1 before the inning ended. Tony's defensive play to secure the first out probably limited the damage.

San Diego clinched the series with a 6–1 victory in Game Four. They put the game away with a four-run rally in the bottom of the eighth. Tony ignited the rally with a leadoff double, a line drive to right center. Trying to protect Tony's ailing right knee, manager Bruce Bochy removed Tony for a pinch runner after the double.

18. "I want more"

Again, champagne sprayed in the Padres' dressing room. Again, Tony declined to partake. "I want more," he said.

The Braves were next up for San Diego. Once more, the Padres were underdogs and their opponent possessed the home field advantage. The National League Championship Series was slated for best-of-seven. The Atlanta coaches knew Tony could be a problem. He had hit well against Atlanta's three best pitchers, Greg Maddux, John Smoltz, and Tom Glavine. For his career, he was batting .455 against Maddux, .452 against Smoltz, and .322 against Glavine.

Tony justified the Atlanta coaches' fears in Game One. He knocked an RBI single off Smoltz to knot the score at 1–1. The game went into extra innings tied, 2–2. Ken Caminiti's solo home run in the top of the tenth provided the winning run for San Diego. Tony went 2-for-5. Game Two was all Kevin Brown. He pitched a three-hit shutout as the Padres won, 3–0. Tony singled for his one hit in four at bats.

Game Three was contested in San Diego. In the bottom of the fifth Atlanta starter Greg Maddux wanted no part of pitching to Tony. Trailing 1–0 to begin the inning, the Padres rallied to tie it, 1–1. Tony then came up with two outs and Padres runners on second and third. First base was open. Maddux walked Tony intentionally to load the bases. The strategy failed when the next batter, Ken Caminiti, singled for a 2–1 Padres lead. The Padres later scored two more runs to win Game Three, 4–1. They now held a commanding three games to none lead in the series, only one victory away from winning the National League pennant. Maddux harbored no regrets after the game about walking Tony. "I'd do it again. I'd do it the next 100 times in a row," he remarked.[13]

The Braves battled back to win Games Four and Five. For once, Maddux scored a success against Tony. In Game Five San Diego trailed 7–4 going into the bottom of the ninth. They quickly made it 7–6 on a two-run homer by reserve catcher Greg Myers. They were two runs away from winning the series. With nobody on and nobody out and their backs against a wall Atlanta brought in Maddux for a rare relief appearance. Maddux secured the first two outs of the inning when Greg Vaughn struck out and Padres second baseman Quilvio Veras grounded out to the shortstop. Maddux next did something he surely didn't intend. He walked Steve Finley, bringing Tony up to the plate. Maddux wriggled out of the jam. He induced Tony to ground out to the first baseman to end Game Five.

The defeats in Games Four and Five forced San Diego to travel back to Atlanta for Game Six. The Padres scored five runs in the top of the sixth to jump to 5–0 lead. Tony contributed two hits to the San Diego offense although neither of his hits led to a run scoring. Tony suffered from fluid on his right knee after Game Five. Again trying to protect Tony's knee and holding a 5–0 lead, Bruce Bochy removed Tony from the game after he batted and grounded to short in the top of the ninth. The Padres brought in their closer, Trevor Hoffman, to seal the win and the National League pennant. Removing Tony from the game failed to save wear and tear on his knee. Instead, he nervously paced in the dugout.[14] Hoffman did his job. He mowed down three Atlanta batters in the bottom of the ninth. With their 5–0 victory in Game Six, the San Diego Padres were headed to the World Series for the first time since 1984.

Consistent with his past practice, Tony laid low for the post-game celebration. Greg Vaughn reported on a scene that he said he would never forget. While San Diego players, coaches, and front office officials engaged in a frenetic celebration, Vaughn spotted Tony sitting quietly, savoring the moment with spouse Alicia, daughter Anisha, and son Anthony.[15] Tony always thought of his family as a team.

The Padres were set to meet the American League champion New York Yankees in the 1998 World Series. It would be an unenviable task. The 1998 Yankees posted an American League regular season record by winning 114 games. They rolled over the Texas Rangers three games straight in the first round of the playoffs. They bested the defending American League champion Cleveland Indians four games to two to win the American League pennant. The 1998 Yankees were notable for the depth and variety of their talent. They had both right-handed and left-handed strength throughout their hitting lineup and pitching staff.

He'd never been inside Yankee Stadium, Tony disclosed. He had driven by it but nothing more.[16] Tony made sure to take in the history of the place prior to Game One in New York. He perused the monuments in the outfield to former Yankee greats—Ruth, Gehrig, DiMaggio, Mantle. He snapped pictures with his camera.

Yankees Game One pitcher David Wells had a fine 1998 regular season, going 18–4. He looked sharp in Game One. His pitches were hitting both corners of the plate. Still, in the first inning Tony greeted Wells by hitting a pitch on the outside corner to the opposite (left) field for a single, though the Padres failed to score. Tony grounded out against Wells in his second at bat in the third. He came up next in the fifth with the score knotted at 2–2. There were two outs. Quilvio Veras was perched on first base after he singled. Tony had collected his first hit of the game against Wells on an inside pitch. He expected Wells to go outside in this

18. "I want more"

at bat. That is what Wells did. Amped up by his first game in Yankee Stadium, Tony hit probably the hardest ball of his career. He smashed a Wells fastball off the right field upper deck for a two-run homer. Tony's shot temporarily silenced the large Yankee Stadium crowd. The Padres were up 4–2. It wasn't to be for the Padres, however. They were leading 5–2 in the seventh when the powerful Yankee lineup plated seven runs. The Yankees defeated San Diego 9–6 in Game One. David Wells praised Tony. "You've got to tip your hat to the guy," Wells said to reporters. "In my mind, he's the best hitter in the game."[17]

In Game Two the Yankees pummeled the Padres, 9–3. The Yanks sent out a 20-game winner, David Cone, for Game Three, contested in San Diego. With the score 0–0 in the bottom of the sixth Tony came up against Cone with Padres pitcher Sterling Hitchcock on first and Quilvio Veras on second. With the count 1–0, Cone threw Tony a hard-breaking splitter. Yankees catcher Joe Girardi placed his mitt low expecting the ball to dive into the dirt after crossing home plate. Tony adjusted to the flight of the ball, placed his hands low, and golfed the ball between first and second for a single. Veras scored from the second. Hitchcock also scored on an error by the Yankees. Tony later scored on a sacrifice fly to propel San Diego to a 3–0 lead. The Padres threatened to climb back into the series. Again, the Yankees lineup was too strong. They scored two runs in the seventh and three in the eighth to win Game Three, 5–4. Tony's 2-for-4 day was to no avail. For a second time, Tony received post-game praise from a Yankees pitcher. "I threw a really good splitter to Tony Gwynn," Cone said. "He did a great job of putting his bat on the ball. That's why he's such an amazing hitter."[18]

The Yankees bested San Diego 3–0 in Game Four to sweep the World Series. Tony had a good series, going 8-for-16. The Padres had the misfortune to bump into outstanding opponents in the 1984 and 1998 World Series. The 1984 Detroit Tigers were one of the better teams of the post–World War II era. The 1998 Yankees are generally regarded as one of the greatest teams of all-time, possibly eclipsed only by the 1927 Yankees of Ruth and Gehrig.

Tony and his teammates "wanted it all" but came up short. Tony lauded San Diego's 1998 season. This team "showed a lot of character," he said to the press. It beat some good clubs to get to the World Series.[19] Tony received a prized gift from Fox Sports broadcaster Keith Olbermann. Aware of Tony's appreciation of baseball history, Olbermann had a recording made of long-time Yankees announcer Bob Sheppard calling out Tony's name in the starting line-up over the Yankee Stadium public address system. Olbermann sent the recording to Tony, who was greatly touched by Olbermann's gesture.[20]

A few days after the World Series the city of San Diego conducted a parade for the National League champion Padres. Some Padres players spoke of the 1998 season to the crowd. Tony emphasized an altogether different point in his remarks. This was a pivotal time in San Diego sports history. Since they entered the major leagues in 1969, the Padres had been playing in a multi-purpose stadium they shared with the NFL's San Diego Chargers. The stadium was located in Mission Valley, an area approximately six miles northeast of downtown San Diego. A 1997 task force report recommended the city build a new baseball stadium downtown along with hotel and retail development. Tony was more to San Diego than a ballplayer. He was a San Diego institutionalist. He was an avid supporter of Proposition C, a referendum to the city's voters to approve $275 million in public spending for the new baseball stadium and surrounding development. In two weeks, Proposition C was coming up for a vote. Referring to the upcoming vote, Tony said to the crowd, "You know what we have to do."[21]

Proposition C passed with nearly 60 percent of the vote. It might have passed in any event but the Padres run to the 1998 World Series didn't hurt. Six years later, the downtown stadium, named Petco Park, opened for baseball.

Chapter 19

The Last 10 Are the Hardest

Tony participated in a memorable event on July 13, 1999, at Fenway Park, Boston. The occasion was the 1999 All-Star game. During his playing days with the Red Sox, Ted Williams feuded with Boston sportswriters and fans. Williams believed no matter the quality of his production at the plate or his performance in the field the Boston writers and fans demanded more. When he inevitably fell short of their expectations, he chafed at their criticism. Now, almost four decades after he retired as an active player, the resentments of years past were either forgiven or forgotten. Major League Baseball invited Williams to the ballpark where he toiled for 19 seasons to throw out the ceremonial first pitch to the 1999 All-Star game.

The Boston crowd roared when a golf cart ferried Williams to the pitcher's mound. Williams responded by tipping his hat to the crowd. National and American League All-Stars crowded around the golf cart to greet Williams, who was generally regarded as the greatest hitter then-living, if not of all time. Retired baseball greats also paid their respects, including Hank Aaron, Bob Gibson, Willie Mays, and Stan Musial. Williams beamed when Tony leaned into the golf cart to shake his hand. Tony presented Ted with the ceremonial first ball.

Ted was closer to Tony than any other current ballplayer, with the possible exception of Boston's All Star shortstop, Nomar Garciaparra. Ted was still unsteady on his feet from a series of strokes. He required assistance to throw the ceremonial ball. Ted and Tony had been through this drill before. Tony assisted Ted when he threw out the ceremonial first pitch for the Padres' 1996 home opener. Ted probably knew he could trust Tony not to steal the limelight. Sure enough, Tony stood as unobtrusively as possible behind Ted, steadying his left side, while Ted lobbed a ball with his right arm to former Boston catcher Carlton Fisk. Hearing the cheers of the Boston crowd touched the 80-year-old Williams. He brushed away tears. "It's the best thing that I've ever been a part of in my whole life," Tony said to *San Diego Union-Tribune* sportswriter Tom Krasovic.[1] Later, Tony said that "We'll never have a moment in baseball like this again."[2]

Not everything went Tony's way during the 1999 season. San Diego is a small-market town, Padres owner John Moores emphasized. Payroll totaled $50 million during the 1998 season, he reported. He was determined to hold payroll to $50 million in 1999. Consequently, the Padres began to shed key personnel. They declined to offer a contract to Ken Caminiti. As a result, Caminiti filed for free agency and signed with the Houston Astros. Steve Finley also became a free agent. He signed with the Arizona Diamondbacks. The Padres traded Greg Vaughn to the Cincinnati Reds for outfielder Reggie Sanders. Sanders was a better defensive player than Vaughn but unlikely to match the home run and RBI production of Vaughn. San Diego's best pitcher, Kevin Brown, was another player lost to free agency. He signed a $105 million, seven-year deal with the Dodgers. In addition, the Padres traded a reliable starting pitcher, Joey Hamilton, to the Toronto Blue Jays.

Adverting to the departure of Caminiti, Finley, Vaughn, Brown, and Hamilton, Tony said, "I think that if you lose five players from a World Series team, you can't expect to still have a World Series club."[3] Tony chastised the Padres front office for taking their time to re-sign Trevor Hoffman, one of the best relief pitchers in baseball. "Quit dinking around," he complained. The Padres signed Hoffman.[4]

Tony began the 1999 season 72 hits shy of 3,000. He knew that, barring injury, he was certain to reach the coveted 3,000 hit threshold during the 1999 season. He got off to a good start. He collected 35 hits in April leaving him 37 short of 3,000. He cooled off the first three weeks of May. Still, he garnered 12 more hits. He was 25 away.

Tony's march to 3,000 went sideways on May 21. He strained his left calf while breaking out of the batter's box after hitting a ground ball. He limped down the first base line. He was out by several feet at first. The injury relegated him to the Disabled List (the DL). He returned to action on June 12. Three days thereafter, he reinjured the calf catching a fly ball. He went back to the DL.

Meanwhile, the Padres caught fire. Mired in last place for most of May and the first half of June, they won a club record 14 in a row between June 18 and July 2. They took six out of eight after the All-Star break. Their hot streak moved them to within two games of first.

Though Tony was out of commission for the better part of June and July, the Padres prepared to celebrate hit number 3,000. They installed 21 large banners off the light ring above the field at Qualcomm Stadium.

19. The Last 10 Are the Hardest

Each banner listed the name of one of the 21 major leaguers who previously attained the 3,000 hit mark. The Padres placed a 22nd banner, which was left blank. It was reserved for Tony's name when he accomplished the historic feat. The residents of San Diego also prepared for hit number 3,000. There were "Tony 3,000" signs posted in windows across the city.[5] Tony and Alicia caught the spirit as well. They hauled a truck trailer next to San Diego's Qualcomm Stadium. The trailer featured an exhibit that included Tony's eight silver bats for capturing the National League batting title, his five Gold Gloves, and his 14 All-Star game rings. The Gwynns entitled their exhibit "The Road to 3,000." They charged a $1 admission fee, with the proceeds being forwarded to the Tony and Alicia Gwynn Foundation.[6]

Tony finally made it back to the lineup on July 19, He accumulated nine more hits between July 20 and 31. He was nine short of 3,000. Though Tony was steadily closing in on 3,000, his stints on the DL slowed the pace. The attention paid to his quest for 3,000, and the length of time taking to achieve it, blew up on July 31. That day, the Padres traded reserve catcher Jim Leyritz to the New York Yankees. Leyritz had been previously with the Yankees from 1990 to 1996. Prior to leaving for New York, Leyritz leveled a blast at Tony. After he was traded to San Diego in 1998, Leyritz noted that he had enjoyed watching Tony prepare for his at bats. But, he asserted, Tony lacks the intangibles. To explain his meaning, he cited another good hitter, Don Mattingly of the Yankees. Mattingly is a team player, Leyritz contended, drawing a contrast to Tony. For example, Leyritz continued, Mattingly stays in the dugout when he is injured. Two other Padres players, whose names were not publicly mentioned, seconded Leyritz's remarks. The controversy evoked memories of 1990 when Mike Pagliarulo and Jack Clark accused Tony of being "selfish."[7]

Tony's teammate, Reggie Sanders, offered a perspective. "When there's a person who's considered 'The Padre' or 'The Cleveland Indian,' I think the younger guys in particular look for that person to be more outspoken."[8] *San Diego Union-Tribune* reporter Tom Krasovic pointed out that Tony rarely socialized off the field with his teammates. He preferred the company of his family.[9]

Tony fired back at Leyritz. During the 1998 season Leyritz helped us some, Tony conceded. But he must be only a role player because he is being traded and he "takes potshots on his way out the door."[10] Tony acknowledged Leyritz was upset when he left a game early while he was on the DL. He left early, he said, because he was driving everyone in the dugout crazy. He had been expecting this, Tony admitted. The focus on his chase for 3,000 had resulted in "unease" on the team. Though not mentioned by Tony, his teammates were likely soured by a eight-game losing streak from July 22 to 31. That knocked them out of range of first place.

Leyritz's criticism appeared to have little effect on Tony's level of play. On August 1, the same day as Leyritz's parting shots were reported publicly, Tony drilled three hits as the Padres pounded the Houston Astros, 10–3. After beating Houston, the Padres left town for a long road trip to St. Louis, Montreal, and New York (to play the Mets). The first stop was August 2–5 against the Cardinals. Almost three dozen of Tony's relatives and friends trekked to St. Louis hoping to witness hit 3,000. Tony's mom, Vendella, accompanied him on the team plane.

Tony was not alone chasing baseball history in St. Louis. The Cardinals' Mark McGwire came into the Padres series with 497 career home runs. He was bidding to become the 16th major league player to hit 500 or more career home runs. In addition, he was trying to reach that mark in the fewest number of at bats in history.

The Padres lost the first game to St. Louis, 6–5. Tony flied out, grounded out, and popped out twice during his first four plate appearances. He managed to grind a single in the ninth inning for hit 2,995. Mark McGwire crunched career homer 498.

Cardinals pitcher Darren Oliver was the star of the second game of the series. He hurled a four-hit shutout as the Cardinals topped the Padres, 6–0. Tony went hitless in four at bats. McGwire managed a single in three at bats. A frustrated Tony said of his struggle to reach the 3,000 hit plateau, "Right now, I just want to get it over with."[11]

Tony busted out the third game of the series before a Busch Stadium crowd of 43,456. The large crowd cheered him before every at bat. He collected three hits. One of those hits was a grand slam home run in the top of the fifth inning to propel the Padres to a 6–3 lead. Even though the grand slam homer put their team behind, the large St. Louis crowd toasted Tony with a standing ovation. The Padres couldn't hold on, however, and they lost another close one, 7–6. Mark McGwire crept toward the 500 milestone with career homer 499.

Rod Carew, who attained 3,000 hits in 1985, told Tony the final 10 hits to get to 3,000 would be the hardest.[12] By now, Tony agreed with Carew. He was sitting at 2,998 career hits. He was capable of notching two hits in the final game of the St. Louis series, He had collected two hits, or more, many times in his career. Yet the pressure was weighing

19. The Last 10 Are the Hardest

on him. A large group of relatives and friends had undertaken the long trip to St. Louis to witness hit 3,000 in person. What's more, he had worked hard at his craft for 18 long major league seasons to reach the cusp of 3,000.

San Diego batting coach Merv Rettenmund indicated Tony was getting out front on the ball, jumping at pitches. "There's a difference," Rettenmund explained, "between concentrating on what you're doing and dwelling on it."[13] Tony had reached the point where he cared little how he got the historic blow. "The objective now is to get two more hits. I don't care if it's a bunt, a blooper, a chink, a home run. Just get it and get back to normal."[14] Like Rettenmund, Alicia noticed the strain on Tony prior to the last game of the St. Louis series. "I have never seen him so nervous in my life," she said.[15]

A crowd of 45,106 attended the final series game on August 5. They cheered for Tony's 3,000th and McGwire's 500th. Tony flied out twice, walked, and grounded out in his first four plate appearances. Mark McGwire provided the fireworks. He crushed career homer 500 in the third inning. He followed with career 501 in the eighth. As he had in the first game of the series, Tony broke through in the ninth inning. He cracked a double to right field to drive in a run. Another run scored on an error to extend a San Diego lead from 6–3 to 8–3. Arriving at second base after his double, Tony tipped his hat to McGwire. McGwire, the Cardinals first baseman, tipped his hat to Tony. The crowd gave the two of them a standing ovation. In his twenty-seven years covering the Cardinals, one St. Louis writer observed, he had never seen St. Louis crowds cheer for an opposing player as they had for Tony Gwynn. San Diego won the fourth game of the series, 10–3.

Tony was one hit from 3,000. He was still feeling the pressure. "One hit to relaxing," he said.[16] He praised the St. Louis fans. He marveled that they cheered for him. He noted they treated his family "like royalty." Despite the tension he was under, Tony was not above poking fun at himself and the retinue of family and friends who were following him around. Noting the nearly three dozen of them who had traveled to St. Louis he asked who is going on to Montreal? "So now," he said with a laugh, "I get to find out who my real friends are."[17]

The Padres flew to Montreal for a four-game set against the Expos. Most of his relatives and friends who traveled to St. Louis were unable to continue to Montreal. Spouse Alicia, mom Vendella, daughter Anisha, and a niece, soldiered on. Son Tony Jr. returned to California to prepare for a baseball tournament. Tony appreciated the large crowds

Tony Gwynn

he encountered in St. Louis. It was a different story in Montreal. Only 13,540 patrons were present at Montreal's Olympic Stadium on August 6. There were 28,460 empty seats.

Padres second baseman Quilvio Veras led off the game with a single against Expos rookie pitcher Dan Smith. Tony batted second. He ran the count to 1–2. Smith threw a slider, low in the zone. As he had so many times before, Tony lowered his hands and his body and adjusted his swing path to the pitch. He slapped a line drive single to center for hit 3,000. Putting aside their frustrations over the attention paid to Tony's march to 3,000, his teammates mobbed him. One of the first to greet him was a woman who bolted out of the stands. She apparently still possessed that Gwynn quickness. It was Tony's mom, Vendella. August 6, 1999, was her 64th birthday. "Happy birthday, Mom,"[18] Tony whispered. Kerwin Danley was the umpire at first. Danley had been Tony's teammate at San Diego State. Danley was conflicted. Should he congratulate his old teammate? Or, would doing so interfere with the neutrality expected of umpires? Tony had a way of recognizing the plight of others. Amidst the celebration, Tony walked over to Danley to shake his hand. Danley hugged him.

Later in the game, back in the dugout, Tony snuck into the tunnel between the dugout and the clubhouse. He dropped to his knees, gazed up at the ceiling, and said, "Dad, we did it."[19] His father never wavered in his confidence in Tony's athletic ability. His father had seen this day coming. Tony wished he had lived to see it. Unbound from the pressure of 3,000, Tony let loose, He smashed three more hits, all singles, for a four-hit game. The Padres won a high-scoring affair, 12–10.

Tony admitted the quest for 3,000 had been more of an ordeal than he expected. It takes "passion" to accumulate this many career hits, he said. And, he added, "I love playing the game."[20]

Atlanta pitcher Greg Maddux mused upon Tony's accomplishment. Of Tony's 3,000 hits, 91 had come against the Atlanta pitching trio of Maddux, John Smoltz, and Ton Glavine. "I just want Tony to realize," jested Maddux, "he couldn't have gotten there without us."[21] On a serious vein, Maddux stated he had never seen a hitter who was so good at hitting good pitches. When Tony's hot, Maddux suggested, maybe the best thing is just throw the ball down the middle of the plate and hope for the best. Pete Rose, who had witnessed Tony's first two major league hits, also complimented Tony. "He's the best pure hitter I ever played against."[22]

Tony knew Dan Smith's name would now be inextricably connected

19. The Last 10 Are the Hardest

to yielding a career hit number 3,000. The next day, when the teams practiced, he pulled Smith aside. "Whether you like it or not," he said, "you are part of a special day for me and my family." He gave Smith a jersey, a bat, and baseballs that he signed. Several weeks later, when the Expos traveled to San Diego, it was "Tony Gwynn 3,000 Hit Poster Night." Tony sent a signed poster to Smith with a note. "To, Dan. It was a good pitch," Tony wrote.[23]

The Padres returned from their long road trip to match up against the Florida Marlins on August 13. A crowd of 48,743 was on hand for a pre-game celebration of Tony's 3,000th hit. The 22nd banner hanging from the light ring, previously blank, now was etched with Tony's name. The Padres replayed Tony's 3,000th hit for the crowd on the big Jumbotron television. Ted Williams offered recorded congratulations. Tony spoke to the crowd. He apologized for notching hit 3,000 on the road instead of at home. He thanked his parents for raising him right.

Tony failed to hit safely his first three at bats. He thrilled the crowd with an RBI single in his fourth at bat. It wasn't enough. The Padres lost, 4–3. Tony was more productive the following evening before a mammoth home crowd of 61,135. He hit two home runs, driving in four, to lead San Diego to a 6–4 triumph. After his second homer the fans yelled for him to come out of the dugout to acknowledge their cheers. Years before, Tony had been reluctant to do so. He feared showing up opposing players. Times had changed. Players routinely came out to take a bow. Tony changed too. He came out of the dugout.[24]

Tony hit consistently throughout the month of August. He suffered a brief setback on August 29. He stroked an RBI single in the fifth inning to increase a San Diego lead from 1–0 to 2–0. He then retired from the game with a bum left knee. Later, the knee was drained of fluid.

Tony carried on the rest of the season despite recurrent knee problems. He was working on a sixteen-game hitting streak on September 22. He was hitless in three at bats. He came out after the fifth inning with a sore knee, ending the streak. He put on another spectacular performance at home during a doubleheader against the Cardinals on September 29. He went 3-for-4 in the first game, scoring two runs. He was 4-for-4 in the second game with two RBIs. Continuing their habit of losing one-run games to the Cardinals, the Padres lost the first tilt 4–3 and the second, 6–5.

The Padres completed their 1999 season on the road against Arizona. Tony clubbed a home run, his 10th of the year, in the second game of the Diamondbacks series on October 1. Once he hit his ninth

Tony Gwynn

Tony was honored as a "Living Legend" by the Louisville Slugger Museum & Factory in 2012 (Used with permission by Louisville Slugger Museum & Factory).

homer, he had set a goal to reach double-digit home runs for the season. He was pleased he attained his objective. The homer was the 133rd of his eighteen-year career. That's the same number of home runs, Tony pointed out, Mark McGwire has hit in just two seasons. He sent an irreverent message to his buddy, McGwire. "So, we're even, dog."[25] Tony pinch hit in the final two games of the season on October 2 and 3. He made out in both at bats.

Tony competed in 111 games in 1999, his lowest number of games of participation since 1983, with the exception of the strike-shortened 1994 season. He batted .338. His injuries limited him to 446 plate appearances, 56 short of the 502 required to qualify for the batting title. It didn't matter. The Rockies Larry Walker was far ahead. He won the title with a .379 average. Along with his 10 homers, Tony had 62 RBIs, 27 doubles, and seven stolen bases. His strikeout ratio was outstanding. He fanned a mere 14 times in 411 at bats, or 446 plate appearances. He lived up to his reputation as the toughest out in baseball.

The Padres finished fourth in the NL West with a 74–86 record. (The division expanded to five teams in 1998 with the addition of the expansion Arizona Diamondbacks.) It was a far cry from their 98–64

19. The Last 10 Are the Hardest

mark in 1998. Their pitching was reliable for the most part. Hitting was their downfall. Their .252 team batting average was the lowest in the majors. The absence of Caminiti, Finley, and Vaughn left too big of a hole in the middle of their lineup.

Tony received a prestigious honor during a World Series game at Yankee Stadium on October 27, 1999. Major League Baseball presented him with the Roberto Clemente Man-of-the-Year award for his charitable work. Alicia deserves the award as much as I do, Tony pointed out.[26] There was little doubt Tony and Alicia donated much of their time to charitable activities. They invited underprivileged children to live in their home. A year later, however, the *San Diego Union-Tribune* published an article critical of some of the Gwynn's charitable endeavors.

The paper reported that there were record-keeping issues with the Tony and Alicia Gwynn Foundation. For example, the paper stated, the foundation had failed to register with the state of California as required by state law. According to the *Union-Tribune*'s piece, records of donations, expenses, and contributions at the foundation were incomplete. Two experts contacted by the paper opined that the foundation appeared to be managed inefficiently. Tony and Alicia acknowledged mistakes, the *Union-Tribune* article continued. They promised to improve management of the foundation.[27]

Encouraged by his strong finish to the 1999 season—the 16-game hitting streak in September, the 7-for-8 doubleheader on September 29, and the 10th home run on October 1—Tony expressed optimism for 2000. Early in Spring Training he announced that he was ready for the regular season to start.[28] His optimism proved unfounded. His left knee was drained of fluid in February 2000. It was drained on several additional occasions thereafter. Moreover, on opening day, April 3, New York pitcher Al Leiter plunked him on the elbow with a fastball. When the ball hit Tony's elbow, "It was a loud noise," said Padres manager Bruce Bochy, "almost like it hit wood."[29]

Tony returned to the starting lineup in short order, but more trouble followed. His ailing left knee kept him out from April 29 to May 16. He was batting an anemic .186. Tony offered a succinct explanation for his lackluster hitting. "I suck,"[30] he said. Tony revived on May 19 against Atlanta. He went 3-for-3 feasting, as he often had, on Atlanta pitching. This time the victim was Atlanta lefthander Terry Mulholland, rather than Maddux, Smoltz, or Glavine. Tony missed the next two games with a sore knee. Then, he hit safely in 18 of his next 20 starts. By June 17, he brought his batting average up to .317. His left knee was drained for the seventh time since mid–February after the June 17 contest.

Tony made his final appearance of the 2000 season on June 23. He had a meaningful last at bat. The Padres and the Reds were tied 7–7 after nine innings. Pinch hitting, Tony led off the top of the 10th. He doubled. Bruce Bochy replaced him with a pinch runner. The Padres scored three runs, stymied the Reds in the bottom half, and won, 10–7.

Draining his left knee, Tony admitted, was no longer helping. His knee felt better when it was drained in years past. This season, he confessed, the pain remained whether the knee was drained or not. He underwent reconstructive knee surgery on June 26 at the Scripps Clinic. Tony's surgeons removed numerous loose particles from his knee. In some areas, the surgeons indicated, cartilage had completely worn away. In those areas, the knee was bone-on-bone. The surgeons reported they sought to induce growth of new cartilage through a series of microfractures on his knee and upper thigh. The results of the microfracture technique were unclear, the surgeons acknowledged, because original cartilage is smooth while induced cartilage has a rougher texture.

There was one welcome piece of news for Tony the spring of 2000. His son, Tony Jr., who had excelled in baseball and basketball for Poway, California, High School, accepted an offer from San Diego State to follow in his father's footsteps and join Coach Jim Dietz's baseball program.

Tony Sr. appeared in but 36 games in 2000. He batted .323, with 12 doubles (a good output for just under one-fifth of a season), and 17 RBIs. Slowed by his left knee, he counted no triples and no stolen bases.

Several new additions performed capably for the Padres in 2000. Third baseman Phil Nevins slugged 31 homers with 107 RBIs. First baseman Ryan Klesko contributed 26 homers with 92 RBIs. Second baseman Bret Boone knocked 19 homers with 74 RBIs. Center fielder Ruben Rivera added 17 homers with 57 RBIs. The team showed potential but was hobbled all season by injuries. At one point, nine of their pitchers were on the DL. When Tony was placed on the DL after his knee surgery, he joined 10 other Padres already on the list. The Padres managed a marginal improvement from 1999. They finished 76–86, two games better than their 1999 record. Despite an improved won-loss record, they finished last in the division.

The Padres looked fit for a winning season in 2001. The question was, would Tony still remain a Padre? Tony's existing contract with the Padres contained a clause wherein the team could pay Tony $2 million and buy out the contract after the 2000 season. Alternately, the Padres

19. The Last 10 Are the Hardest

could renew the agreement and pay Tony $6 million in 2001. The Padres elected to buy out the contract. On October 31, 2000, Tony became a free agent for the first time in his career. He sent differing signals concerning his intentions. He hinted at signing with an American League team because its designated hitter rule could offer him an opportunity to save wear and tear on his knees. Other times, he insisted he was a National League guy and intended to keep playing in right field. After several weeks of back-and-forth negotiations, a deal was struck. Tony was, after all, "Mr. Padre." He noted that "This is where I wanted to be and I knew that and they [the Padres] knew that too."[31]

The Padres and Tony agreed to a one-year contract. The contract guaranteed Tony a 2001 salary of $1 million. He would receive another $1 million through a series of deferred payments to be made from 2003 to 2007. Given the uncertainties with Tony's left knee, the Padres doubted his durability. The new contract reflected that concern. It included additional bonuses based on Tony's number of plate appearances. For example, he would be paid $1.6 million for 400 to 599 plate appearances or $3.7 million for 600 or more appearances.

After once again declining to take advantage of free agency, Tony reminisced about his decision to remain with one team during his career. He believed it brought stability to his family. "You can't worry about everybody else and how much money they're making,," he added. If so, you will be "ticked off every year."[32] When Tony applied principles to others, he was usually careful to apply those principles to himself. Thus, he noted, "I'm greedy too." Nonetheless, he concluded, you should just worry about taking care "of yourself and your family."[33]

It soon became apparent Tony was unlikely to receive bonuses for plate appearances. He was scratched from a Spring Training game on March 12 because of discomfort in his surgically-repaired left knee. A few days afterward, he admitted he was unlikely to be healthy enough to last a full nine-inning game in 2001. He predicted he was likely to be removed from games prior to the seventh inning.[34] One development did please Tony. The Padres signed free agent Rickey Henderson. Tony and many of his teammates enjoyed Henderson's freewheeling, if sometimes eccentric, approach to the game. Also, Henderson kept himself in top condition. That was why he was still playing professional baseball 22 seasons after he broke into the major leagues.

The Padres opened on April 2 at San Francisco's Candlestick Park. Tony managed, barely, to make it past seven innings. He hit a single in the eighth and then Bruce Bochy replaced him with a pinch runner.

Tony Gwynn

The Padres lost the opener, 3–2. Two days later Tony was unable to go because of problems with the left knee. He walked into Bochy's office. The knee is "shaky," he said.[35] He had the best outing of his 2001 season on April 17. He slashed a double, a triple, and a single against the Colorado Rockies. The triple, on a curving liner down the right field line, was his first in four years. At one point during the game, he felt a pull in his right hamstring while rounding first base.

The sore hamstring sidelined Tony for three weeks. He reinjured it on May 9, his forty-first birthday. The walls were closing in, and Tony knew it. He always thought he wanted to retire by fading into the sunset and not suck at the end of his career. With his mounting injuries he could see that "sucking" was around the corner. Many athletes agonize over the transition from professional sports competition to a new occupation. In contrast, Tony had formulated a plan. On May 28, San Diego State announced its long-time head baseball coach, Jim Dietz, intended to retire at the conclusion of the 2002 college baseball season. Tony expressed a strong interest in succeeding Dietz. On June 28, he announced 2001 would constitute his final season in professional baseball.[36]

The first week of September, Tony hand delivered his resume to San Diego State Athletic Director Rick Bay. It was a foregone conclusion Tony would get the job. When he indicated his interest, applications from other candidates dried up. Tony wanted to keep it professional, nonetheless. He showed up on the San Diego State campus in a suit and tie. State made it official on September 20, 2001, introducing Tony as their new head baseball coach. Tony agreed to work under Dietz as a volunteer coach during the 2002 season so he could benefit from a year of on-the-job training. He would take over from Dietz effective July 1, 2002. Once he became head coach, San Diego State agreed to pay him $100,000 a year for three years.

Tony's chronically-sore left knee relegated him to a pinch hitter role during the months of July, August, September, and October. There were a few exceptions. He started in right field on July 19 against Arizona. He went 1-for-3. Rickey Henderson replaced him in right after his final at bat, a strikeout, in the bottom of the fourth. He started in right again in Pittsburgh against the Pirates on August 11. Some 39,388 fans attended the game at Pittsburgh's new PNC Park. Possibly because it was Tony's final season, it was the largest crowd at PNC Park to that point in the season. Tony stepped up. He doubled and scored a run in the top of the second. With the score tied 2–2 in the top of the sixth, he

19. The Last 10 Are the Hardest

cracked a two-run homer (his only one of the season) into the right field stands to give the Padres a 4–2 advantage. He came out of the game for a defensive replacement in the bottom half. The Padres won, 6–2.

After the Pittsburgh game, he was batting a robust .389 for the year. He could still hit. He just couldn't run. Matters were made worse because his right knee was giving him trouble too. Pieces of cartilage had been drained from it. Tony announced the right knee would require surgery at the end of the 2001 season. He wasn't sure when he injured it but thought it was during the Pittsburgh game.

The Pittsburgh game was Tony's last in the field. He pinch-hit the rest of the way. He was sometimes effective as a pinch hitter but the role did not fit him well. He had trouble finding his rhythm when he batted just once a game. Without being in the field, he fidgeted around in the dugout between his at bats. His batting average slowly declined. He pinch-hit 12 times in August, edging out three hits. He pinch-hit 21 times in September with four hits. One of the four hits was timely. On September 22 he pinch-hit against the Giants in the bottom of the seventh. The Padres trailed, 2–0. They loaded the bases. Bochy inserted Tony as a pinch hitter. Tony punched a single to right, driving in two, and tying the game. The Padres won the contest, 4–3.

The Giants series in San Diego from September 21–23 were supposed to be Tony's final home games of his career. The September 11, 2001, terrorist attacks altered the schedule. Major League Baseball shut down for a week after the attacks. The home games in San Diego canceled during the shutdown were rescheduled to the first week of October.

While Tony's career was winding down, Rickey Henderson was engaged in a historic effort. On October 2 against the Dodgers, Henderson tied Ty Cobb's record for career runs scored (2,245). Henderson promised to slide across home plate when he broke the record. He broke it the next day when he hit a home run. He kept his promise. He slid across home plate.

There was more. In San Diego's second-to-last game on October 6, Henderson slashed career hit number 2,999. That day, Tony had one of his more effective pinch-hit appearances. He hit a double, driving in a run, as the Padres whacked the Rockies, 10–4. The double would prove to be Tony's last major league hit.

Tony's final game of his career was on October 7. Arriving at San Diego's Qualcomm Stadium, Tony announced to a security guard, "I'm ready." Yeah, for your last major league game, the guard suggested. "No,"

Tony Gwynn

Tony responded, for the San Diego Chargers game. Tony was an avid sports fan. He lugged around a television so he could watch the first half of the Chargers game as they were playing against the Cleveland Browns in the Eastern time zone, three hours ahead of California time.[37]

Rickey Henderson offered to sit out, leaving the stage to Tony. It would have been a significant concession. Henderson would have had to wait another season to attain 3,000 hits, assuming a major league team would add a 43-year-old player to their roster. Tony talked him out of it. Henderson wasted no time before a home crowd of 60,603. Batting leadoff in the bottom of the first, he hit a blooper to right field that he stretched into a double. After a celebration, he scored the first run of the game on a single by Ryan Klesko. Then, he came out of the lineup.

The Padres strung out Tony's final plate appearance to the ninth inning. He pinch hit with the Padres hopelessly behind the Rockies, 14–5. He wanted to slice a single to the 5.5 hole in his last major league at bat. He was slightly off in his timing. He grounded out to short.

From his gaudy perch at .389 on August 11, Tony's average declined to .324 at the end of the season. But he batted above .300 for the 19th consecutive year, a National League record. The only player ahead of him was the American League's Ty Cobb with 23.

The Padres showed modest improvement over the 2000 season. At one point in May, they held sole possession of first place. They hovered near the .500 mark most of the year. They fell back at the end, finishing at 79–83, good for fourth place in the NL West.

The Padres honored Tony in a post-game ceremony. San Diego Mayor Dick Murphy announced the address of the new downtown baseball stadium as 19 Tony Gwynn Drive.[38]

Tony finished with a .338 career batting average, the highest of any player who began their career after World War II. He recorded 3,141 hits, 135 homers, 543 doubles, 85 triples, 1,138 RBIs, 319 stolen bases, and only 434 strikeouts in 10,232 plate appearances. He reached 3,000 hits in fewer at bats and fewer games than any other player except Ty Cobb and Nap Lajoie.

When the Padres called up Tony to the majors in July 1982, their clubhouse manager, Whitey Wietelmann, assigned him uniform number 19. Wietelmann implored him not to disgrace number 19. He hadn't.

Chapter 20

Coach Gwynn

Now, "real life begins." So said Tony of his post-playing days.[1] He knew what he was talking about. Tony was one of the few major leaguers to shine his own shoes and buy his own bats. But, otherwise, the San Diego Padres attended to his every baseball-related need. The Padres employ a staff of hundreds. The staff oversee maintenance of the stadium and playing field, ticketing, scouting, computer technology, accounting and finance, marketing, media relations, community outreach, and arranging for transportation and hotels at road games. In contrast, the San Diego State baseball program slid by with several coaches and a support staff of roughly a dozen. That is why Jim Dietz, head coach since 1972, personally performed many of the functions necessary to a baseball operation. As Dietz's designated successor, Tony had much to learn. In one 2002 practice the netting used to protect a batting practice pitcher from line drives broke. Tony admitted he had no clue how to fix it.[2]

Jim Dietz assigned Tony two primary responsibilities for the 2002 season—charting pitches during games and serving as a hitting instructor. One of Tony's strengths, however, was fundraising. For years he and Alicia raised money for their charitable foundation. Furthermore, he could access funds based on his name recognition, particularly in southern California, and his cordial relationship with Padres owner John Moores. The San Diego State baseball program was not self-financing. In 2002 the university allocated the program an expense budget of approximately $60,000. Travel costs alone exceeded $100,000. Jim Dietz and his staff scrambled to raise the funds to keep the program afloat. Tony took it upon himself at his final major league game to bring in money for San Diego State baseball. He signed bats, gloves, game programs, and other apparel to sell to the fans. The proceeds were dispensed to San Diego State.

Tony envisioned the installation of a new electronic scoreboard for Tony Gwynn Stadium. He expected the new scoreboard, with its replay capability, would enhance the fan experience and increase attendance at San Diego State games, which averaged slightly under 400 a game. The final contract Tony signed with the Padres provided for a series of deferred salary payments to be disbursed from 2003 to 2007. He approached John Moores for an advance on his deferred payments. Moores agreed. Tony thus contributed approximately $100,000 of his own money toward the new scoreboard. Eventually, he raised $1 million for the project. At first, San Diego State lacked the internal expertise to operate the scoreboard's graphics. Tony agreed to pay from his own funds a staff of vendors to run the scoreboard until the school could develop sufficient expertise.

The scoreboard was in place for State's 2002 home opener. The year prior the opener drew a crowd of 398. In 2002, a crowd of 1,507 showed up. One factor was curiosity about Tony, who was in the midst of an unusual transition from perennial major league All-Star to college coach. But another factor may have been publicity concerning the new scoreboard.

Jim Dietz fielded a respectable team in 2002. They finished with a 44–27 record. The Aztecs were members of the Mountain West Conference (MWC). In 2002 the conference consisted of eight teams but only six sponsored a baseball program—San Diego State, New Mexico, Utah, Brigham Young University (BYU), Air Force, and the University Nevada, Las Vegas (UNLV). San Diego State won the MWC regular season title with a 20–10 mark. Though a worthwhile accomplishment, the title was of little consequence to obtaining a bid to the NCAA tournament. The NCAA awarded an automatic bid only to the winner of the post-regular season double-elimination MWC tournament. San Diego State faltered in the tournament. They reached the final undefeated only to lose twice to BYU. Since its formation in 1998, no MWC baseball team had received an at-large bid to the NCAA. The conference was lightly regarded nationally. One rating service put it no better than 23rd in the country. Despite its regular season championship and its 44–27 record, State failed to receive a bid to the NCAA tournament.

Tony succeeded Dietz on July 1, 2002. Before he was allowed to recruit, he had to pass a test on NCAA rules. He missed passing the test on the first two tries by one question. He passed on his third attempt. He received bad news from Alicia while he was on a recruiting trip in July 2002. His friend Ted Williams passed away. Tony was not surprised. He knew Ted had been in bad shape.

Some college baseball observers doubted Tony's long-term commit-

20. Coach Gwynn

ment to coaching. Tony's son Tony Jr. was a star center fielder for San Diego State. At the conclusion of the 2003 season, Tony Jr. would become eligible for the MLB draft. He was widely expected to be picked in one of the early rounds. The skeptics expected Tony to lose interest in coaching after his son left the college ranks. Others suggested that Tony's intelligence, attention to detail, and knowledge of the game would make him a prime candidate for a front office job with the Padres or another major league team. Still others noted Tony had secured a position with ESPN as a color announcer for baseball games broadcast by the network. These critics imagined broadcasting was the direction Tony was likely to be headed. Lastly, there was a long-held belief that great ballplayers made for bad coaches. They were, according to this school of thought, too talented compared to their players. Success had come too easy for them. Inevitably, their frustration with their players would convince them to exit the coaching profession.

Prior to the 2003 college baseball season, Tony and his coaches conducted a series of batting clinics for youngsters ages 9–17. Tony thought of himself as a teacher. It gratified him when a young player improved because of his instruction. He delivered a message to his critics after holding the clinics. If they had watched me direct these clinics, he said, they would realize "I love what I'm doing."[3]

Jim Dietz led San Diego State to the NCAA tournament eight times between 1979 and 1991. (Tony was a member of two of Dietz's tournament teams.) Each time State was knocked out in the NCAA regionals. Dietz's squad had failed to qualify for the NCAA eleven straight seasons. Tony harbored ambitions to forge State into a national power—a team that regularly qualified for the NCAA tournament, won in the regionals, and earned a berth in the College World Series in Omaha. He installed a sign in the clubhouse that read, "The Road to Omaha Always Starts Through This Door."[4]

To burnish State's national credentials and improve their chances of gaining an at-large bid to the NCAA tournament, Tony decided to strengthen the team's nonconference schedule. Under Dietz State had performed well against nonconference foes such as Western Kentucky, Southern Utah, and Cal State-Riverside. The victories over low-ranked teams did little to impress NCAA tournament selection officials. Tony scheduled several top-25 ranked opponents for the 2003 season. Dietz disagreed with Tony's plan. In fact, it didn't begin well. The Aztecs opened with a three-game series against No. 8–ranked Arizona State. They lost all three. Later in the season, they took on No. 13 University of

Miami. They were swept three straight. They lost to Long Beach State, at the time ranked No. 8.

Jim Dietz regularly brought his team into conference play with a winning record. Tony's 2003 team staggered in at 7–15. Losing hit Tony hard. He generally was able to get past it when he was a player. Losing was different to Tony when he was a coach. As a coach, he knew he was responsible for 35 or 40 players not just himself. That responsibility intensified his sense of conscientiousness. Thus, as he admitted, "I can't let it go."[5]

He wasted little time exhibiting his frustration. He was tossed by the umpires in his ninth game as coach. Trailing the University of Santa Clara 9–6, Tony came out of the dugout in the ninth inning to announce a lineup change. The NCAA recently had issued a missive to umpires to more strictly enforce a rule governing the attire worn by college coaches. The rule required any coach on the field to wear team colors. The weather was cool so Tony came out wearing a black jacket. The home plate umpire insisted he should have been wearing red. Tony protested. The umpire indicated he was going to write Tony up. Tony responded he would write a report on the umpire, whereupon he was ejected from the game. Tony was correct, however. San Diego State's team color was black, not red. Tony couldn't understand why the umpires failed to check for the correct team color prior to the game.

Going into conference play, the Aztec were last in the MWC in team batting average and home runs. In Tony's opinion Aztec batters seemed to lose their focus with runners in scoring position. The relief corps blew several leads in the late innings. The team made the same mistakes on the basepaths and on defense. In one game Tony asked the No. 2 batter in his lineup to lay down a sacrifice bunt. His player grew visibly distraught. Tony was mystified. Why? he asked. Well, his player replied, when he played in high school he batted No. 3 so no one ever asked him to bunt. After one loss, Tony walked outside and pleaded, "Help me, Lord. Help me."[6]

The Aztecs rebounded to an 18–12 record in the MWC, good enough to tie for second. Tony believed their demanding nonconference schedule could pay off in the conference tournament. It almost did. They lost to UNLV in the finals. It was another frustrating defeat. They were leading 8–1 when UNLV scored 10 runs in the bottom of the sixth. UNLV won, 14–9.

San Diego State finished the year 29–32 overall. On the plus side, attendance at home games more than doubled from just under 400 fans

20. Coach Gwynn

per game in 2002 to nearly 900 in 2003. Part of the reason for increased attendance was Tony's "rock star" status, in the words of one reporter. He was besieged by autograph seekers both at home and on the road.[7]

Prior to the 2004 season, Tony hatched another scheme to raise money for San Diego State. The Padres' new downtown stadium, Petco Park, was originally slated to open in time for the 2002 season. Political disputes and litigation delayed the stadium's opening until 2004. Tony proposed Petco open not with the Padres' first 2004 home game but with a four-day weekend of college baseball. He invited seven other college teams to join San Diego State for a series of games between Thursday, March 11, and Sunday, March 14. San Diego State competed against the University of Houston in Petco's first game. State won, 4–0. The game drew a crowd of 40,106. It was the largest crowd in history to attend a college baseball game. LSU and Tulane established the previous record when they performed before 27,763 in the New Orleans Superdome. The four days of college baseball at Petco drew 105,500 fans. The event raised $1 million for San Diego State baseball.

Tony was thrown out of a college game for wearing a jacket probably like this one. An umpire contended red was the team color. The umpire was wrong (Stan Lui/SDSU Athletics).

The Aztecs again took it on the chin in nonconference play. They went 10–17. They scored one notable success the first weekend of March. They took two of three from a previously undefeated and No. 22–ranked North Carolina State team. Tony increasingly was adopting the tactics that coaches use to motivate their players. Before one game against the Wolfpack, he grabbed an armful of bats and threw them on the ground. "See them bounce," he said to his team. "Those bats have some hits in them." The gambit appeared to work. The Aztecs stroked 10 hits in a 7–4 victory.[8]

State battled all season for the MWC regular season crown. They pulled it out on the last day. They were tied with UNLV for first place. State finished their game first. They trounced Utah, 18–2. Meanwhile, UNLV was leading New Mexico 4–1 going into the ninth inning. New Mexico staged a ninth inning rally to beat UNLV 5–4, handing the title to San Diego State.

State won one, lost one, and then swept through the loser's bracket to reach the 2004 MWC tournament final. They lost the final 6–3 to UNLV. Tony was hopeful State would receive an at-large bid from the NCAA. They had forged a 35–29 record while competing against strong nonconference competition. Once again, the NCAA snubbed the Mountain West Conference. State failed to secure an at-large berth. Tony found one source of consolation. He was named the 2004 MWC Coach-of-the-Year.

On September 4, 2004, prior to a game against the Colorado Rockies, the Padres retired Tony's uniform number, 19. "I just want to take a second to thank those who helped me get on top of that wall [in the outfield where his uniform number was displayed] because you don't get there by yourself," Tony said to a crowd of 42,716.[9]

Tony hoped for a turnaround during the 2005 and 2006 seasons. Instead, San Diego State finished with losing overall records both years. The team endured a particularly frustrating stretch in 2006 when they lost 14 in a row. Their 2006 nonconference schedule was rated the fourth toughest in the country. "I'm still having fun," Tony reported.[10] Competing against nationally-ranked teams, however, drove up home attendance. State opened at home against No. 1 Texas in 2005 for a three-game series. The first game of the series drew a school record crowd of 2,857. The three games drew 6,359 fans total.

At one point during the 2005 season Tony's frustrations with the MWC and the inability of its teams to secure at-large bids to the NCAA tournament boiled over. A mid–March three game series between State and Air Force in Colorado Springs was snowed out. Air Force was traveling to San Diego a month later for a three-game set against the Aztecs. Tony scheduled six games, three consecutive doubleheaders in three days, to make up the canceled games. At the request of the Air Force

20. Coach Gwynn

coach, the MWC administration cut the series from six games to four. Tony blasted the decision. Part of his frustration could have been that the Aztecs likely would have won all six games against a weak Air Force team. In fact, they did beat Air Force in the four games that were scheduled. "We're getting screwed," Tony said. "The conference should make them play six. That's the rules. It's a joke, An absolute joke. You want to know why this conference gets no respect in baseball? It's because of stuff like this."[11]

The MWC suspended Tony one game for his remarks. He served his suspension during a home game against UNLV. He found a way to watch. The roof of the university's racquetball courts overlook Tony Gwynn Stadium. Tony perched himself in a folding chair to take in the UNLV game. State won, 7–3. His players praised him afterward. "We kind of wanted to do this for him because he was just trying to stick up for us," said Aztecs shortstop James Guerrero.[12]

Tony's three-year contract to coach San Diego State expired after the 2005 season. The university signed him to another three-year contract, still paying him $100,000 a year. Thus far, Tony's squads had been unable to secure an NCAA tournament bid. "This has been more difficult than I thought," Tony admitted.[13] Still, there were positives which persuaded State to retain him. Home attendance was way up. Tony knew how to raise money. He also proved the doubters wrong about his long-term commitment to college coaching. When ESPN offered him a job to announce baseball full-time. Tony turned it down. "I'm going to miss it, but I am a coach first,"[14] he said. He continued to retain another announcing job. After college baseball season ended, he worked San Diego Padres games for a local television station, Channel 4. More important, it was obvious Tony had a positive influence on his players. Through good times and bad, he spread the Tony Gwynn gospel to his players: Do it right. Do it with class. Prior to team practices, he would sit down with various players and ask them about their lives and their families. Then, he would say, "Let's go to work."[15]

During a game against BYU one of Tony's players hit a walk-off home run. His player stood at home plate admiring the ball as it arced over the outfield wall. Tony brought up the incident in a post-game meeting with his team. He was mad. It wasn't so much that his player had shown up the opposing team. It was something else. Act like you have been there before, he emphasized to his players. In other words, take success in stride. To amplify his point, he kicked a hole in the clubhouse door at Tony Gwyn Stadium. The hole remained the rest of that season.[16]

Tony Gwynn

Once a player has retired from the major leagues for five years, they are eligible for election to the Baseball Hall of Fame. Thus, Tony became eligible on the 2006 ballot. Players are voted into the Hall by a vote of the Baseball Writers Association of America or they can be selected by a veteran's committee. Players are elected by the writers if they receive a "yes" vote on 75 percent or more of the ballots. Tony was nervous about the vote. On an intellectual level, he knew was a shoo-in for election with his 3,141 hits, .338 career batting average, and eight National League batting crowns. But Tony was a high achiever. Until he achieved the honor, he worried. On January 8, 2007, one day before the 2006 election results were scheduled to be announced, Tony's players bucked him up at a team practice. "Hall of Fame, Hall of Fame," they shouted.[17]

The telephone call came shortly after 10:00 a.m., Pacific time. "You're in," Jack O'Connor, Secretary-Treasurer of the Baseball Writers Association of America, informed Tony. He had been selected for the Hall on 97.6 percent of the ballots. It was one of the largest percentage votes in history. Surrounded by family, Tony cried.

The next day, he was feted at a ceremony at Petco. The players arrived wearing their black San Diego State uniforms. They sang the school fight song. His election was again honored before a San Diego State game at Petco in March. Jane Forbes Clark, chairperson of the Hall of Fame, attended the proceedings. She placed in perspective the magnitude of Tony's accomplishment. There are 16,000 players who have competed in the major leagues, she informed the crowd, but only 198 have been elected to the Hall of Fame.[18]

In July 2007 the Padres dedicated a statue of Tony outside Petco Park. It depicted a left-handed swinging Tony aiming for the "5.5 hole." The base of the statue bore a quote from Tony's father, "Work hard and good things will happen." Tony announced, "It's perfect."[19] Greg Maddux, a pitcher Tony often tormented but who was now a member of the Padres pitching staff, said of the statue, "It's cool."[20]

Tony and long-time Baltimore Oriole Cal Ripken were inducted into the Hall of Fame on July 29, 2007. Possibly because of both Tony's and Ripken's long-time associations with their respective teams, a record crowd of 75,000 turned out for the induction ceremony. Tony was garbed in suit and tie for his induction speech. He thanked his youth baseball and basketball coaches, Jim Dietz and Tim Vezie, who coached him at San Diego State, Bobby Tolan, Ted Williams, and Alicia "who allowed me to chase my dreams" and "spend all the time I could to be the best baseball player I could be." He discussed his approach to the

20. Coach Gwynn

game. "I'm a big believer," he said, "that when you sign on the dotted line there's a responsibility to the people who watch baseball to make good decisions and show people how things are supposed to be done."[21]

Tony recognized April 15, 2007, would represent the 60th anniversary of Jackie Robinson's first major league game. He directed the installation of Robinson's uniform number, 42, on a sign above the right field wall of Tony Gwynn Stadium. He explained Robinson's legacy to his players. His players knew some of the Jackie Robinson story. They knew he was the first African American player in the major leagues. They knew he endured abuse. They did not know all the details. Tony filled them in. He described the death threats, the racial epithets hurled from dugouts and the stands, the brushback pitches thrown at Robinson's head, the refusal of service at restaurants and hotels. You could see a "light" go on in the eyes of his players, Tony said, when he told them about Jackie Robinson, for they realized their troubles "paled in comparison" to Robinson's. Tony emphasized that as long as he was the head coach at San Diego State his players would learn about Jackie Robinson. Let's hope, he added, that "human decency never goes out of style."[22]

Brandishing his impeccable major league credentials. Tony attempted to recruit some of the nation's top high school players. Under NCAA rules, a high school senior could sign a letter of intent with a college but, if they were later taken in the MLB draft, they could instead opt to go pro. Or, they could attend college in which event they could again become eligible for the draft after three years. Tony signed a highly-touted shortstop, Matt Bush, in 2004. Bush went pro after he was the No. 1 pick in the 2004 draft taken by, of all teams, the San Diego Padres. Tony obtained a commitment in 2005 from Henry Sanchez, a hard-hitting first baseman. Sanchez elected to go pro after being selected by the Minnesota Twins. Like all college coaches, Tony competed with major league scouts for talent. The trick to college recruiting was to sign the best high school players unlikely to be taken in the draft or who preferred three years of college ball to the minor leagues. Alternately, you could spot those players who, as Jack McKeon had said, possessed that upside potential others did not see.

Tony lost several players to the draft or to graduation after the 2006 season. Consequently, in 2007, he brought in a large recruiting class—28 players. His recruiting class impressed *Baseball America*. The biweekly magazine rated San Diego State No. 33 in the country in its preseason rankings. Blunt as usual, Tony disagreed with *Baseball America*. His team didn't deserve that ranking, he contended.

Tony Gwynn

Still, his 2007 team improved on the 2005 and 2006 seasons. They plowed through their stiff nonconference schedule with a winning record, 15–11. It was the first tine one of Tony's teams entered MWC play with a winning won-loss mark. The Aztecs swept a doubleheader from Air Force on April 22 to run their record to 27–17. A prime reason for the team's improvement over previous seasons was the pitching staff. The staff posted ERAs above 6.00 in 2005 and 2006. Their ERA sat at 3.64 after the Air Force doubleheader. The Aztecs could use five starters. Also, as their closer, they had found that high school player with an upside others did not see. His name was Stephen Strasburg. He was tall, six-foot-five. He attended high school in Santee, California, 22 miles from San Diego. He came out of high school weighing 245 pounds. He sported a credible fastball at 90 miles per hour. The knock on Strasburg was that he was considered soft, not a fierce competitor. Tony's pitching coach, Rusty Filter, lobbied to recruit Strasburg. Tony was uncertain about Strasburg but agreed to follow Filter's advice.

Strasburg bore down in college. He worked as hard, if not harder, than anyone on the San Diego State team. He brought his weight down to 215. If anything, his competitive fire needed to be restrained, not encouraged. In 2007 his fastball gained speed. He went 1–3 on the year with seven saves. His losing won-loss record was misleading. He registered a 2.43 ERA. He struck out 47 batters in 37 innings of pitching. He was named MWC co-freshman of the year.

San Diego State collapsed after they swept the doubleheader against Air Force. They lost 13 of their final 15 games. Their bats went dead. They were knocked out of the MWC tournament. They failed to qualify for the NCAA for the 16th consecutive season.

Tony promoted Strasburg from reliever to starter for the 2008 season. Strasburg's fastball was improving in both velocity and location. One day, Tony Jr., now an outfielder for the Milwaukee Brewers, attended a pre-season San Diego State practice. Tony suggested his son take a few swings against one of his pitchers. Tony Jr. struck out. The pitcher was Strasburg. Tony Jr. knew he had been had. He shot a knowing look at his dad. His dad was laughing.

Strasburg began to dominate college hitters. His fastball was approaching 100 miles per hour. He struck out nine in eight innings against Utah on March 20. He fanned 12 against Houston on March 28. He was the winning pitcher in both games. His performance in another game against Utah on April 11 made him a national sensation. He struck out 23 Utah batters, yielding one hit, in a 1–0 Aztec victory. In his next

20. Coach Gwynn

start he clocked 13 strikeouts while surrendering only four hits as State trounced UNLV, 17–1. A week later he pitched a 13-strikeout complete game victory over Texas Christian University while yielding one hit and one run. (TCU joined the MWC in 2005.) He was tied for the national NCAA Division lead in strikeouts with 99 for the season.

For the first time in Tony' coaching career his team was ranked in the top 25. They finished tied for second in the MWC with a 16–8 record. Reporters and pro scouts from about the country flocked to TCU's Lipton Field in Houston to watch Strasburg pitch in the MWC tournament. State won their first game of the tourney, and lost in their second. Strasburg pitched in neither game, much to the consternation of the assembled media and scouts. Tony refused to indulge them. Strasburg said he didn't feel right so Tony held him out. Strasburg, whom Tony called "Strassy," pitched in State's third game of the tournament.[23] He pitched well. He gave up only one run. The Aztec batters failed to support him. They lost to Utah, 1–0. They finished 31–28 overall. Once more, the NCAA snubbed them when it announced at-large bids. Strasburg was 8–3 on the year. He recorded 133 strikeouts in 97⅓ innings with a 1.57 ERA. He was the lone college player selected for the 2008 U.S. Olympic baseball team. The rest of the squad consisted of minor league players. Strasburg and his Olympic teammates earned a bronze medal at the 2008 Olympics in Beijing.

Tony signed a third three-year contract with San Diego State in the summer of 2008. "I love what I do," he proclaimed. More than winning, he observed, he wanted to teach his players "to get out there and be part of your community."[24]

Tony may have failed to perceive Strasburg's potential, coming out of high school, but he knew about fame. In 2009, Strasburg was going to have it. He was the consensus choice to be the No. 1 pick in the 2009 MLB draft. He was touted as possibly the greatest college pitcher of all time. He was bound to be hounded all season by scouts, fans, and the media. Tony tried to put the issue in perspective for Strasburg. Wouldn't you rather be a player people pay attention to than one who is ignored? he argued. Knowing there would be an obsession over Strasburg's 2009 season pitching statistics, Tony advised him to focus more on working hard rather than the results.[25]

In one 2009 game he propounded to Strasburg the Tony Gwynn gospel. Strasburg yielded a ground ball that slid by a diving Aztec second baseman for a hit. Strasburg thought his second baseman had made a half-hearted stab at the ball. To Strasburg the batter should have been out. He moped on the mound. Tony spoke to him after the inning. Tony praised Strasburg for pitching his way out of trouble. Then, he informed Strasburg that the ball to the second baseman was a hit. Forget about the second baseman Tony told Strasburg. His message was: be objective about yourself. In another game Strasburg was distracted by a large array of radar guns behind home plate that were pointing at him when he pitched. "It comes with the territory," Tony explained.[26]

Tony and his coaches were careful with Strasburg's pitch counts. The coaching staff usually lifted him in the seventh or eighth inning. They allowed him to pitch only two complete games during the regular season, one of them a no-hitter. Tony knew the stakes. He understood the fame and fortune awaiting Strasburg in the major leagues. He was taking no chances whether it hurt his team or not. Strasburg is "not going to leave his arm" at San Diego State, Tony declared.[27]

Strasburg lived up to the hype despite the pitch count restrictions. He struck out 10 or more batters in 10 of the 12 regular season games he pitched. He breezed through with a 12–0 record. He set an NCAA record for most strikeouts per inning. In 2009, he struck out 195 batters in 109 innings. Fans filled up college stadiums to watch him work. They wore T-shirts emblazoned on the back with Strasburg's name and his uniform number, 37.

In one 2009 road game Tony was reminded of the fickleness of fame. He was used to signing autographs for fans the moment he stepped off the team bus. As usual, he spotted a group of autograph hounds waiting outside the bus. When he got out, they rolled past him. They were looking for Stephen Strasburg.[28]

The MWC featured a strong slate of teams in 2009. San Diego State finished the MWC with a 15–9 record. It was only good enough for fourth place behind TCU, New Mexico, and BYU. Strasburg pitched State to a 2–1 victory in their first game of the MWC tourney. They next defeated Utah 9–8 to reach the final. Because the tournament was double-elimination they needed to win but one game in the final for an automatic bid to the NCAA tournament. Instead, Utah beat them twice. Through a combination of a strong nonconference schedule, a 40–21 record, and, possibly, the attention focused on Stephen Strasburg, State was awarded an at-large bid to the NCAA tournament, fulfilling one of Tony's goals when he became head coach. At-large bids were important because anything could happen in a double-elimination conference tournament. That is why Tony was so focused on the point.

State was assigned to a tough regional. The other three teams were

20. Coach Gwynn

No. 7 Virginia, defending national champion, Fresno State, and the No. 1 team in the country, the University of California at Irvine. In State's first game of the regional Virginia beat Strasburg, 5–1. It was his only loss of the season. According to the Cavaliers' head coach, they practiced for Strasburg's fastball, on occasion clocked at 102 miles per hour, by batting against a pitching machine placed 30 feet from home plate.[29] State defeated Fresno State in their second game behind the pitching of their second-best starter, Tyler Lavigne, and the relief pitching of future major leaguer Addison Reed. It was their first victory in the NCAA tournament since 1990, attaining another one of Tony's objectives as a head coach. But, after Strasburg, Lavigne, and Reed, State's pitching slacked off. They lacked the pitching depth to hang with No. 1–ranked UC Irvine. They lost 14–3, eliminating them from the NCAA tournament.

Consistent with pre-season predictions Strasburg was the No. 1 pick in the MLB draft. He was taken by the Washington Nationals. He received a four-year, $15.1 million dollar contract which included a $7.5 million signing bonus. He heeded Tony's advice to get out in the community. Upon signing his contract, he donated $41,000 to the San Diego State baseball program. In later years, he co-sponsored with Tony a fun run to raise money for State's baseball team.

The advice Tony provided him meant something to Strasburg. Coach Gwynn was like a "second father" to me, he said.[30] If anything, Strasburg's mother topped him. Muhammad Ali might have been the greatest, she asserted, but Tony Gwynn is "the second greatest."[31] Strasburg pitched his first major league game against the Pittsburgh Pirates on June 8, 2010. He pitched the Nationals to a 5–2 win. He pitched seven innings, striking out 14. Tony traveled across the country to attend. He sat with the Strasburg family.

Later Strasburg's mother presented Tony with a picture of a young Stephen Strasburg wearing a San Diego Padres batting helmet and tee shirt. Tony placed the picture in his office underneath Tony Gwynn Stadium. He loved to tease visitors by pointing to the picture. Guess who that is? he would say. Invariably, the visitor had no idea. That's Stephen Strasburg, Tony would say, followed by his high-pitched cackle.[32]

The Aztecs regressed in 2010. They finished at 28–28. They hosted the 2010 MWC tournament on their home field. It didn't matter. They lost two straight.

Tony's health took an adverse turn in August 2010. Alicia noted a bulge forming on his right cheek. Doctors performed a biopsy. It was cancer. The cancer was situated in the parotid gland, one of the glands that supplies saliva to the mouth. The cancer was found at the exact spot where for decades Tony held his smokeless chewing tobacco. He encountered other physical problems as well. His weight ballooned to more than 300 pounds. He suffered from three bulging disks in his back.

Doctors removed as much of the cancer as they could during surgery. They were forced to work around a facial nerve that controls face and eye movements. The rest of the cancer would hopefully be killed by a seven to eight-week regimen of chemotherapy and radiation. To prevent head movements during radiation, technicians placed a mask over Tony's face. He couldn't stand the mask. He was claustrophobic. Thereafter, technicians cut larger eyeholes in the mask, piped in jazz music during treatments, and gave Tony a sedative. He successfully pushed through the treatments. Like many cancer patients, he rang a bell after his final treatment. Unlike most cancer patients, he brought the mask home to remind him of his ordeal. For a time after his rounds of chemotherapy and radiation, Tony was unable to smile. He couldn't close his right eye. He had grown a moustache but the right side disappeared leaving only half a moustache. If he could have, he would have laughed.[33]

Tony's doctors doubted a connection between parotid cancer, a rare form of cancer, and smokeless chewing tobacco. Tony was less certain. It seemed too much of a coincidence to find cancer where he regularly used chewing tobacco. The opinion of his doctors was the generally-accepted view in 2010. A little noted study in a 1986 issue of the medical journal *Head and Neck*, however, reported a possible connection between parotid cancer and chewing tobacco.[34]

In any event, Tony had known he needed to kick his tobacco habit. He had one benign growth on his cheek removed in 1991 and another in 2007. His family urged him to stop. He couldn't. The addiction was too strong; the cravings too overwhelming. He would sneak out of the house at night to purchase smokeless. The store clerks unsuccessfully tried to talk him out of it.

Tony's inability to stop chewing would not have surprised researchers at the National Institute of Health. A January 1986 statement issued by the NIH declared: "The continued use of smokeless tobacco even by those who experience serious adverse health consequences attests to its addicting powers." The user of smokeless, the NIH statement continued, seeks to maintain blood levels "bounded on the high side by toxic effects and on the low side by the onset of withdrawal symptoms."[35]

Tony underwent surgery in February 2011 to repair the bulging disks

20. Coach Gwynn

in his back. He brought his weight down. He missed the first two months of the 2011 season. Assistant Coach Mark Martinez ran the team in Tony's absence. Laden with freshmen, the team struggled through a murderous nonconference schedule that included No. 3 Oklahoma, No. 4 Vanderbilt, No. 5 UCLA, No. 14 California, and No. 15 Arkansas. Again, they were knocked out of the MWC tournament. They completed the season with a 23–36 record.

Tony entered into another three-year contract with San Diego State a few weeks after the conclusion of the 2011 season. Several months later, the parotid cancer returned. Doctors had protected the facial nerve on the right side of Tony's face during the 2010 surgery. They were forced to be more aggressive upon the cancer's return. They removed the facial nerve for better access to the cancer cells. They replaced the original nerve with grafts from Tony' neck. The surgery lasted 14 hours. Tony and Alicia were hopeful the doctors had found all the cancer. Tony returned to coaching in March 2012. He left a few weeks later suffering from blood clots in his legs. The clots were possibly related to the 14-hour surgery.

San Diego State still had a young team in 2012. They had 15 sophomores and 12 freshmen. They finished 26–34. They reached the MWC tournament finals but lost to New Mexico so, once again, they missed the NCAA tournament.

Meanwhile, John Moores announced he

Tony attending to a basket of baseballs while coaching at San Diego State (SDSU Athletics).

intended to sell his majority interest in the San Diego Padres. Tony associated with an ownership group led by Hollywood producer Thomas Tull. Tull failed in his bid to secure the team. During the course of negotiations to sell the team, it was revealed that Tony owed the IRS $400,000 in back taxes.[36] Tony indicated he was extinguishing the debt with installment payments. On occasion, it appeared Tony's focus on baseball, public speaking, and charity work deflected his attention from his personal financial affairs. The IRS debt was another example.

For the most part, Tony was able to coach full-time in 2013. One day he was annoyed with the Aztecs batting practice. He stepped up to the plate to hit against a batting practice pitcher. He took the first pitch. Then, he laced line drives to every corner of the ballpark. See, he pointed out to his players, he had been sitting down and he could hit like that. If his players had not focused on it before, they now realized why their coach had been elected to the Hall of Fame.[37] Tony's 2013 team finished 15–15 in conference play. After a loss in the conference tournament they caught fire. They rolled through the loser's bracket to the finals. They defeated New Mexico twice to win the MWC tournament championship and thus secure an automatic bid to the NCAA tournament. Their losing streak in the NCAA regionals continued. They lost 5–3 to eventual national champ UCLA and 6–3 to their cross-town rival, the University of San Diego.

Tony's 2014 team appeared to be his best yet. On March 17, they defeated Purdue 6–5 to run their season record to 16–4. A week later Tony requested a medical leave of absence. "I'm doing good," he claimed.[38] He sat out the balance of the season. The Aztecs carried on with Mark Martinez in charge. They sought to retain Tony's presence in spirit if not in fact. "Every day what we strive for is to do things right. That's something Coach Gwynn instills in all of us as baseball players and men," said San Diego State catcher Brad Haynal in reference to the Tony Gwynn gospel.[39] They telephoned Tony when they won games and sang the Aztec fight song. Mark Martinez found a Tony Gwynn bobblehead. He placed it in the San Diego State dugout. The players bounced the bobblehead for good luck. On occasion the players would raise their arms and yell, "T.G."[40]

State won the MWC tournament for the second straight season. Again, they were unable to get past the NCAA regionals. Although they had not yet qualified for the College World Series, Tony's vision for San Diego State baseball was coming closer to fruition. *San Diego Union-Tribune* writer Kevin Acee previously had been sharply critical

20. Coach Gwynn

of Tony's leadership of the team. They were underperforming, Acee contended. They were not as successful as other southern California teams such as the University of San Diego. But Acee expressed a different view after State's second consecutive appearance in the NCAA tournament. "We can finally say the Aztecs have reached the place where they belong," he wrote in the June 1, 2014, edition of the paper. San Diego State, he predicted, "might remain in college baseball's upper echelon for a while."[41]

On June 11, San Diego State announced it had agreed to a one-year contract with Tony to continue as head coach. The university also announced it had promoted Mark Martinez from Assistant Head Coach to Executive Head Coach. Neither the school nor Tony provided a public comment on the status of Tony's health.

Despite the silence from San Diego State and Tony, the one-year contract instead of the usual three-year agreement combined with the promotion of Martinez should have offered clues. Tony's parotid cancer had returned a third time. He beat it twice. Now, it was spreading. He was in and out of the hospital. He was dying. He knew it. He declined last-resort treatments. He retained the ability to laugh at himself. Sometimes, Alicia later reported, he would fall asleep in front of the television. When he awoke, he would announce, "I'm still here."[42] He died during the early morning hours of June 16, 2014. He was fifty-four years old.

Epilogue

Tony liked mingling with people. At the same time, he was a private person. He did not like being the center of attention. Accordingly, few in San Diego or the baseball community knew the severity of his illness. Thus, the initial reaction to his death was disbelief. Next, came the tributes.

As to be expected, obituaries in newspapers and sports-related publications such as *Sports Illustrated* cited Tony's achievements during his major league career—a .338 career batting average, 3,141 career hits, eight National League batting titles, five Gold Gloves, 19 consecutive .300 seasons, the close call with a .400 batting average in 1994, 15 times a National League All-Star, the 97.6 percent first ballot vote electing him to the Hall of Fame. Trevor Hoffman told the *San Diego Tribune* that Tony "revolutionized" video in baseball.[1] In a broadcast for the *Major League Network*, John Smoltz, against whom Tony batted .444 for his career, said he tried every pitch in his arsenal, including a knuckleball, to try to get Tony out. "What he was so good at," Smoltz added, "was he recognized anything you were trying to do. And he saw it quicker than anyone else."[2]

Tony's ability to hit with two strikes in the count, where a pitcher holds a significant advantage, was reported on by MLB.com. Since records have been kept (beginning in the early 1990s) MLB.com noted, Tony far and away compiled the highest batting average—.302—with a two-strike count. His nearest competitor was 40 points lower, Wade Boggs at .262.[3]

More telling than the recitation of baseball statistics were the accolades for Tony Gwynn, the person. Tom Verducci of *Sports Illustrated* wrote that Tony "was an ambassador not just for the game of baseball but for all mankind."[4]

In Rich Wolfe's 2014 book *He Left His Heart in San Diego*, the *San Diego Union-Tribune*'s Bill Plaschke asserted Tony was "unmatched as a human being" for he possessed "a unique combination of greatness and

Epilogue

grace, toughness and kindness, heavenly skills and earthly touch." Furthermore, his locker was "a refuge for everyone" with "all welcome, all equal."[5] Mark Martinez, an assistant coach under Tony at San Diego State since 2005 and his successor as head coach, said Tony taught more than baseball for "He taught his core value. Do it right. He taught players to respect the game, to respect people, and do it with class."[6]

Tony's friend and former teammate, Jerald Clark, explained Tony's devotion to performing for fans and to acceding to their requests for autographs: According to Clark Tony would say,

> I have to entertain these people. These people are coming out to watch a baseball game. A lot of people are going to work every day. They have kids. They're not like making a lot of money. They're struggling. But they're spending their hard-earned money to come out and watch us entertain them.[7]

Barry Bonds lamented that he failed to heed Tony's advice. "He kept telling me to be nice. But I was so deep into being controversial. I said to hell with it. It's sad I did that."[8]

There were references to Tony's great laugh and his sense of humor. Ed Graney of the *Las Vegas Review-Journal* attempted to describe Tony's laugh. "Infectious. Bellowing. Incredible." Also, it was "Hearty. Warm. Comfortable. Welcoming."[9]

Clint Hurdle competed in the major leagues from 1977 to 1987, and later managed minor and major league teams. He relayed a story illustrating Tony's combination of self-confidence with self-deprecation. Hurdle encountered Tony at a game late in Tony's major league career. You have been hot [at the plate] for "like 18 years," Hurdle said to Tony. Thereafter, Hurdle continued, whenever he and Tony saw each other Tony would introduce himself as "hot for 18 years," and then he would laugh.[10]

C.J. Saylor, one of Tony's former players at San Diego State, noted he once asked Coach Gwynn if the San Diego State public address system could play a Lil Wayne tune that included the line "Ballin' Like Tony Gwynn" when he stepped up to bat. No, Tony told him, because you are not "half the player" I was. The signature Tony Gwynn laugh followed.[11]

Inevitably, the reminiscences on Tony's life turned to the issue of his long-time use of smokeless tobacco, possibly a contributing cause to his death. Upon learning of Tony's passing from cancer, Stephen Strasburg, Addison Reed, and Bruce Bochy vowed to quit using smokeless. Cities with major league teams began to ban use of smokeless on the field. San Francisco, Chicago, and New York were among the first to

Epilogue

enact bans. In light of Tony's death, the Major League Collective Bargaining Agreement was amended in 2016 to bar the use of smokeless at games or team functions by players who entered the major leagues after the 2016 season. In May 2016 the Gwynn family filed a wrongful death lawsuit against U.S. Smokeless Tobacco, Inc., Ltd., and its corporate parent, Altria. The family announced they filed the lawsuit primarily to increase public awareness of the risks of using smokeless. Two years later, the suit was settled. The terms of the settlement remain confidential.

Tony's life was repeatedly honored at baseball stadiums and other venues. On June 16, 2014, the day Tony died, the Padres were in Seattle for a night game against the Mariners. The Mariners painted a 19, Tony's uniform number, at the 5.5 hole between shortstop and third base where Tony had collected so many hits during his career. Five days later, more than 400 attended a funeral for Tony at the Conrad Prebys Student Center on the campus of San Diego State. One of Alicia's brothers, Clarence Cureton, officiated. "Tony loved his family," said Cureton. "He loved the very idea of family."[12]

A crowd of 23,229 attended a June 26, 2014, celebration of Tony's life at Petco Park. The Padres displayed Tony's career highlights on the stadium's Jumbotron. At one point during the proceedings, the fans broke into a chant of "Tony, Tony, Tony."[13]

San Diego State honored Tony's life at its 2015 season home opener on February 13. Tony's brother Chris, himself an alum of the San Diego State baseball program, spoke to the crowd. Tony's daughter, Anisha, sang the National Anthem. When Tony's number, 19, was unveiled on the right field wall, the crowd of 2,519 rose for a standing ovation. On Father's Day, 2015, roughly a year after Tony died, Tony Jr. effected another form of tribute to his dad. He uncorked a walk-off home run in the bottom of the ninth to seal a victory for his team, the Triple A Syracuse Chiefs. "It's been a hard week. I'd be lying if I said anything different," said Tony Jr. Sounding very much like his father, he also declared, "But there's still a job to do and that's something I take very seriously."[14]

On October 29, 2015, the county of San Diego dedicated a section of Interstate 15, located in the northeast sector of the county, as "Tony Gwynn Memorial Freeway." Fittingly, the section named for Tony intersects with the Ted Williams Parkway. A San Diego County supervisor spoke at the dedication ceremonies. Tony could have decided to leave San Diego for another city, the supervisor indicated, but, instead, he stayed.[15]

Epilogue

From February 26–28, 2016, San Diego State and the University of San Diego co-hosted the inaugural Tony Gwynn Classic, an eight-team early season college baseball tournament. San Diego State, the University of San Diego, Arizona, Kentucky, Tulane, Nebraska, the University of California at Santa Barbara, and Bryant University participated. A University of San Diego baseball announcer apparently first proposed the idea. When it was presented to Tony, he loved it. "He talked about it all the time," said Alicia.[16] The purpose of the tournament was to bring in college baseball teams from across the country to compete in a tournament atmosphere that resembled a post-season NCAA regional. The University of California at Santa Barbara took the first Tony Gwynn Classic by defeating the University of San Diego, 9–3, in the final.

The July 2016 Major League All-Star game was held at San Diego's Petco Park. Prior to the game, Major League Baseball announced that, henceforth, the winner of the National League batting crown would be designated the Tony Gwynn National League Batting Champion. Likewise, the American League winner would be known as the Rod Carew American League Batting Champion.

On May 19, 2017, the city of Poway, California, where Tony had resided with his family, unveiled a bronze statue of Tony. The statue was cast by Seth Vandable, a sculptor from Texas. Several local businesses underwrote $100,000 for labor and constructions costs and numerous individuals contributed another $200,000 toward the additional costs

Sculptor Seth Vandable cast this statue of Tony holding his daughter Anisha. The statue was dedicated in 2017 in Poway, California (Seth Vandable).

Epilogue

for the statue. It depicted Tony, wearing his baseball uniform, waving to a crowd with his left arm while cradling daughter Anisha with his right. The statue included the inscription, "Family Man. Athlete. Powegian. Friend. Legend." Tony's statue at Petco Park featured a quote from his father, "Work hard and good things will happen." Similarly, Vandable's work contained a quote from Tony, "Remember these two things: play hard and have fun."[17] Sportscaster Dick Enberg was among the speakers at the unveiling. Enberg had worked with Tony broadcasting San Diego Padres games on local television. "In my 60 years of broadcasting," Enberg said, "there's been only a very few who matched athletic greatness with extraordinary goodness." One was John Wooden. Another was Tony Gwynn.[18]

In one sentence during an interview with the *Washington Post*, Stephen Strasburg probably encapsulated Tony's life as well as anyone. "This is a guy," Strasburg observed, "who put other people before himself."[19]

Chapter Notes

Chapter 1

1. Union High School (Gallatin, TN) Yearbooks, 1949–1952 (courtesy Sumner County, Tennessee, Archives).
2. Tony Gwynn with Roger Vaughn, *The Art of Hitting* (New York: GT Publishing, 1998); Rich Wolfe, *He Left His Heart in San Diego* (Lone Wolf Press, 2014), as told by Tony Gwynn to Bill Staples, 12.
3. Wolfe, as told by Tony Gwynn, 15.
4. *Ibid.*, 17.
5. *Ibid.*, 12–13.
6. *Ibid.*, 17–18.
7. *Ibid.*, 13.
8. *Ibid.*, 19–20.
9. *Ibid.*, 17.
10. Tony Gwynn, Hall of Fame Induction Speech, July 29, 2007, genius.com-tony-gwynn-hall-of-fame-induction-speech.
11. Tony Gwynn and Jim Geschke, *Tony!* (Chicago: Contemporary, 1986), 20–21.
12. *Ibid.*, 18.
13. Gwynn with Vaughn, *The Art of Hitting*, 36.

Chapter 2

1. Wolfe, *He Left His Heart in San Diego*, as told by Tony Gwynn, 21.
2. George Will, *Men at Work: The Craft of Baseball* (New York: Macmillan, 1990), 228.
3. Ted Williams and John Underwood, *The Science of Hitting* (New York: Simon & Schuster, 1986), 7.
4. Wolfe, *He Left His Heart in San Diego*, as told by Tony Gwynn, 24.
5. Gwynn and Geschke, *Tony!*, 26.
6. *Ibid.*, 29.
7. *Ibid.*, 25.
8. "Path to Hall Began in L.B.," *Long Beach Press–Telegram*, July 26, 2007, https://www.presstelegram.com>2007/07/26>path-to-hall-began-in-l.b.
9. Gwynn and Vaughn, *The Art of Hitting*, 35.
10. Gwynn and Geschke, *Tony!*, 28.
11. Wolfe, *He Left His Heart in San Diego*, as told by Tony Gwynn, 28.
12. Kirk Kenney, "Things About Gwynn," *San Diego Union-Tribune*, May 9, 2000.

Chapter 3

1. Wolfe, *He Left His Heart in San Diego*, as told by Tim Vezie, 43.
2. Gwynn and Geschke, *Tony!*, 32.
3. *Ibid.*
4. Wolfe, *He Left His Heart in San Diego*, as told by Bobby Meacham, 40.
5. Andrew Lawrence, "Tony Gwynn's Last Days: Cancer, Tobacco, and the Death of a Legend," *Sports Illustrated*, June 2, 2016, www.si.com/mlb/2016/06/02/tony-gwynn-cancer-san-diego-padres.
6. Gwynn and Geschke, *Tony!*, 33.
7. *Ibid.*
8. Richard Hoffer, "Fear of Failure: His Lifetime Average is .335—and—Climbing," *Sports Illustrated*, September 18, 1995, vault.si.com/1995/09/18/fear-of-failure-his-lifetime-average-is-.335-and-climbing.
9. Williams and Underwood, *The Science of Hitting*, 24.

Notes—Chapters 4, 5, 6 and 7

10. Wolfe, *He Left His Heart in San Diego*, as told by Jim Dietz, 50.
11. Buster Olney, "Tony's Burden," *San Diego Union-Tribune*, March 23, 1994.
12. Wolfe, *He Left His Heart in San Diego*, as told by Nick Canepa, 127.
13. Gwynn and Geschke, *Tony!*, 14.
14. Steve Dolan, "In 8 Years There Were Standout Players and Big Wins But Many Headaches Too," *Los Angeles Times*, February 28, 1987, Pro Quest Newspapers.
15. Wolfe, *He Left His Heart in San Diego*, as told by Nick Harsh, 35.

Chapter 4

1. Wolfe, *He Left His Heart in San Diego*, as told by Jack McKeon, 141.
2. Jack McKeon and Kevin Kernan, *I'm Just Getting Started: Baseball's Best Storyteller on Old School Baseball, Defying the Odds, and Good Cigars* (Chicago: Triumph, 2005), 80.
3. Wolfe, *He Left His Heart in San Diego*, as told by John Maffei, 60.
4. Ken Gerdau, *Daily Aztec* (San Diego State University), Tony Gwynn Commemorative Issue, May 4, 2016.
5. McKeon and Kernan, *I'm Just Getting Started*, 78.
6. Wolfe, *He Left His Heart in San Diego*, as told by Jack McKeon, 141.

Chapter 5

1. Gwynn and Vaughn, *The Art of Hitting*, 38.
2. Daniel A. Russell, "Why Aluminum Bats Can Perform Better Than Wood Bats," paper prepared for Penn State University, www.acs.psu.edu/d.russell/bats/alumwood.html.
3. Gwynn and Vaughn, *The Art of Hitting*, 41.
4. Tony Gwynn and Jim Rosenthal, *Tony Gwynn's Total Baseball Player: Winning Techniques for Hitting, Fielding, and Baserunning* (New York: St. Martin's Press, 1992), 9.
5. Gwynn and Vaughn, *The Art of Hitting*, 45.

6. Bill Plaschke, "The Book on Bowa," *Los Angeles Times*, August 8, 1987, Pro Quest Newspapers; Benjamin Hill, "Gwynn's Quick Ascent Precludes Storied Career," *MLB.com*, January 9, 2007, www.mlb.com/y2007/m01/d09/c151028.jsp.
7. Wolfe, *He Left His Heart in San Diego*, as told by John Kruk, 84.
8. . Gwynn and Geschke, *Tony!*, 43.
9. *Ibid.*, 43–44.
10. Author Interview with Jack McKeon, October 18, 2021.

Chapter 6

1. David Porter and Joe Naiman, *The San Diego Padres Encyclopedia* (Champaign: Sports Publishing, 2002), 195.
2. Bob Chandler with Bill Swank, *Bob Chandler's Tales from the San Diego Padres Dugout: A Collection of the Greatest Padres Stories Ever Told* (New York: Sports Publishing, 2006), 157.
3. Gwynn and Rosenthal, *Tony Gwynn's Total Baseball Player*, 94.
4. *Ibid.*, 2.
5. Wolfe, *He Left His Heart in San Diego*, as told by Jack McKeon, 143.
6. Kirk Kenney, "Things About Gwynn," *San Diego Union-Tribune*, May 10, 2010.
7. Phil Collier, "Gwynn Debut Impressive But Padres Lose 5th Anyway," *San Diego Union*, July 20, 1982.
8. Tom Verducci, "Single Minded as They Closed in on Magic Hit Number 3,000: Tony Gwynn and Wade Boggs Looked Back on Eerily Similar Careers That Established Them as the Top Contact Hitters of Their Time," *Sports Illustrated*, August 9, 1999, vault.si.com/1999 08/09/single-minded-as-they-close-in-on-magic-hit.
9. Gwynn and Geschke, *Tony!*, 48–49.
10. "Path to Hall Began in L.B.," *Long Beach Press-Telegram*, July 26, 2007.

Chapter 7

1. Gwynn and Geschke, *Tony!*, 50; Dick Williams and Bill Plaschke, *No More Mr.*

Notes—Chapters 8, 9 and 10

Nice Guy: A Life of Hardball (San Diego: Harcourt, Brace, Jovanich, 1990), 236.
2. Hoffer, "Fear of Failure," *Sports Illustrated*, September 18, 1995.
3. Chris Jenkins, "The Hit Parade," *San Diego Union-Tribune*, July 29, 1997.
4. Williams and Underwood, *The Science of Hitting*, 19.
5. Gwynn and Geschke, *Tony!,* 57.
6. Wolfe, *He Left His Heart in San Diego*, as told by Jack McKeon, 143.
7. Wolfe, *He Left His Heart in San Diego*, as told by Bill Center, 218.

Chapter 8

1. Steve Wulf, "The Beast Team in Baseball: The Menagerie Known as the San Diego Padres Zoo Has Been Devouring National League Opponents," *Sports Illustrated*, April 16, 1984, vault.si.com.vault/1984/04/16-the-beast-team-in-basball.
2. Chandler and Swank, *Tales from the San Diego Padres Dugout*, 92.
3. Tom Cushman, "Final Blast Loudest One for Padres," *San Diego Evening Tribune*, July 21, 1984.
4. Gwynn and Geschke, *Tony!*, 64.
5. Chris Mortense, "McSherry Calls Brawl the Worst He Has Ever Seen," *Atlanta Constitution*, August 13, 1984.
6. Gerry Fraley, "Torre Blaming 'Idiot' Williams," *Atlanta Constitution*, August 13, 1984.
7. *Ibid.*
8. "Gathering Assorted Items of Baseball History and Trivia," January 4, 2011, https://miscbaseball.wordpress.com/2011/01/04/2051/.
9. Porter and Naiman, *San Diego Padres Encyclopedia*, 90.

Chapter 9

1. A.J. Perez, "The Chicago Cubs Billy Goat Curse Explained," *USA Today*, October 16, 2016, https://www.usatoday,com/story/sports/mlb/2016/10/25/chicago-cubs-billy-goat-curse-explained/92715898.

2. Porter and Naiman, *San Diego Padres Encyclopedia*, 94.
3. Steve Wulf, "You've Got to Hand It to the Padres," *Sports Illustrated*, October 15, 1984, https://vault.si.com/vault/1984/10/15.
4. Chandler and Swank, *Tales from the San Diego Padres Dugout*, 98.
5. Wulf, "You've Got to Hand It to the Padres," *Sports Illustrated*, October 15, 1984.
6. *Ibid.*
7. Porter and Naiman, *San Diego Padres Encyclopedia*, 97.
8. Wulf, "You've Got to Hand it to the Padres," *Sports Illustrated*, October 15, 1984.
9. *Ibid.*

Chapter 10

1. Mark Kreidler, "Gwynn Hits the Jackpot in 1984," *San Diego Union*, April 9, 1985.
2. *Ibid.*
3. Chris Jenkins, "The Hit Parade," *San Diego Union-Tribune*, July 29, 2007.
4. Bob Nightengale, "Report: Wiggins' Death AIDS-Related," *Tampa Bay Times*, January 14, 1991, https://www.tampabay.com/archive/1991/01/14/report-wiggins-death-aids-related.
5. Phil Collier, "Tony Beats Chris, But Padres Tie," *San Diego Union*, April 6, 1985.
6. Gwynn and Geschke, *Tony!*, 90.
7. Phil Collier, "Gwynn, Templeton Would Welcome Drug-Testing Plan," *San Diego Union*, March 2, 1986.
8. Jamie Dial, "A Fresh Breeze Cools the Desert Air," *Sports Illustrated*, March 10, 1986, vault.si.com/vault/1986/03/10/a-fresh-breeze-cools-the-desert-air.
9. *Ibid.*
10. Barry Bloom, "Padres Win in a 'Laugher,'" *San Diego Evening Tribune*, May 29, 1986.
11. Williams and Plaschke, *No More Mr. Nice Guy*, 235.
12. Eric Stephen, "An Appreciation of Tony Gwynn Moments Against the Dodgers," *SB Nation*, May 9, 2020, www.truebluela.com/2020/5/9/2123034/tony-gwyyn-happy-birthday-dodgers.

13. Mark Kreidler, "Gwynn's 4 Hits, 5 Steals, Can't Save Padres," *San Diego Union*, September 21, 1986.
14. David Hill, "Los Angeles Dodgers: Bob Welch—the Man to K Tony Gwynn Three Times in One Game," May 9, 2020, *Call to the Pen*, https://calltothepen.com/2020/05/09/los-angeles-dodgers-bob-welch-the-man-to-k-tony-gwynn-three-times-in-one-game.
15. Tom McMillan, "Gwynn Shows He's a Complete Player in Loss," *San Diego Union*, August 28, 1986.
16. *Ibid*.
17. Chris Jenkins, "The Hit Parade," *San Diego Union-Tribune*, July 29, 2007.
18. Bob Slocum, "Gold Glove Nice Catch for Improved Gwynn," *San Diego Evening Tribune*, December 3, 1986.

Chapter 11

1. Ron Firmite, "Padre with a Passion," *Sports Illustrated*, May 4, 1987, vault.si/vault/1987/05/04/padre-with-a-passion-his-young-teams-struggles-have-forced-manager-larry-bowa-to-temper-his-fury-with-patience.
2. Mark Kreidler, "Gwynn, Bowa: Padres Suspect," *San Diego Union*, March 13, 1987.
3. Ed Zieralski, "Victory Is Tribute to Whitson, Gwynn," *San Diego Evening Tribune*, May 11, 1987.
4. Tom Friend, "San Diego's Gwynn Files for Bankruptcy," *Los Angeles Times*, May 24, 1987, Pro Quest Newspapers.
5. Mark Kreidler, "'Gwynn's Wife Says, Yes, He Can," *San Diego Union*, July 16, 1987.
6. Nick Canepa, "This .400 Talk Drives Gwynn Crazy," *San Diego Evening Tribune*, July 18, 1987.
7. Kreidler, "Gwynn's Wife Says, Yes, He Can," *San Diego Union*, July 16, 1987.
8. *Ibid*.
9. Phil Collier, "Gwynn Stars as Padres Roll on 5-for-5 Night, Helps Club Win 5th in a Row," *San Diego Union*, August 12, 1987.
10. Bob Slocum, "Gwynn Gives Padres a High 5-for-5," *San Diego Evening Tribune*, August 12, 1987.
11. *Ibid*.
12. Sharon Robb, "Chris Gwynn Hopes to Match Brother's Success in Baseball," *Orlando Sun-Sentinel*, June 15, 1985, https://www.com/news/fl-xpm-1985-06-15-8501240005-story-html.
13. Will, *Men at Work*, 169.
14. Rick Davis, "It Was a Stellar Season for Gwynn," *San Diego Evening Tribune*, October 5, 1987.

Chapter 12

1. Barry Lorge, *San Diego Union*, March 16, 1988.
2. Bob Slocum, "Padres Batty While Hitting Streak Still on Hold," *San Diego Evening Tribune*, April 18, 1988.
3. *Ibid*.
4. Bob Slocum, "Gwynn Still Stumped Over His Slump," *San Diego Evening Tribune*, April 23, 1988.
5. *Ibid*.
6. Kevin Kernan, "Gwynn Wants an Indoor Cage," *San Diego Union*, May 1, 1988.
7. Kevin Kernan, "Hawk Blanks Phils on 4 Hits," *San Diego Union*, June 1, 1988.
8. Bob Slocum, "Gwynn Says No to No-Hitter," *San Diego Evening Tribune*, June 7, 1988.
9. *Ibid*.
10. Gwynn and Vaughn, *The Art of Hitting*, 120.
11. *Ibid*., 121.
12. Barry Bloom, "Hot Gwynn Still Isn't Feeling Right," *San Diego Evening Tribune*, July 15, 1988.
13. Porter and Naiman, *San Diego Padres Encyclopedia*, 117.
14. Barry Bloom, "Gwynn Has Decision on His Hands," *San Diego Evening Tribune*, October 1, 1988.
15. Kevin Kernan, "Gwynn's Title Part of a Sweet Finish," *San Diego Union*, October 3, 1988.
16. Kervin Kernan, "Batting Cage Sweet Music to Gwynn," *San Diego Union*, April 5, 1989.
17. Steve Wulf, "Back in the Saddle," *Sports Illustrated*, April 5, 1989, vault.si.com/vault/1989/04/05/702464.
18. Rick Davis, "Gwynn Gets Thumb

Notes—Chapter 13

and Padres Play Dumb," *San Diego Evening Tribune*, August 5, 1989.

19. Mark Kreidler, "Gwynn Big Hit Right to the End," *San Diego Union*, October 2, 1989.

20. *Ibid.*

21. *Ibid.*

22. Barry Bloom, "How the West Was Lost," *San Diego Evening Tribune*, October 2, 1989.

Chapter 13

1. Steve Wulf, "Power to the Padres," *Sports Illustrated*, April 16, 1990, https://vault.si.com/>vault>1990/04/16/west-nl-power-to-the-padres.

2. Wayne Lockwood, "Major Leagues," *San Diego Union*, May 17, 1990.

3. Bob Nightengale, "Criticism Catches Gwynn Off Guard Baseball: Four-Time Batting Champion Shows the Strain of Teammates' Remarks After San Diego Loses to Montreal," *Los Angeles Times*, May 24, 1990, Pro Quest Newspapers.

4. Kevin Kernan, "Gwynn Defends Play After Taking a Quote from Pags Personally," *San Diego Union*, May 23, 1990.

5. *Ibid.*

6. Barry Bloom, "Clark Gets Gwynn Riled Up Again," *San Diego Evening Tribune*, March 4, 1991.

7. Tim Kurkjian, "Beginning Again: After a Nightmarish 1990, The Padres' Tony Gwynn Seeks a Season of Redemption," *Sports Illustrated*, March 11, 1991, vault/si.comvault/1991/03/11/beginning-again-after-a-nightmarish-1990-the-padres-tony-gwynn-seeks-a-seson-of-redemption.

8. Kevin Kernan, "Padres Meet Challenge in N.Y., 5–4," *San Diego Union*, May 25, 1990.

9. Nick Canepa, "Mr. Pags Should Direct His Rags at Someone Else," *San Diego Evening Tribune*, May 26, 1990.

10. *Ibid.*

11. Kevin Kernan, "Gwynn Gets Through Toughest Days, Looks Ahead," *San Diego Union*, May 26, 1990.

12. Tim Kurkjian, "San Diego Hits a Sour Note," *Sports Illustrated*, August 6, 1990, vault/si.com/vault/1990/08/06/san-diego-hits-a-sour-note.

13. *Ibid.*

14. Geoff Edgars, "Roseanne on the Day She Shrieked 'The Star Spangled Banner,' Grabbed Her Crotch, and Earned a Rebuke from President Bush: The Comedian Talks About the Moment That Changed Her Life 25 Years Ago," *Washington Post*, July 23, 2015, Pro Quest Newspapers.

15. Bill Center, "Roseanne Is Sorry She Didn't Sing So Good," *San Diego Union*, July 28, 1990.

16. Kurkjian, "San Diego Hits a Sour Note," *Sports Illustrated*, August 6, 1990.

17. Kurkjian, "Beginning Again," *Sports Illustrated*, March 11, 1991.

18. Claire Smith, "His Uniform Changes But Clark Doesn't," *New York Times*, March 3, 1991, Pro Quest Newspapers.

19. Barry Bloom, "It's Time for the Padres to Back Gwynn," *San Diego Evening Tribune*, September 15, 1990.

20. *Ibid.*

21. Kevin Kernan, "Fate Fingers Gwynn," *San Diego Union*, September 16, 1990.

22. Kurkjian, "Beginning Again," *Sports Illustrated*, March 11, 1991.

23. Kevin Kernan, "Padres Say Worker Hung Gwynn Doll," *San Diego Union*, September 21, 1990.

24. Bob Nightengale, "From Gwynn, Laughter Springs Baseball: Padre Outfielder Puts Year of Troubles Behind Him," *Los Angeles Times*, March 1, 1992, Pro Quest Newspapers.

25. Tom Friend, "Tony Gwynn Returns After Facing Cancer," *ESPN.com*, www.espn.com/espn/otl/newsstory/?id=6257656.

26. Kurkjian, "Beginning Again," *Sports Illustrated*, March 11, 1991.

27. Bob Nightengale, "Gwynn Rips Clark, Cites 'Jealousy,'" *Orlando Sun-Sentinel*, March 5, 1991, https://www.sun-sentinel.com/news/fl-xpm-1191-03-05-9101120006-story.html.

28. Nightengale, "From Gwynn, Laughter Springs Baseball," *Los Angeles Times*, March 1, 1991.

Notes—Chapters 14 and 15

29. Kurkjian, "Beginning Again," *Sports Illustrated*, March 11, 1991.
30. Nick Canepa, "Gwynn Still Baffled by Jack's Knife," *San Diego Evening Tribune*, April 4, 1991.
31. Kevin Kernan, "Gwynn Plans to Keep His Sense of Humor," *San Diego Union*, March 1, 1991.
32. *Ibid.*
33. Jeff Sullivan, "The Time Tony Gwynn's Teammates Thought He Was Selfish," *SB Nation*, https://www.sbnation.com/2011/6/28/2247559/tony-gwynn-san-diego-padres.

Chapter 14

1. Tony Gwynn, Louisville Slugger Legends Award Question and Answer Session, November 9, 2012 (courtesy Louisville Slugger Museum & Factory).
2. *Ibid.*
3. Wolfe, *He Left His Heart in San Diego*, as told by Chris Jenkins, 153.
4. *Ibid.*
5. *Ibid.*
6. Chris Jenkins, "So What's Next, Padres Office Furniture?" *San Diego Union-Tribune*, October 27, 1992.
7. Porter and Naiman, *San Diego Padres Encyclopedia*, 133.
8. Gwynn and Rosenthal, *Tony Gwynn's Total Baseball Player*, Foreword by Willie Davis, vii.
9. *Ibid.*, 39.
10. *Ibid.*, 47.
11. Wolfe, *He Left His Heart in San Diego*, as told by Dale Ratermann, 159.
12. Kevin Kernan, "Gwynn's Fifth Hit a Winner," *San Diego Union-Tribune*, May 1, 1993.
13. *Ibid.*
14. Kevin Kernan, "Gwynn Has No Regrets About Missing the Cycle," *San Diego Union-Tribune*, June 12, 1993.
15. Kevin Kernan, "Gwynn's 3-Run Double Caps 5-Run Rally in 9th," *San Diego Union-Tribune*, June 12, 1993.
16. Porter and Naiman, *San Diego Padres Encyclopedia*, 135.
17. Dave Sheinin, "Fire Sale in San Diego Leaves Fans, Players Steaming," *Washington Post*, July 5, 1993, Pro Quest Newspaper.
18. Alan Solomon, "Padres' Gwynn 'Touched' by Ovation at Wrigley Field," *Chicago Tribune*, July 28, 1993, Pro Quest Newspapers.
19. Wayne Lockwood, "Through Season of Turmoil Gwynn Still Gwynn," *San Diego Union-Tribune*, July 30, 1993.
20. Buster Olney, "Gwynn's Sixth Hit Sets Stage for Winning Squeeze in 12th," *San Diego Union-Tribune*, August 5, 1993.
21. Kevin Kernan, "2001: A Gwynn Odyssey," *San Diego Union-Tribune*, August 7, 1993.
22. *Ibid.*
23. Buster Olney, "Gwynn Is Angry Over Weight Talk," *San Diego Union-Tribune*, September 12, 1993.
24. Jerry Magee, "More Than a Great Hitter, Gwynn Was a Civic Treasure," *San Diego Union-Tribune*, June 22, 2014.
25. Scoop Malinowski, "Biofile: The Tony Gwynn Interview, 1993," *MLB.com*, https://www.mlb.com/news/story/tony-gwynn-biofile-interview-1993.
26. Gwynn and Vaughn, *The Art of Hitting*, 132.

Chapter 15

1. Buster Olney, "Gwynn Just Happy to Be Back in the Lineup," *San Diego Union-Tribune*, April 13, 1994.
2. A.J. Cassavelli, "Was Gwynn's Quest MLB's Last Run at .400?" *MLB.com*, May 8, 2020, www.mlb.com/news/featured/tony-gwynn-and-the-.400-batting-average-chase.
3. Buster Olney, "Gwynn Makes Phillis Pay for Knockdown," *San Diego Union-Tribune*, April 25, 1994.
4. Buster Olney, "Gwynn Is Four Shy of Double-Play High," *San Diego Union-Tribune*, June 16, 1994.
5. Buster Olney, "Gwynn Lamenting Another Game That Somehow Got Away," *San Diego Union-Tribune*, June 25, 1994.
6. Buster Olney, "Speaking His Mind," *San Diego Union-Tribune*, August 5, 1994.

7. Buster Olney, "Williams Return to the Show Is an All-Around Success," *San Diego Union-Tribune*, June 18, 1994.
8. Olney, "Speaking His Mind," *San Diego Union-Tribune*, August 9, 1994.
9. Buster Olney, "Gwynn Lands in Center Field After Tough Trip," *San Diego Union-Tribune*, July 12, 1994.
10. Buster Olney, "Gwynn's Flirt With .400 Continues as Padres Win," *San Diego Union-Tribune*, July 3, 1994; Josie Karp, "Star Treatment for Tony, Son, 3 Padres Left Out in the Cold," *San Diego Union-Tribune*, July 4, 1994.
11. Bill Center, "World Series Blast Rated No. 1 on Hit Parade," *San Diego Union-Tribune*, October 7, 2001.
12. Buster Olney, "McGriff, Gwynn Shine Brightest of All the Stars," *San Diego Union-Tribune*, July 13, 1994.
13. Buster Olney, "All Kidding Aside, Gwynn, Williams Help Each Other," *San Diego Union-Tribune*, August 3, 1994.
14. Buster Olney, "Speaking His Mind," *San Diego Union-Tribune*, August 9, 1994.
15. Buster Olney, "Padres Follow Rettenmund Lead," *San Diego Union-Tribune*, July 18, 1994.
16. Samantha Stevenson, "In the Shadow of .400 Gwynn Is Forced to Wait," *New York Times*, August 24, 1994, Pro Quest Newspapers.
17. Buster Olney, "Gwynn Swings Wonder Bat in Race to .400," *San Diego Union-Tribune*, August 8, 1994.
18. *Ibid.*
19. Buster Olney, "Gwynn Falls in .400 Bid—For Now," *San Diego Union-Tribune*, August 12, 1994.
20. Buster Olney, "Gwynn's .400 Bid Cut Short," *San Diego Union-Tribune*, September 15, 1994.
21. Wolfe, *He Left His Heart in San Diego*, as told by Merv Rettenmund, 215.
22. A.J. Cassavelli, "Was Gwynn's Quest MLB's Last Real Run at .400?" *MLB.com*, May 8, 2020, https://www.mlb.com/news/featured/tony-gwynn-and-the-400-batting-average-chase.
23. Chandler and Swank, *Bob Chandler's Tales from the San Diego Padres Dugout*, 173.

Chapter 16

1. Williams and Underwood, *The Science of Hitting*, 9.
2. Tom Krasovic, "Kings of Swing," *San Diego Union-Tribune*, April 25, 1995.
3. *Silverman v. Major League Player Relations Committee*, 880 F.Supp. 246 (S.D.N.Y. 1995).
4. Bill Littlefield, "ESPN's Tim Kurkjian Remembers Tony Gwynn," WBUR, June 14, 2014, https://www.wbur.org./onlyagame/2014/06/21/tony-gwynn-kurkjian; Wolfe, *He Left His Heart in San Diego*, as told by Denny Matthews, 217.
5. Nick Canepa, "Beatles Wouldn't Be Enough to Lure Dubious Fans to Park," *San Diego Union-Tribune*, May 23, 1995.
6. *Ibid.*
7. Tom Krasovic, "Fan Abuse Erases Pre-Game Goodwill for Angry Roberts," *San Diego Union-Tribune*, April 22, 1994.
8. Tom Krasovic, "Gwynn Is Up Early to Get Taste of How Coors Field Plays," *San Diego Union-Tribune*, May 2, 1995.
9. Bill Center, "Hard Work and 'Magical Hands'—Attention to Detail Helped Gwynn Achieve Greatness," *San Diego Union-Tribune*, January 10, 2007.
10. Tom Maloney, "Gwynn Finds Swing, But Average Slumps," *San Diego Union-Tribune*, May 25, 1995.
11. Wolfe, *He Left His Heart in San Diego*, as told by Larry Lucchino, 150.
12. Tom Krasovic, "Caminiti's 2 Homers, 5 RBI Sink Dodgers," *San Diego Union-Tribune*, June 29, 1995.
13. Tom Krasovic, "Dr. Gwynn Does Surgery on Astros," *San Diego Union-Tribune*, August 1, 1995.
14. Tom Krasovic, "Bad Toe, Worse Swings Have Tony in a Dark Mood," *San Diego Union-Tribune*, September 9, 1995.
15. *Ibid.*
16. Tom Krasovic, "New Padres Come to Old End But Eager for 'Next Year,'" *San Diego Union-Tribune*, October 2, 1995.
17. *Ibid.*
18. Mark Sauer, "Tony Gwynn—San Diego's Favorite Son," *San Diego Union-Tribune*, September 27, 1998.
19. *Ibid.*
20. *Ibid.*

21. Bryce Miller, "'Loose Cannon' Jim Dietz Shaped Hall-Worthy Legacy at San Diego State," *San Diego Union-Tribune*, October 12, 2019.
22. Wayne Lockwood, "Moores Give $3 Million for Field," *San Diego Union-Tribune*, March 30, 1996.
23. Tom Verducci, "Bat Man," *Sports Illustrated*, July 28, 1997, https://vault.si.com/vault/1997/07/28/bat-man.
24. Tom Krasovic, "Talking with Tony," *San Diego Union-Tribune*, March 29, 1996.
25. Tom Krasovic, "Gwynn's Homer Is Winner in Ninth," *San Diego Union-Tribune*, June 9, 1996.
26. Chandler and Swank, *Bob Chandler's Tales from the San Diego Padres Dugout*, 118.
27. Tom Verducci, "What Is Rickey Henderson Doing in Newark?" *Sports Illustrated*, June 23, 2003, https://vault.si.com/vault/2003/06/23/what-is-rickey-henderson-doing-in-newark.
28. Wolfe, *He Left His Heart in San Diego*, as told by Bill Center, 217.
29. Paula Mascari-Bott, "Batting Titles He's Got," *San Diego Union-Tribune*, September 16, 1996.
30. Bill Center, "Gwynn Relishes His Hit No. 2,560," *San Diego Union-Tribune*, September 29, 1996.
31. Chandler and Swank, *Bob Chandler's Tales from the San Diego Padres Dugout*, 122.
32. Tom Friend, "Another Gwynn Gives Padres Title," *New York Times*, September 29, 1996, Pro Quest Newspapers.
33. Tom Krasovic and Bill Center, "T. Gwynn Glad He Didn't Jump Ship," *San Diego Union-Tribune*, October 1, 1996.
34. Tom Verducci, "Totally Juiced," *Sports Illustrated*, June 3, 2002, https://vault.si.com>2002/06/03/totally-juiced.
35. Bob Nightengale, "Steroids Become an Issue in Baseball: Many Fear Performance-Enhancing Drug Is Becoming Prevalent and Something Must Be Done," *Los Angeles Times*, July 15, 1995, Pro Quest Newspapers.

Chapter 17

1. Tom Krasovic, "Tony Happy to Stand on His Own Two Feet," *San Diego Union-Tribune*, February 19, 1997.
2. Tom Krasovic, "Gwynn Aging Eyes Not as Keen But His Bat Is," *San Diego Union-Tribune*, July 13, 1997.
3. Tom Krasovic, "Gwynn Treads Surely Toward Career Power Year," *San Diego Union-Tribune*, May 13, 1997.
4. Wayne Lockwood, "Forget Robinson Hoopla," *San Diego Union-Tribune*, April 19, 1997.
5. Bill Center, "Tony Gets His Wish to Stay in San Diego," *San Diego Union-Tribune*, April 6, 1997.
6. Tom Krasovic, "Gwynn Treads Surely Toward Career Power Year," *San Diego Union-Tribune*, May 13, 1997.
7. Ibid.
8. Tom Verducci, "Bat Man," *Sports Illustrated*, July 28, 1997.
9. Bill Center, "Ted, Tony Form Mutual Admiration Society," *San Diego Union-Tribune*, June 9, 1997.
10. Ibid.
11. Tom Krasovic, "Gwynn Slams Door on Dodgers," *San Diego Union-Tribune*, June 17, 1997.
12. Tom Krasovic, "Gwynn Says Robinson's Travails Eased His Own," *San Diego Union-Tribune*, July 19, 1997.
13. Verducci, "Bat Man," *Sports Illustrated*, July 28, 1997.
14. Michael J. Schell, *Baseball's All-Time Best Hitters: How Statistics Can Level the Playing Field* (Princeton: Princeton University Press, 1999); Wayne Lockwood, "In One Man's Laboratory Gwynn Is the Best Ever," *San Diego Union-Tribune*, July 26, 1997.
15. Wolfe, *He Left His Heart in San Diego*, as told by Michael Schell, 137.
16. Tom Krasovic, "Gwynn Attains Individual Goal With 200th Hit," *San Diego Union-Tribune*, September 14, 1997.
17. Bill Center, "A Race to the Finish," *San Diego Union-Tribune*, September 17, 1997.
18. Tom Cashman, "Yes, Mr. Mays, That's T. Gwynn as in Eight-Time NL Batting Champ," *San Diego Union-Tribune*, September 29, 1997.

19. *Ibid.*
20. Chandler and Swank, *Tales from the San Diego Padres Dugout*, 175.

Chapter 18

1. Gwynn and Vaughn, *The Art of Hitting*, 8.
2. *Ibid.*, 9.
3. *Ibid.*
4. *Ibid.*, 63.
5. *Ibid.*, 73.
6. *Ibid.*, 94.
7. Bill Center, "Gwynn Slump Reaches New Depths," *San Diego Union-Tribune*, July 13, 1998.
8. Tom Krasovic, "Teammates Know How Gwynn Feels," *San Diego Union-Tribune*, July 17, 1998.
9. Tom Krasovic, "Gwynn Sees Red Against Nomo, Sees Ball Well Against Mets," *San Diego Union-Tribune*, July 30, 1998.
10. Bill Center, "Gwynn Goes on DL With Aching Achilles," *San Diego Union-Tribune*, August 14, 1998.
11. Tom Krasovic, "Gwynn Has His Playoff Game Face," *San Diego Union-Tribune*, September 25, 1998.
12. Wayne Lockwood, "Tony Calls Third Title Best of All," *San Diego Union-Tribune*, September 13, 1998.
13. Chris Jenkins, "Turnabout for Pitchers," *San Diego Union-Tribune*, October 11, 1998.
14. Bill Center, "Hurts So Good," *San Diego Union-Tribune*, October 15, 1998.
15. Bob Nightengale, "Mr. Padres' All-Star Game: Tony Gwynn's Impact Resonates in San Diego," *USA Today Sports*, July 10, 2006, usa.today.com/story/sports/mlb/columnist-bob-nightengale.
16. William Rhoden, "Honoring His Father's Instructions," *New York Times*, October 17, 1998.
17. Stan McNeal, "Gwynn Would Trade Home Run, Other Hits, Any Day," *San Diego Union-Tribune*, October 18, 1998.
18. Tom Krasovic and Bill Center, "Yankees on Brink of Something Good," *San Diego Union-Tribune*, October 21, 1998.
19. Mick McGrane, "Noble Pursuit—Gwynn Hits .500 But He Can't Lift Padres Alone," *San Diego Union-Tribune*, October 22, 1998.
20. Chandler and Swank, *Tales from the San Diego Padres Dugout*, 176.
21. Tony Perry, "Padre Euphoria Could Sway Stadium Vote," *Los Angeles Times*, October 24, 1998, Pro Quest Newspapers.

Chapter 19

1. Tom Krasovic, "Extra Week Just Adds Frustration to Gwynn's Woes," *San Diego Union-Tribune*, July 16, 1999.
2. "Baseball—2016," *San Diego Union-Tribune*, March 20, 2016.
3. Bill Center, "Countdown to Spring Training: 10 Days," *San Diego Union-Tribune*, February 8, 1999.
4. Tom Krasovic, "Gwynn Scolds Padres," *San Diego Union-Tribune*, February 20, 1999.
5. Jeff McDonald, "Tony Gwynn Hits Warm Spot in San Diego Hearts," *San Diego Union-Tribune*, August 2, 1999.
6. *Ibid.*
7. Tom Krasovic, "Leyritz Takes Shot at Gwynn on the Way Out," *San Diego Union-Tribune*, August 1, 1999.
8. Tom Cushman, "Tony Lets His Bat Do the Talking, and It Shouts," *San Diego Union-Tribune*, August 2, 1999.
9. Tom Krasovic, "Gwynn Relates to Mac With All the Attention," *San Diego Union-Tribune*, August 3, 1999.
10. Tom Krasovic, "Leyritz Takes Shot at Gwynn on the Way Out," *San Diego Union-Tribune*, August 1, 1999.
11. Mike Eisenbath, "Gwynn Isn't Choosy: He Just Wants the Chase to Be Over With," *St. Louis Post-Dispatch*, August 5, 1999.
12. Tom Krasovic, "Classic T-Shot—Gwynn 3,000th Launches 4-for-5 Night, Brings Relief," *San Diego Union-Tribune*, August 7, 1999.
13. Bill Center, "Tony Busts Out, Shares Thrills with Mac," *San Diego Union-Tribune*, August 5, 1999.
14. Eisenbath, "Gwynn Isn't Choosy: He Just Wants Chase to Be Over," *St. Louis Post-Dispatch*, August 5, 1999.

Notes—Chapter 20

15. Tom Krasovic, "Gwynn Decided to Put Some Memorabilia in Hall Way," *San Diego Union-Tribune*, August 8, 1999.

16. Bill Center, "Now Tony Will Try to Do It for Mom," *San Diego Union-Tribune*, August 6, 1999.

17. Vahe Gregorian, "Nerves Conquer Gwynn Psyche, Slow Chase to Mark," *St. Louis Post-Dispatch*, August 6, 1999.

18. George Diaz, "Gwynn Sticks to Same Plot," *Indianapolis Star*, August 7, 1999.

19. Bob Nightengale, "Mr. Padre's All-Star Game: Tony Gwynn's Impact Still Resonates in San Diego," *USA Today*, July 10, 2016.

20. Murray Chass, "Another Day, Another Milestone," *New York Times*, August 7, 1999.

21. Bill Center, "Besting the Best," *San Diego Union-Tribune*, August 8, 1999.

22. Kevin Acee, "A Rosey Start," *San Diego Union-Tribune*, August 8, 1999.

23. Chris Jenkins, "The Hit Parade," *San Diego Union-Tribune*, July 29, 2007.

24. Bill Center, "Gwynn Homers Twice in Victory," *San Diego Union-Tribune*, August 15, 1999.

25. Tom Krasovic, "Gwynn's Homer a Splash as Williams Again Sizzles," *San Diego Union-Tribune*, October 2, 1999.

26. Tom Krasovic, "Gwynn Gets Clemente Award," *San Diego Union-Tribune*, October 27, 1999.

27. David Washburn and David Hasemeyer, "Cracks in the Gwynn Foundation," *San Diego Union-Tribune*, December 13, 2000.

28. Tom Krasovic, "Gwynn Thinking Contact—Not Contract," *San Diego Union-Tribune*, February 20, 2020.

29. Tom Krasovic, "Bell Tolls Late for Padres in Opening Day Loss," *San Diego Union-Tribune*, April 4, 2000.

30. Tom Krasovic, "Lopez Gets a Reprieve as Tony Goes on DL," *San Diego Union-Tribune*, May 1, 2000.

31. Tom Krasovic, "Deal Assures Gwynn Will Return for 20th Season," *San Diego Union-Tribune*, December 8, 2000.

32. Tom Krasovic, "Wind Up Tony and He Just Plays," *San Diego Union-Tribune*, February 28, 2001.

33. *Ibid.*

34. Tom Krasovic, "Gwynn Expects to Be Sitting in the Late Innings," *San Diego Union-Tribune*, March 14, 2001.

35. Tom Krasovic, "Knee 'Shaky' So Gwynn Sits Out," *San Diego Union-Tribune*, April 9, 2001.

36. Tom Krasovic, "I Miss This Game Already," *San Diego Union-Tribune*, June 29, 2000.

37. Bill Center, "His Day: Loving It and Leaving It," *San Diego Union-Tribune*, October 8, 2001.

38. Porter and Naiman, *San Diego Padres Encyclopedia*, 173.

Chapter 20

1. Tom Krasovic, "Pirate Fans Cheer Gwynn's First Homer," *San Diego Union-Tribune*, August 12, 2001.

2. Kevin Acee, "The Rookie," *San Diego Union-Tribune*, February 4, 2002.

3. Kirk Kenney, "Look Who's Coaching," *San Diego Union-Tribune*, November 16, 2002.

4. Bernie Wilson, "Omaha Is the Goal," *Los Angeles Times*, January 25, 2004, Pro Quest Newspapers.

5. Nick Canepa, "Gwynn Finds Job Is a Grind," *San Diego Union-Tribune*, April 15, 2003.

6. Kirk Kenney, "Never Give In," *San Diego Union-Tribune*, June 29, 2003.

7. Wolfe, *He Left His Heart in San Diego*, as told by Kirk Kenney, 67.

8. Kirk Kenney, "SDSU Bats Bounce Back in Win," *San Diego Union-Tribune*, March 7, 2004.

9. Jeff Ristine, "Padres Give No. 19 a Place of Honor," *San Diego Union-Tribune*, September 5, 2004.

10. Nick Canepa, "Why Can't Gwynn Win at SDSU?" *San Diego Union-Tribune*, March 22, 2006.

11. Kirk Kenney, "Gwynn Irked by Series Cutback," *San Diego Union-Tribune*, April 22, 2005.

12. Kirk Kenney, "Aztecs Get the Red Out, Win One for Suspended Gwynn," *San Diego Union-Tribune*, April 30, 2005.

13. Nick Canepa, "Gwynn Finds Job Is

a Grind," *San Diego Union-Tribune*, April 15, 2003.

14. Jay Posner, "Gwynn Gives Up ESPN Gig But Still on Padres Telecasts," *San Diego Union-Tribune*, February 10, 2006.

15. Brad Haymal, Tony Gwynn Commemorative Issue, *Daily Aztec*, May 4, 2016.

16. Scott Miller, "Stephen Strasburg's Father-Son Bond with Tony Gwynn Made Him an MLB Star," *Bleacher Report*, July 12, 2016, https//bleacherreport.com/MLB.

17. Chandler and Swank, *Bob Chandler's Tales From the San Diego Padres Dugout*, 179.

18. Kirk Kenney, "Honoring Tony," *San Diego Union-Tribune*, March 11, 2007.

19. Tom Krasovic, "Bronze Statue a 'Perfect' Likeness," *San Diego Union-Tribune*, July 22, 2007.

20. *Ibid*.

21. Tony Gwynn, Hall of Fame Induction Speech.

22. Kirk Kenney, "Jackie's Lessons," *San Diego Union-Tribune*, April 14, 2007.

23. Kirk Kenney, "Aztecs Battle Back Late to No Avail in 13-Inning Loss to BYU," *San Diego Union-Tribune*, May 12, 2007.

24. Kirk Kenney, "Gwynn to Helm SDSU for Three More Years," *San Diego Union-Tribune*, November 6, 2008.

25. Kirk Kenney, "Things About Gwynn," *San Diego Union-Tribune*, May 10, 2020.

26. Damin Esper, "Aztecs Strasburg Mows Down Santa Clara," *San Diego Union-Tribune*, May 2, 2009.

27. Tim Sullivan, "Strasburg's Hot Stuff Creates Some Interesting Dilemmas," *San Diego Union-Tribune*, February 28, 2009.

28. Kirk Kenney, "Things About Gwynn," *San Diego Union-Tribune*, May 10, 2020.

29. Tim Sullivan, "Ace Can't Do It Solo," *San Diego Union-Tribune*, May 30, 2009.

30. Scott Miller, "Stephen Strasburg's Father-Son Bond," *Bleacher Report*, July 12, 2016.

31. *Ibid*.

32. *Ibid*.

33. Tom Friend, "Tony Gwynn Returns After Facing Cancer," *ESPN.com*, March 25, 2011, www.espn.com/espn/otl/news/story?id=6257656.

34. Heather G. Stockwell and Gary H. Lyman, "Impact of Smoking and Smokeless Tobacco on the Risk of Head and Neck Cancer," *Head and Neck Surgery*, Volume 9, No. 2, November/December 1986.

35. National Institute of Health, "Health Implications of Smokeless Tobacco Use," Consensus Development Conference Statement, January 13–15, 1986.

36. Ken Stone, "Poway's Gwynn Owes IRS More Than $400,000," *Poway Patch*, June 9, 2012.

37. Justin Gheorge, Tony Gwynn Commemorative Issue, *Daily Aztec*, May 4, 2016.

38. Kirk Kenney, "SDSU's Absent Gwynn Says 'I'm Doing Good,'" *San Diego Union-Tribune*, April 23, 2014.

39. Kevin Acee, "Gwynn Presence Strong as Aztecs Keep Rolling," *San Diego Union-Tribune*, May 30, 2014.

40. *Ibid*.

41. Kevin Acee, "SDSU Finally Reaching Its Baseball Potential," *San Diego Union-Tribune*, June 1, 2014.

42. Kirk Kenney, "No. 1 Tony Gwynn," *San Diego Union-Tribune*, December 28, 2014.

Epilogue

1. Chris Jenkins, "Mr. Padre–Hall of Famer Stood Out Both On and Off the Field," *San Diego Union-Tribune*, June 17, 2014.

2. Bill Bender, "Remembering Tony Gwynn and His Ability to Hit the Best of the Best," *Sporting News*, June 16, 2019, https://www.sportingnews.com/us/mlb.

3. A.J. Cassavelli, "19 Facts About the Wonderful Career of Gwynn," *MLB.com*, May 8, 2020, https://www.mlb.com/news/19-facts-about-the-career-of-tony-gwynn.

4. Tom Verducci, "Tony Gwynn Was

a Joy to Watch at the Plate and in Life," *Sports Illustrated*, June 16, 2014, www.si.com/mlb.2014/06/16/tony-gwynn-obituary-san-diego-padres-hall-of-fame.

5. Wolfe, *He Left His Heart in San Diego*, as told by Bill Plaschke, 103.

6. Wolfe, *He Left His Heart in San Diego*, as told by Mark Martinez, 207.

7. Wolfe, *He Left His Heart in San Diego*, as told by Jerald Clark, 197–198.

8. Nightengale, "Mr. Padre's All-Star Game: Tony Gwynn's Impact Still Resonates in San Diego," *USA Today*, July 10, 2016.

9. Ed Graney, "Tony Gwynn Never Consumed by Big League Attitude," *Las Vegas Review-Journal*, www.review/journal.com/sports/sportscolumns/edgraney/tony-gwynn-never-consumed-by-big-league-attitude.

10. Bill Brink, "Remembering Tony Gwynn," *Pittsburgh Post-Gazette*, June 18, 2014, https://www.post-gazette.com/Blogs//Pirates-Blog/2014/06/18/remembering-tony-gwynn-Polanco/stories/201406180246.

11. C.J. Saylor, Tony Gwynn Commemorative Issue, *Daily Aztec*, May 4, 2015.

12. Bill Center, "San Diego State Hosts Private Tony Gwynn Service," June 22, 2014, padres/mlbblogs.com/san-diego-state-hosts-private-tony-gwynn-service.

13. Chris Jenkins, "'Live Like Tony' 20,000 Plus Bid Farewell to Mr. Padre," *San Diego Union-Tribune*, June 27, 2014.

14. Chuck Schilken, "Tony, Jr., Honors His Late Dad With Walk-Off Hit on Father's Day," *Los Angeles Times*, June 22, 2015, https://www.latimes.com/sports/sportsnow/tony-gwynn-jr-father's-day-20150622-story.

15. J. Harry Jones, "Stretch of I-15 Named in Honor of Padres No. 19," *San Diego Union-Tribune*, October 20, 2015.

16. Kirk Kenney, "Gwynn's Legacy Now Reaches Further," *San Diego Union-Tribune*, June 16, 2015.

17. Tony Gwynn Memorial Website/Poway/CA/poway.org>Tony-Gwynn-Memorial.

18. J. Harry Jones, "Tony Gwynn Honored by Statue in Poway," *San Diego Union-Tribune*, May 19, 2017.

19. Adam Kilgore, "Stephen Strasburg Grateful for Time with Tony," *Washington Post*, June 18, 2014, Pro Quest Newspapers.

Bibliography

Books

Bowa, Larry, and Barry M. Bloom. *Larry Bowa: I Still Hate to Lose.* Champaign: Sports Publishing, 2004.

Chandler, Bob, and Bill Swank. *Tales from the San Diego Padres Dugout: A Collection of the Greatest Padres Stories Ever Told.* New York: Sports Publishing, 2006.

Gwynn, Tony, and Jim Geschke. *Tony!* Chicago: Contemporary, 1986.

Gwynn, Tony, and Jim Rosenthal. *Tony Gwynn's Total Baseball Player: Winning Techniques for Hitting, Fielding, and Baserunning.* New York: St. Martin's Press, 1992.

Gwynn, Tony, and Roger Vaughan. *The Art of Hitting.* New York: GT Publishing, 1998.

Lewin, Josh. *You Never Forget Your First: Ballplayers Recall Their Big League Debut.* Herndon: Potomac, 2005.

McKeon, Jack, and Kevin Kernan. *I'm Just Getting Started: Baseball's Best Storyteller on Old School Baseball, Defying the Odds, and Good Cigars.* Chicago: Triumph, 2005.

Plummer, Joe. *Growing Up with Tony Gwynn: A Lifetime of Swinging for the Fences.* San Diego: Montezuma, 2015.

Porter, David, and Joe Naiman. *The San Diego Padres Encyclopedia.* Champaign: Sports Publishing, 2002.

Schell, Michael J. *Baseball's All-Time Best Hitters: How Statistics Can Level the Playing Field.* Princeton: Princeton University Press, 1999.

Seidel, Michael. *Ted Williams: A Baseball Life.* Chicago: Contemporary, 1991.

Will, George F. *Men at Work: The Craft of Baseball.* New York: Macmillan, 1990.

Williams, Dick, and Bill Plaschke. *No More Mr. Nice Guy: A Life of Hardball.* San Diego: Harcourt, Brace, Jovanovich, 1990.

Williams, Ted, and John Underwood. *The Science of Hitting.* New York: Simon & Schuster, 1986.

Wolfe, Rich. *He Left His Heart in San Diego.* Lone Wolf Press, 2014.

Newspapers and Magazines

Amarillo Globe-News
Atlanta Constitution
Baseball America
Boston Globe
Chicago Tribune
Cincinnati Enquirer
Cincinnati Post
Daily Aztec
Fort Wayne Journal Gazette
Fort Wayne News-Sentinel
Indianapolis Star
Las Vegas Review-Journal
Long Beach Press-Telegram
Los Angeles Times
New York Times
Orlando Sun-Sentinel
Philadelphia Inquirer
Pittsburgh Post-Gazette
St. Louis Post-Dispatch
San Diego Evening Tribune
San Diego Union
San Diego Union-Tribune
Sporting News
Sports Illustrated
Tampa Bay Times
USA Today
Washington Post

Bibliography

Online Sources

Baseball Archives, SDSU Athletics
baseball-reference.com
espn.com
MLB.com
newspapers.com
ProQuest Historical Newspapers
thebaseballcube.com
thedailyaztec.com

Index

Acee, Kevin 168–169
Ainge, Danny 14, 16
Air Force Academy 158–159, 162
All-Star Games 41, 65, 73, 84–85, 98–99, 110, 123, 132, 139
all-time best hitters 124
Alou, Moises 100, 134
aluminum bats 23, 25
Amarillo Double A team 25, 28, 38, 40
Arizona Diamondbacks 131, 133, 140, 145, 146, 150
Arizona State University 155
The Art of Hitting 129, 131
Ashby, Andy 101, 120, 134
Associated Press reporter 81
Atlanta Braves 30, 33–34, 57, 66, 73, 80, 83, 117, 121, 126, 132, 134–135, 147
Atlanta–San Diego Brawl 42–44
Ausmus, Brad home run 101

back taxes 168
Bagwell, Jeff 97
Ballin' Like Tony Gwynn 171
bankruptcy 64, 78
banners for 3,000th hit 140–141, 145
batting cage 69, 72
batting tees 28, 87, 129
batting title races 61, 71–72, 73–75, 92, 111, 116, 118, 126–127
Barr, Roseanne, National Anthem 79–80
Baseball America ranking 161
Baseball Hall of Fame 1, 63, 91–92, 168; Tony's induction into and speech 160–161
Baseball Writers Association of America 160
Bay, Rick 113, 150
Baylor, Don 91, 124
Bere, Jason 99–100
Bevacqua, Kurt 43, 51

Bochy, Bruce 41, 52, 60, 111, 115, 117, 134, 136, 147–149, 151, 171
Bonds, Barry 171
Booker, Greg 24, 42
Boros, Steve 58, 61–62
Bowa, Larry 62–63, 65–69, 71
Branch Rickey Award 112
breaking up no-hitters 54, 69
Brigham Young University (BYU) 13, 18, 159, 164
Brown, Kevin 130, 134–135, 140
Browning, Tom 69
Burkhead, Curtis 15
Bush, George H.W. 79–80
Butler, Brett 123

Caminiti, Ken 106, 110–111, 117–120, 124, 126, 132–133, 135, 140, 147
cancer 166; first return 167; second return 168
Canepo, Nick 78
"Captain Video" 35, 101
"Captain's Wheel" 28
career in youth sports 6–7
Carew, Rod 8, 65, 106, 142, 173
Carter, Joe 76
cassette recorder 9–10, 35
Center, Bill 116
Chandler, Bob 47, 105
charity work 93, 112–113, 147, 153
chasing .400 64–65, 83, 99–101, 103–106, 122–124
chewing tobacco habit 15, 33, 58, 70, 166, 171; Gwynn family's lawsuit 172; operation on cheek 81
Chicago Cubs 38, 45, 51, 53, 62, 71, 92, 103, 110, 130–131
Chicago Tribune 90
Chicago White Sox 54, 57, 97, 99
Cincinnati Reds 1, 35–36, 40, 56, 69, 72–74, 76, 78–79, 116, 130, 132, 148

Index

Clark, Jack 72, 76–78, 80, 82, 126, 141
Clark, Jerald 171
Clark, Will 74–75, 91, 100; as Tony, Jr.'s favorite player 99
Clemens, Roger 132
Clinton tax plan 86
Cobb, Ty 31–32, 56, 91, 118, 124–125, 127, 151–152
Coleman, Jerry 22
college baseball career 14–17, 19
college basketball career 13–14, 16–19; 55-foot shot 18
Colorado Rockies 91–92, 97, 101, 115–118, 123–124, 126, 132, 150–151, 158
Cone, David 99
contentious Padres team meeting 77–78
contracts signed with Padres 21, 94, 121, 148–149
Costas, Bob 106
Cox, Bobby 126

Daal, Omar 89
Davis, Willie 8, 87, 129
defensive play 21, 57, 88; throws out runner at home 60; throws out runner at second base 109; throws out runner at third in a 1996 playoff game 134; throws out three runners in one game 60–61; throws out two runners in All-Star game 85; work with House 28; work with McCullough 26; World Series miscues 52–53
Detroit Tigers 50–53
Dietz, Jim 14–18, 113, 148, 150, 153–156, 160
doodling on bats 116
Durham, Leon 48–49
Dye, Bobby 14

Eckersley, Dennis 129–130
ejections by umpires 24–25, as a college coach 156; by Joe West 68; by rookie ump 73
Elias Sports Bureau 103
emphasis on family 93; celebrates Padres 1998 pennant with family 136; family is a team 121; loved the idea of family 172; preferred to socialize with family 141
Enberg, Dick 174
ESPN 153, 155, 159

Father Ryan High School 3
Feeney, Chubb 44, 71

Filter, Rusty 162
final major league game 151–152
final major league hit 151
Finley, Steve 106, 111–112, 115, 117, 120, 123, 131, 133–135, 140, 147
"fire sale" trades 86–89
first major league game 31
first major league home run 33
Fishers, Indiana home 87–88
5-for-5 games 64, 66, 88, 90, 95, 131
5.5 hole 31, 69, 95, 110–111, 117, 126, 131, 152, 160, 172
5 stolen base games 40, 59
Flannery, Tim 31, 49, 50, 63, 65
Florida Marlins 89, 114, 124, 126, 130, 145
Forbes Clark, Jane 160
free agent 149
Freeman, Dick 80; lawsuit by Padres fans 90; letter to season ticketholders 87–88
Fregosi, Jim 98

Gaines, Smokey 14, 16, 18–19, 92
Galarraga, Andres 92, 111, 116
Gallatin, Tennessee 3
Garvey, Steve 34, 36, 38, 47–52, 62
Gibson, Kirk 50–52
Glavine, Tom 135, 144, 147
"glory hog" 6, 78
Gold Glove 61, 64, 81, 83, 85, 141
Gossage, Rich ("Goose") 39, 44, 50, 52, 62
Graney, Ed 171
Gwynn, Alicia 29–30, 34, 64, 78, 86, 91, 93, 143, 147, 154, 167, 169; believes Tony can hit .400 65; celebrates 1998 pennant 136; describes effect of disfigured Tony Gwynn doll on Tony 80; discloses Tony's support of college baseball classic 173; encourages Tony to stick with basketball 18; founds music promotion company 87; marriage to Tony 19; meeting Tony 11–12; notices growth on Tony's cheek 165; teasing Tony to get a hit 112; urges Tony to keep battling against a slump 70; videotapes Tony's at bats 35
Gwynn, Anisha 65, 143; birth 57; celebrating Padres 1998 pennant with Tony 136; Poway statue 174; sings National Anthem 172
Gwynn, Anthony Keith, Jr. (son) 65, 100, 143; assents to father's pre-game

Index

speech 98; birth 34; celebrating Padres 1998 pennant 136; encourages father not to worry about bankruptcy 64; father predicts Phillies will try to hit him with a pitch 96; father predicts son could make the major leagues 102; home run after father's death 172; recruited by San Diego State 148; star for San Diego State baseball team 155; travels with father to 1994 All-Star game 99

Gwynn, Charles, Jr. ("Junior") 4, 8, 12, 16, 56, 160, 174; college athletic career 9; expertise throwing breaking pitches 6; playing H-O-R-S-E with Tony 5; playing tennis against Tony 7

Gwynn, Charles, Sr. 5, 7, 61; brags on sons' athletic accomplishments 32; encourages sons to "work hard and good things will happen" 6; informs Tony to shine his own shoes 37; proficiency in athletics 3; purchases *The Science of Hitting* 8; Tony acknowledgment to his father after 3,000th hit 144; urges Tony to leave the Padres 93; as warehouse supervisor 4

Gwynn, Chris 4, 6, 32; acquired by Padres 114; home run ends Padres 1995 division title hopes 111; home run wins 1996 division title for Padres 117; promotion to major leagues 66; speech at San Diego State memorial for Tony 172; star for San Diego State baseball team 56

Gwynn, Vendella 5–7; accompanies Tony on team plane 142; advises Tony to stick with baseball 11; baking pecan pies 93; bolts out of stands after Tony's 3,000th hit 144; proficiency in athletics 3

Harris, Josh 1–2
Hartgraves, Dean 110
Hawaii Triple A Team 29–30, 34
Haymal, Brad 168
Henderson, Rickey 114, 120, 150; breaks Cobb's runs scored record 151; career hit 3,000 152; comparison to Yogi Berra 115–116
Hershiser, Orel 54, 64
hit No. 1,000 69
hit No. 2,000 91
hit No. 3,000 144
hitting slumps 35, 69–70, 109, 132

hitting streaks 33, 36, 70, 145
Hoffman, Trevor 115, 117, 134, 136, 140; credit to Tony for inventing video 170
Hornsby, Rogers 112, 118, 124
House, Tom 28, 57
Houston Astros 20, 73, 103, 104, 106, 108, 110, 121, 134, 140, 142
Howard, Frank 22, 27
Hoyt, LaMarr 54, 56–57, 62
Hurdle, Clint 171

Indiana Pacers 88
Indianapolis Colts pep talk 88
indoor batting cage 69, 72
injuries 17, 33–34, 66, 68–69, 80–81, 85, 110, 115, 120, 123, 125, 130, 132–133, 140, 147, 150; knee injuries and surgeries 83, 86, 92, 95, 112, 125, 131, 136, 145, 147–151
inside the park home run 24, 123
intentional walk 48, 91, 123–124, 126, 135

Jack Murphy Stadium 21, 30, 47–48, 70–72, 80–81, 84, 89–91, 93, 96, 108, 120, 126
jersey retired by Padres 158
Joyner, Wally 114, 120, 133

Keeler, Wee Willie 91, 124
kidney stone 125
Krasovic, Tom 140, 141
Kreidler, Mark 60, 62
Kroc, Joan 39, 71, 79
Kroc, Ray 27–28, 39
Kruk, John 24–25, 59, 63, 70–71

La Russa, Tony 123
Las Vegas Triple A team 34–35, 38, 55, 62
Lasorda, Tommy 59, 111, 117
the laugh 25, 32, 82, 165, 171
Law, Vance 58
Leyland, Jim 124, 126
Leyritz, Jim 141–142
Lockwood, Wayne 121
Long, Bill 20
Long Beach 14–15, 18, 21, 33, 48, 94
Long Beach Tech High School 19–21, 23, 32, 50
Los Angeles Dodgers 5, 8, 29, 35, 54–56, 59–60, 64, 66, 73, 78, 83, 89, 93, 97, 103, 110–112, 114, 116–117, 119, 123, 133, 140
Los Angeles Rams 4

Index

Los Angeles Times 82
Louisville Slugger bat 1, 84

Maddux, Greg 132; 147; admires Tony's Petco statue 160; jokes about Tony's success against Atlanta starters 144; outguessed by Tony 122; walks Tony in playoff game 135
Major League Players Association 22, 63, 94, 101
Major League seasons 31–34; 1983 34–36; 1984 39–45; 1985 54–57; 1986 59–61; 1987 63–69; 1988 68–72; 1989 72–75; 1990 76–81; 1991 83; 1992 85–86; 1993 88–92; 1994 95–104; 1995 108–112; 1996 114–118; 1997 120–128; 1998 130–134; 1999 140–147; 2000 147–148; 2001 149–152
Marichal, Juan 5
Martinez, Mark 167–169, 171
Mason, Roger 63
McCullough, Clyde 26, 28, 33, 37, 57
McGriff, Fred 86–87, 90, 99, 121
McGwire, Mark 104, 142–143, 146
McKeon, Jack 27, 38–39, 42, 62–63, 82, 161; drafts Tony 21; exits team meeting 77; praised by Tony 71; praises Tony's dedication 37; resigns as Padres manager 79; sends Tony to winter instructional camp 26; takes over as Padres manager 69; urges Tony to take weight off shoulders 70; watches Tony in exhibition game 20
McReynolds, Kevin 20, 38–39, 40–41, 48
McSherry, John 43–44
Meacham, Bobby 14–15, 17, 21
Merrill, Robert 79
Mike Ivy bat 24
Mr. Padre 82, 88, 118, 149
Monge, Sid 31
Montague, Ed 74–75
Montreal Expos 40, 70, 76, 117, 121, 143–145
Moores, John 106, 113, 140, 153–154, 167
Morgan, Joe 84
Morris, Jack 50–51, 53
Mountain West Conference (MWC) 154, 156, 158–159, 162–165, 167
Musial, Stan 66, 91, 112, 139
MVP Voting 53, 67

National Institute of Health 166
National Labor Relations Board (NLRB) 107

Nettles, Graig 39–40, 43, 51–52, 62
New York Mets 59–60, 76–78, 88–89, 101–102, 109, 131, 136–137, 141
New York Yankees 21, 39, 72, 76–77, 136–137, 141
"Nine Grains of Pain" bat 103, 108
1981 Draft 19–21
North Carolina State University 157
Northwest League 21, 24–25

Oakland A's 28, 123
Olbermann, Keith 137–138
Orosco, Jesse 59

Pacific Coast Athletic Association (PCAA) 13–14
Padres Scholars 109, 112
Padres uniform No. 19 history 31
Padres uniforms 21, 22, 82
Paglaruilo, Mike 76–78, 126, 141
Palmeiro, Rafael 71–72
parent influence 93–94
Pearl High School 3
Petco Park 138, 157, 160, 172–174
Philadelphia Phillies 31–32, 76, 90, 95–96, 98, 102, 111, 131
Piazza, Mike 111, 116
Picciolo, Rob 108
Pittsburgh Pirates 39, 41, 53, 70, 85, 121, 150–151, 165
Plantier, Phil 101–102, 104
Plaschke, Bill 170
player strikes 22, 27, 101, 103, 107–109
Players Association 22, 58, 63, 94, 101–102, 107
Playoff Series Cubs 46–50; 1996 versus St. Louis 119; 1998 versus Atlanta 135–136; 1998 versus Houston 134
power surge 121
praise by Yankee pitchers 137
pre-game speech 98
Proposition C 138

Qualcomm Stadium 126, 133, 140–141, 151

racial incident 25
Rader, Doug 30
Raines, Tim 54, 61, 63, 127
reluctance to acknowledge cheers 66, 89, 145
Rettenmund, Merv 97, 99–100, 105, 130, 143

Index

Riggleman, Jim 89–90, 92, 95, 97–98, 100–101
Ripken, Cal 85, 100, 160
Rippley, Steve 42
"The Road to 3,000" 141
Roberto Clemente Award 147
Robinson, Jackie 4, 161
Rose, Pete 8, 31, 56, 82; handshake with Tony 32; Tony best pure hitter 144; Tony breaks up no-hitters 70; Tony demurs from Rose career hit celebration 57
Rosenthal, Jim 87
Ruffin, Bruce 91
Rule 5 Draft 29
Rule 9 118
Russell, Bill 117

St. Louis Cardinals 28, 35, 70, 88, 96, 109, 115, 119, 122–123, 129–130, 133, 142–143, 148
San Diego Evening Tribune 78
San Diego Padres franchise history 21–22
San Diego Padres uniform No. 19 history 31
San Diego School of Baseball 37, 70
San Diego State coach 150; coach-of-the-year 158; contracts signed 150, 159, 163, 167, 169; ejected by umpire 156; electronic scoreboard 153–154; kicked hole in a door 159; NCAA tournaments 164–165, 168; recruiting problems 161; suspended by Mountain West Conference 159; volunteer coach 153
San Diego State coach seasons: 2003 155–157; 2004 157–158; 2005 158–159; 2006 158; 2007 162; 2008 162–163; 2009 163, 2010 165; 2011 167; 2012 167; 2013 168; 2014 168 164–165, 168
San Diego Union 32, 54, 58, 60–62, 65
San Diego Union-Tribune 87, 116, 121, 139, 141, 147, 168
San Francisco Giants 5, 33, 63, 68, 73–74, 90–91, 97, 110, 117, 120, 124, 131, 149, 151
Sandberg, Ryne 49–50, 53
Sanders, Reggie 140–141
Santiago, Benito 63, 66–67, 72, 76, 87
Saylor, C.J. 171
Schell, Michael 124–125
Schilling, Curt 96
The Science of Hitting 8–9, 16, 36, 84, 106, 129

Scrub Chubb sign 71
selfish controversy 76–78, 141
Sheffield, Gary 86–87, 89–90, 97
Show, Eric 30, 54, 77
Silver Bat Award 53, 141
Silver Slugger Award 64
Silverado Park 5, 8
six-hit game 90–91
Smith, Dan 144–45
Smith, Lee 47, 48
Smoltz, John 135, 144, 147, 170
Solomon, Alan 90
Sotomayor, Sonia 107
Sporting News 61
Sports Illustrated 39, 47, 72, 76, 119, 124, 170
spring training: 1982 (invited to camp) 28–29; 1983 34; 1986 Williams holdout 58; 1987 (pessimism about team) 62; 1988 (joke on reporter and fans) 68; 1991 (feud with Clark) 81–82; 1994 (tape notes to locker) 99; 1995 (after 1994 strike) 108; 1997 127; 1998 (comes to camp early) 130; 2000 147; 2001 (scratched from game) 149
statue at Petco Park 160
Strasburg, Stephen: living with fame 163; praise for Tony 174; quits chewing tobacco 171; senior year won-loss record 164; strikes out 23 Utah batters 162; Tony as "second father" to 165
"Stump Tony Gwynn" 86
Sutcliffe, Rick 46, 49

Tanner, Chuck 41
teammate drug issues 55, 57–58, 119
Templeton, Garry 39–40, 73, 77, 81
Texas Christian University (TCU) 163–164
three consecutive home run game 63
three strikeout game 60
Tolan, Bobby 23–24, 160
Tony and Alicia Gwynn Foundation 141, 147
Tony-Chris Home Run Contest 56
Tony Gwynn doll 80
Tony Gwynn gospel/principles 1, 2, 7, 93, 159, 161, 163–164, 168, 171
Tony Gwynn Stadium 113, 121, 153, 159, 161, 165
Tony Gwynn's Total Baseball Player: Winning Techniques for Hitting, Fielding, and Baserunning 28
Torre, Joe 43–44, 87

Index

tributes to Tony 170; All-Star game 171; Bonds 171; Clark 171; Enberg 174; funeral 172; Graney 171; Hoffman 170; Hurdle 171, Martinez 171; Memorial Freeway 172; Petco Park 172; Plaschke 170–171; Poway statue 173–174; San Diego State 172; Saylor 171; Seattle 172; Smoltz 170; Strasburg 174; Tony Gwynn Classic 173; Verducci 170
"turn and burn" 110, 114, 121

underprivileged children 113, 147
University of Houston 157, 162
University of Miami 156
University of Nevada, Las Vegas 16, 156–159, 163
University of New Mexico 158, 164–165
University of Santa Clara 156
University of Texas 163–164
University of Utah 158, 162–164
U.S. Smokeless Tobacco 172

Valenzuala, Fernando 41, 55, 106–107, 112
Vandable, Seth 173–174
Vaughan, Roger 129
Vaughn, Greg 115, 124, 130, 133–136, 140, 147
Veras, Quilvio 126, 135–137, 144
Verducci, Tom 119, 124, 170
Vezie, Tim 13–14, 57, 160
videotaping 35–36, 58, 70, 90, 93, 96, 100–101, 125, 170
Virgil, Ozzie 42, 58

Wagner, Honus 112, 118, 127
Walk, Bob 70
Walker, Larry 123–124, 126–127
Walla Walla Class A team 21–25, 28
Washington Nationals 165
weight issue 16, 77, 92, 100, 166
Welch, Bob 60
Werner, Tom 79, 90, 106–107
West, David 90

West, Joe 68–69, 73, 121
Western Athletic Conference (WAC) 13–15, 18–19
Whitman College 25
Whitson, Ed 34, 42, 51, 72
Wietelmann, Whitey 31, 152
wiffle ball 5, 6, 96, 129
Wiggins, Alan 36, 38–39, 41–42, 47–52, 59, 63, 78; catalyst for 1984 Padres offense 44; drug relapse and death 55; drug use 33; minor league career 29; remained friends with Tony 56; steals five bases in a game 40
Will, George 67, 79
Williams, Dick 27–28, 31, 33, 37–39, 47, 62; argument with Joe Torre 44; contract dispute with Padres 58; ejected in Atlanta 42; praises Tony's hustle 29
Williams, Eddie 97–98, 100–102, 109
Williams, Ted 6, 8, 65, 82, 103, 124; admired by Tony's father 4; attention to his bats 16–17; authors foreword to Tony's book 129; batting advice 9; on batting practice 36; congratulates Tony on 3,000th hit 145; credited by Tony for his 1997 season 128; death 154; encourages Tony to bat .400 122; inside pitch and baseball history 106; introduced to Tony 84–85; Ted Williams Parkway 172; telling Tony to "let it go" 120; thanked by Tony in Hall of Fame speech 160; throws out ceremonial first pitches with Tony 114, 139; Tony buys Williams' book 16
Wilson, Bill 80
winter ball 34, 37
Wolfe, Rich 170
World Series home run by Tony 137
World Series, 1984 50–53
World Series, 1998 136–137
Wrigley Field 33, 46, 90, 103, 125
Wynne, Marvell 63, 72

Yankee Stadium 136–137, 147

www.ingramcontent.com/pod-product-compliance
Ingram Content Group UK Ltd.
Pitfield, Milton Keynes, MK11 3LW, UK
UKHW042009140426
5217IPUK00015B/1072